The Victorian Literature Handbook

Literature and Culture Handbooks

General Editors: Philip Tew and Steven Barfield

Literature and Culture Handbooks are an innovative series of guides to major periods, topics and authors in British and American literature and culture. Designed to provide a comprehensive, one-stop resource for literature students, each handbook provides the essential information and guidance needed from the beginning of a course through to developing more advanced knowledge and skills.

The Eighteenth Century Literature Handbook
Edited by Gary Day and Bridget Keegan

The Medieval British Literature Handbook
Edited by Daniel T. Kline

The Modernism Handbook
Edited by Philip Tew, Steven Barfield and Alex Murray

The Post-war British Literature Handbook
Edited by Katherine Cockin and Jago Morrison

The Renaissance Literature Handbook
Edited by Susan Bruce and Rebecca Steinberger

The Seventeenth-Century Literature Handbook
Edited by Robert C. Evans and Eric Sterling

The Shakespeare Handbook
Edited by Andrew Hiscock and Stephen Longstaffe

The Victorian Literature Handbook

Edited by

Alexandra Warwick

and

Martin Willis

continuum

Continuum
The Tower Building
11 York Road
London SE1 7NX

80 Maiden Lane, Suite 704
New York
NY 10038

www.continuumbooks.com

British Library Cataloguing-in-Publication Data
A catalogue record for this book is available from the British Library.

ISBN: 978-0-8264-9576-1 (hardback)
         978-0-8264-9577-8 (paperback)

Library of Congress Cataloging-in-Publication Data
A catalog record is available from the Library of Congress.

Typeset by Kenneth Burnley, Wirral, Cheshire.
Printed and bound in Great Britain by Cromwell Press Ltd, Trowbridge, Wiltshire

Contents

Contents

Detailed Table of Contents

List of Illustrations

General Editors' Introduction

The Continuum *Literature and Culture Handbooks* series aims to support both students new to an area of study and those at a more advanced stage, offering guidance with regard to the major periods, topics and authors relevant to the study of various aspects of British and American literature and culture. The series is designed with an international audience in mind, based on research into today's students in a global educational setting. Each volume is concerned with either a particular historical phase or an even more specific context such as a major author study. All of the chosen areas represent established subject matter for literary study in schools, colleges and universities, all are both widely taught and the subject of ongoing research and scholarship. Each handbook provides a comprehensive, one-stop resource for literature students, offering essential information and guidance needed at the beginning of a course through to more advanced knowledge and skills for the student more familiar with the particular topic. These volumes reflect current research and scholarship, teaching methods and strategies, and also provide an outline of essential historical contexts. Written in clear language by leading internationally acknowledged academics, each book provides the following:

- introduction to authors, texts, historical and cultural context
- guides to key critics, concepts and topics
- introduction to critical approaches, changes in the canon and new conceptual and theoretical issues, such as gender and ethnicity
- case studies in reading literary and theoretical and critical texts
- annotated bibliography (including websites), timeline and glossary of critical terms.

The series as a whole has drawn its inspiration and structure largely from the latest principles of textbook design employed in other disciplines and subjects, creating an unusual and distinctive approach for the undergraduate arts and humanities field. This structure is designed to be user-friendly and it is intended that the layout can be easily navigated, with various points of cross-reference. Such clarity and straightforward approach should help students understand the material and guide them through the increasing academic difficulty of complex critical and theoretical approaches to Literary Studies. Thse handbooks serve as gateways to the particular field that is explored.

All volumes make use of a 'progressive learning strategy', rather than the traditional chronological approach to the subject under discussion in order to relate more closely to the learning process of the student. This means that the particular volume offers material that will aid the student to approach the period or topic confidently in the classroom for the very first time (for example, glossaries, historical context, key topics and critics), as well as material that helps the student develop more advanced skills (learning how to respond actively to selected primary texts and analyse and engage with modern critical arguments in relation to such texts). Each volume includes a specially commissioned new critical essay by a leading authority in the field discussing current debates and contexts. The progression in the contents mirrors the progress of the undergraduate student from beginner to a more advanced level. Each volume is aimed primarily at undergraduate students, intending to offer itself as both a guide and a reference text that will reflect the advances in academic studies in its subject matter, useful to both students and staff (the latter may find the appendix on pedagogy particularly helpful).

We realize that students in the twenty-first century are faced with numerous challenges and demands; it is our intention that the Handbook series should empower its readers to become effective and efficient in their studies.

Philip Tew and Steven Barfield

1 Introduction: Defining Victorian

Alexandra Warwick and Martin Willis

Chapter Overview	
Victorian Timeline: 1830–1901	6

All attempts to regard history as a series of distinct chronological periods are beset with difficulty, most simply because the continuities between one 'age' and another are strong, and because the rates of change in different areas of society and culture vary. In discussing nineteenth-century Britain the problems of periodization are especially acute. It was the first time that an age self-consciously named itself: it was the Victorians who called themselves Victorians, identifying their period with the figure and reign of the queen. Although all chronological distinctions are to some extent arbitrary, the nomination of this period relies on the chance length of a single lifetime. Had Victoria died mid-century, then her reign might well have been seen as a short coda to the eighteenth century and the Industrial Revolution. As it is, the sense of 'Victorian' has even expanded, to such an extent that whole nineteenth century is sometimes popularly thought of as Victorian, even though close to 40 years of it were over before she ascended the throne. As the turn of the century was celebrated on 1 January 1901, Victoria's death only 21 days later seemed to provide a symbolic break. With her passing it appeared to some people that the old age was over, and the much-anticipated new world of the twentieth century could begin. To others it suggested a less optimistic loss of established certainties and values.

Of course the writing careers of Victorian authors did not end with similar convenience, nor did they necessarily begin at, or near, the moment of Victoria's accession in June 1837. This provides the first problem of periodization: how to deal with writers such as William Wordsworth, whose career

continued as Victoria came to the throne, or Arthur Conan Doyle, extra-
ordinarily popular with the Victorians, who wrote deep into the twentieth
century? If Victorian only indicates a historical period, then it is simple enough
to regard both of these writers as Victorian; one who became so in 1837 and
one who stopped being so in 1901. Yet this seems a reductive and overly paradigmatic way to view the complexities of a writing life, or indeed the life of
any individual who made a contribution to Victorian society. The Victorians
themselves – or at least those in positions of political and cultural influence –
appear to have felt similarly; Alfred Tennyson, after all, became the Victorians'
most cherished Poet Laureate, despite having completed some of his most
important poetry in the 1820s and early 1830s.

Simply put, such challenges to the periodizing orthodoxy reveal how
necessary it is to be flexible with beginnings and endings, recognizing that
moments of change are more often periods of transition. More than that,
however, the unsustainability of the dates of the Victorian period when placed
under pressure by the actualities of Victorian lives suggests that there is a
range of meanings for 'Victorian' that goes beyond the chronological. In fact
the self-evident historical period we could draw upon to define Victorian is
very easily disrupted by the many ideological, social, cultural, economic,
political and familial connotations of the term that have made the meaning of
Victorian complex, contradictory and contested.

It is these other meanings of Victorian that make its usage in literary scholarship a matter of contention. For Victorian has come to stand for a myriad
very different, sometimes opposing, representations of the past. In the first
instance this is understandable: the Victorian period (as a set of inclusive
dates) lasted a long time (near to 64 years), and was subject to a pace of change
not previously experienced. The Victorians of the 1890s were very different to
the Victorians of the 1830s. Moreover, the differences apparent across the
period have given rise to a variable set of values and characteristics, all of
which can be argued to be more or less true of one version of Victorian or
another. A further complication also exists: literary and cultural critics and
historians have, in the twentieth and twenty-first centuries, defined and re-
defined Victorian as part of an ongoing debate over its meanings, so that there
are not only different definitions of Victorian but also significant shifts in the
characteristics of these definitions. As though to add to these complications,
the debates over meanings have also led to re-evaluations of the temporal
boundaries themselves; Victorian is no longer necessarily book-ended by the
years 1837 and 1901 but may extend beyond them or be restricted within them.

There are a number of literary critics who argue that the connotations of the
term Victorian should lead us to discount (at least to some extent) the arbitrary
dates of 1837 and 1901. Robin Gilmour, for example, in his survey of the intellectual and cultural contexts of the Victorians, begins his own analysis in 1830

and ends it in 1890, identifying those opening and concluding years as bracketing what was otherwise a cohesive, if not entirely homogenous, set of cultural values. Gilmour also regards the Victorian period as existing within an outlying identifiable period that began with the Battle of Waterloo in 1815 and ended with the Battle of the Somme in 1916. Philip Davis, author of *The Oxford English Literary History* for the Victorian period, also recognizes a longer historical continuity within which the Victorian period sits: from the end of the Napoleonic War (1815) to the beginning of the First World War (1914). However, while his own reading of the Victorian period begins, like Gilmour's, in 1830, it ends in 1880. For Davis, the period from 1880 to 1901 signals a shift towards a more aesthetic literary culture dominated by pessimism and fragmentation that does not fit easily with his understanding of Victorian as representative of optimism and progress.

Such curtailed versions of what constitutes the Victorian period, and concomitantly what the term Victorian signifies, can be contested. Gilmour, for one, does accept that it is possible to argue that the meanings of Victorian encapsulate both the confidence of the mid-nineteenth century and the anxiety and crisis that overshadow its final two decades. Similarly, J. B. Bullen argues that the word Victorian came to be used in opposition to Edwardian and does therefore connote all of the changing values of the period up to the beginning of the twentieth century. In this reading of the term Victorian represents the largely positive characteristics of progress, civilization, discovery and optimism as well as the more negative associations of the age with repressive morality, restraint and prudence.

As should be obvious there is no present critical consensus on the meaning of Victorian; nor should the scholarly debate be characterized as a journey towards a more truthful, even all-encompassing definition. Although the term Victorian is now applied to a far greater number of writers, thinkers and cultural phenomena than even 30 years ago (many more women writers, marginal scientific practices and sexual identities, for example, are regarded as importantly contributing to the meaning of Victorian) their relative centrality to, or marginalization from, a constantly contested and slippery definition remains in flux. Despite this, Victorian critics are in agreement on one thing: that the term Victorian must be used cautiously and self-consciously in literary scholarship. Since, to greater and lesser extents, all scholarly considerations of Victorian writing are also always interventions in the debate over the meaning of Victorian it is the responsibility of the critic to articulate clearly their own understanding of that ever mutating and elusive adjective.

*   *   *

Each of the contributors to *The Victorian Literature Handbook* have, in their own ways, offered a definition of Victorian, and the *Handbook* as a whole describes a number of the many connotations of that term. Nevertheless, a comprehensive view of Victorian writing is not to be found here. Necessarily, selection leads to both inclusion and exclusion and while the constitution of certain encyclopaedic chapters means that there is some discussion of a tremendous range of literary texts, authors and contexts, there remains a number that have either been left out or considered only briefly. In part this is due to the objectives of the *Handbook*. It is the intention of the following chapters primarily to offer a series of interesting encounters with Victorian writing to the undergraduate student considering Victorian literature for the first time, and also to the more advanced student aiming to enhance their knowledge of the period and its writing. The final chapters, the Appendix and the Further Reading, however, will also interest those who wish to gain some secondary research or teaching expertise in Victorian literature, as well as the Victorian critic wishing to maintain a view of the current critical landscape. Nevertheless, with the student audience firmly in mind, the *Handbook* opens with a series of introductory chapters, proceeds to focused case studies of literary texts, as well as the critical, theoretical and historical contexts in which they might be placed, before offering some more specialized, yet still accessible, concluding discussions.

The *Handbook* works on the principle of an increasing pedagogic sophistication and engagement with the field of Victorian literary study as one chapter gives way to another. The first chapters offer foundational knowledge both broad and narrow; comprehensive historical contexts and short entries on major authors, institutions and events (Chapters 2 and 3). These act as introductions to a closer analysis of selected literary texts and critical works (Chapters 4 and 5). Chapter 6 revisits more explicitly some of the conceptual understandings of Victorian writing implicitly in play in the previous chapters, and provides a coda to the final four chapters. These analyse, in turn, changes in the literary canon (Chapter 7) and critical approaches to the period and its literature (Chapter 8) that have made Victorian studies such a vibrant field of inquiry for over half a century. Chapter 9 considers one of the most important methodologies within the field and one of its greatest strengths, its interdisciplinarity, while the concluding chapter offers a reflective and speculative view of the current and future critical landscape. Each of these chapters is supported by a select bibliography to be found at the end of the book, organized into clearly themed and annotated sections. Finally, the Appendix details the present position of Victorian studies within the university, offering both a statistical and synthesizing view of academic curricula from institutions around the world.

The choices made in deciding on the content of these chapters were premised on the *Handbook*'s proposed utility. The literary texts selected for close reading are drawn from the traditional canon of Victorian literature and exemplify something of the equal importance of Victorian prose, poetry and drama. These texts are widely taught to undergraduate students and are the subject of many published critical analyses. An engagement with them in the *Handbook*, then, can be supplemented by extensively available wider reading. This is also true of the critical texts chosen for analysis in the fourth chapter; they have become canonical works of scholarship in their own right. Yet the very fact that these are critical works respected and used by Victorian critics means that not only are they widely available for *Handbook* readers, but that there are other and different interpretations of their strengths and weaknesses in book reviews and scholarly surveys to place alongside the views presented here. Overall, the *Handbook* aims not to be bound by its own covers: it invites readers, most especially those new to Victorian literary study, to engage with the continuing debates on Victorian literature and culture by taking account of other voices offering alternative views. It is no matter of coincidence that *The Victorian Literature Handbook* is called a *Handbook*: it is not meant for passive reading but as an aid to actual involvement in an endlessly fascinating period of Britain's literary history.

Victorian Timeline, 1830–1901

Literary	*Historical*	*Cultural*
1830 Alfred Tennyson, *Poems, Chiefly Lyrical* William Cobbett, *Rural Rides* Charles Lyell, *Principles of Geology*	**June** Death of George IV; accession of his brother as William IV **July** Revolution in Paris leads to the election of Louis Philippe as King of France; liberal revolts in Italy, Belgium, Germany and Poland **August** General Election, Tories under Wellington elected; agrarian riots against enclosure and threshing machines **September** Huskisson killed by Stephenson's Rocket at the opening of Liverpool to Manchester railway **November** Wellington resigns, succeeded by Earl Grey; Palmerston appointed Foreign Secretary	
1831 Thomas Love Peacock, *Crotchet Castle* Alfred Tennyson, *Poems*	**March** First Parliamentary Reform Bill passes Commons, defeated in Committee **April** General Election, Whig reformers victorious **October** Second Reform Bill defeated in Lords **December** Third Reform Bill introduced	British Association for the Advancement of Science formed; James Clark Ross discovers magnetic north pole; Charles Darwin sets out on the *Beagle*
1832	**February** Cholera outbreak in London **April** Third Reform Bill passes Lords **June** Reform Bill approved: rotten and pocket boroughs abolished, constituencies created in new towns, franchise extended to select property owners	

Literary	*Historical*	*Cultural*
1833 Robert Browning, *Pauline* Thomas Carlyle, *Sartor Resartus* Edward Bulwer-Lytton, *Last Days of Pompeii* John Henry Newman, *Tracts for the Times* (which inaugurates the Oxford movement)	**August** Factory Act abolishes work for children under nine, limits working day to nine hours for under-13s, inspectors appointed	
1834	**March** Report of Royal Commission on Poor Law; Tolpuddle Martyrs sentenced to seven years transportation **August** Abolition of slavery in British Empire; Poor Law Amendment Act sets up workhouses **December** Peel becomes PM	Charles Babbage's analytical engine; Hansom cab; Houses of Parliament destroyed by fire
1835 Robert Browning, *Paracelsus* William Wordsworth, *Yarrow Revisited*		
1836 Charles Dickens, *Sketches by Boz*, begins *Pickwick Papers* Frederick Marryat, *Mr Midshipman Easy*	**August** Marriage Act, registration of births, marriages and deaths becomes compulsory	University of London founded; reduction in stamp duty increases sale of newspapers; London Bridge to Deptford railway opens
1837 Thomas Carlyle, *French Revolution* Charles Dickens, *Oliver Twist* Benjamin Disraeli, *Venetia*	**February** London Working Men's Association proposes 'charter' of democratic reforms to parliament **June** Death of William IV, accession of Victoria **July** General Election, Disraeli elected MP	National Gallery opens; Morse code and electric telegraph used; Euston Station opens

Literary	Historical	Cultural
1838 Charles Dickens, *Nicholas Nickelby* Gideon Mantell, *The Wonders of Geology*	**May** People's Charter printed **June** Victoria's coronation **July** Irish Poor Law **September** Tolpuddle martyrs pardoned and returned to Britain; Cobden founds Anti-Corn Law League **October** First Afghan War (until 1842) **December** Boers on great trek defeat Zulus at Blood River	Fox Talbot photographic prints; first train service London to Birmingham; first steam crossing of Atlantic
1839 Charles Darwin, *Journal of Researches* W. M. Thackeray, *Catherine* Thomas Carlyle, *Chartism*	**February** Chartist national convention **March** Anti-Corn Law League **April** Belgian independence and neutrality **June** First Chartist petition to parliament, rejected **July** First Opium War Chartist riots in Birmingham **November** Chartist riots in Newport, 24 killed	J. W. M. Turner, *The Fighting Temeraire*; Britain backs Turkey in the Eastern Question; Isambard Kingdom Brunel's Temple Meads railway station opened
1840 William Whewell, *Philosophy of the Inductive Sciences*	**February** Victoria marries Albert **June** Assassination attempt on Victoria **September** British warships bombard Egyptian army in Beirut **November** British seize Acre	Charles Barry levels and paves Trafalgar Square, and begins work on rebuilding the Houses of Parliament; penny post; first railway timetables
1841 *Punch* first published Charles Dickens, *The Old Curiosity Shop* Thomas Carlyle, *On Heroes and Hero-Worship*	**May** New Zealand declared British colony	London Library founded; Kew Gardens opened to public; Thomas Cook railway excursions begin; Census begins recording women's occupations

Literary	Historical	Cultural
1842 *Illustrated London News* first published Alfred Tennyson, *Collected Poems* Robert Browning, *Dramatic Lyrics* Charles Dickens, *American Notes* William Wordsworth, *Poems Chiefly of Early and Late Years*	**January** Hong Kong acquired by Britain **May** Parliament rejects second Chartist petition Peel re-introduces income tax **June** Victoria's first train journey **July** Chadwick's *Report on the Sanitary Condition of the Labouring Population* presented to Lords **August** Mines Act, women and children no longer to work underground; 'Plug Riots'; Chartists and Anti-Corn Law protestors attempt general strike in North Midlands; Manchester garrisoned with 2,000 troops in anticipation of Chartist riots; Second Afghan War	
1843 John Ruskin, *Modern Painters (Volume 1)* Charles Dickens, *A Christmas Carol* Thomas Carlyle, *Past and Present* J. S. Mill, *System of Logic*	**March** Opening of Thames tunnel by Brunel **April** Gambia becomes British colony **May** Natal becomes British colony **September** Victoria and Albert make first royal visit to France since 1520 **December** Basutoland made protectorate	Wordsworth made Poet Laureate; Theatre Regulation Act ends patent monopoly; Brunel's *Great Britain* launched
1844 Benjamin Disraeli, *Coningsby* Charles Dickens, *Martin Chuzzlewit* Robert Chambers, *Vestiges of the Natural History of Creation* Elizabeth Barrett, *Poems*	**June** Tsar Nicholas in London discusses possible break up of Ottoman Empire; Factory Act; 12-hour day for women, six-hour day for children aged 8–13 **July** Bank Charter Act regulates issue of bank notes **December** Rochdale pioneers open first co-operative retail shop	J. W. M Turner, *Rain, Steam and Speed*

	Literary	Historical	Cultural
1845	Benjamin Disraeli, *Sybil, or the two nations* Edgar Allen Poe, *Tales of Mystery and Imagination*	**September** Potato blight in Ireland, Irish Famine begins **December** Tories split over repeal of Corn Laws issue	A. H. Layard begins excavations at Nimrud and Nineveh; Victoria Park, first public park, opens in East End of London; 'Railway fever' financial speculation; John Franklin's expedition sets off for North Pole
1846	Edward Lear, *Book of Nonsense* Charles Dickens, *Dombey and Son*	**January** First of Public Health Acts for state aid for Irish famine **May** Repeal of Corn Laws	Mendelssohn, *Elijah*; first public parks in provincial city open in Manchester
1847	Charlotte Brontë, *Jane Eyre* Anne Brontë, *Agnes Grey* Emily Brontë, *Wuthering Heights* Benjamin Disraeli, *Tancred* Alfred Tennyson, *The Princess*	**June** Factory Act: 10-hour day for women and children aged 13–18 **July** General Election	Chloroform first used as an anaesthetic by J. Y. Simpson
1848	T. B. Macaulay, *History of England* (completed 1861) J. S. Mill, *Principles of Public Economy* Elizabeth Gaskell, *Mary Barton* Charles Dickens, *Dombey and Son* W. M. Thackeray, *Vanity Fair* Anne Brontë, *The Tenant of Wildfell Hall* J. A. Froude, *The Nemesis of Faith* Karl Marx and Friedrich Engels, *The Communist Manifesto*	**April** Chartist demonstration, Wellington organizes defence of London with 170,000 special constables; third Chartist petition presented **July** Cholera outbreak; Public Health Act sets up Board of Health	Pre-Raphaelite Brotherhood formed; first railway bookstall (in Euston); gold discovered in California; revolutions in France, Italy, Hungary, Austria and Germany

	Literary	Historical	Cultural
1849	John Ruskin, *Seven Lamps of Architecture* Matthew Arnold, *The Strayed Reveller and other Poems* Charles Dickens, *David Copperfield* A. H. Layard, *Nineveh and Its Remains* Henry Mayhew, *London Labour and the London Poor* Charlotte Brontë, *Shirley*	**February** Disraeli becomes Conservative leader in the Commons **March** Punjab annexed **June** Cholera outbreak, 14,000 dead by October	First bowler hat sold; Stephenson bridge over the Tyne; rail bridge over the Menai Straits
1850	Charles Kingsley, *Yeast, Alton Locke* Alfred Tennyson, *In Memoriam* Herbert Spencer, *Social Statistics* D. G. Rossetti, 'The Blessed Damozel' E. B. Browning, *Sonnets from the Portuguese* William Wordsworth, *The Prelude*	**June** Peel dies after fall from horse **August** Representative government given to South Australia, Victoria and Tasmania; Irish Tenant League established	Millais, 'Christ in the House of his Parents'; Dickens begins the periodical *Household Words*; Tennyson becomes Poet Laureate; Public Libraries Act establishes lending libraries
1851	John Ruskin, *The Stones of Venice*	**February** Australian gold rush begins **May** Opening of Great Exhibition (until October)	William Thomson (later Lord Kelvin) publishes work on the laws of conservation of energy
1852	W. M. Thackeray, *Henry Esmond*	**June** Representative government for New Zealand **September** Death of Wellington	Completion of King's Cross, Lewis Cubitt; James Joseph Sylvester develops theory of calculus; Livingstone begins voyage up the Zambesi; second empire established in France, under Napoleon II
1853	Matthew Arnold, *Poems* Elizabeth Gaskell, *Cranford* Charlotte Brontë, *Villette* Charles Dickens, *Bleak House*	**April** Gladstone's first Free Trade budget **September** British ships in the Dardanelles to defend Constantinople **October** Turkey declares war on Russia	

Literary	Historical	Cultural
1854 Tennyson, 'The Charge of the Light Brigade' Charles Dickens, *Hard Times* Coventry Patmore, 'The Angel in the House'	**March** Treaty of Constantinople (Britain, France and Turkey); Britain declares war on Russia (Crimean War) **April** Cholera in London 10,000 deaths, Snow identifies water-borne transmission **June** Victoria opens Crystal Palace in Sydenham	Brunel's Paddington station completed; London Working Men's College founded
1855 Charles Kingsley, *Westward Ho!* Anthony Trollope, *The Warden* Elizabeth Gaskell, *North and South* W. M. Thackeray, *The Rose and the Ring* Alfred Tennyson, *Maud and other Poems* Robert Browning, *Men and Women*	Crimean War continues **June** Stamp Duty abolished on newspapers	
1856	**February** Armistice signed with Russia, fighting ends in the Crimea, last troops leave in July	
1857 E. B. Browning, *Aurora Leigh* Charlotte Brontë, *The Professor* George Eliot, *Scenes of Clerical Life* Charles Dickens, *Little Dorrit* Thomas Hughes, *Tom Brown's Schooldays* Anthony Trollope, *Barchester Towers* Dinah Mary Mulock, *John Halifax, Gentleman*	**May** Start of the Indian Mutiny **August** Matrimonial Causes Act sets up divorce courts for England and Wales **November** Financial crisis in the City because of failure of US banks over railway speculation	Reading Room of the British Museum opens; Richard Burton and Jon Speke set out in search of the equatorial lakes of Africa; discovery of Neanderthal Man; Victoria and Albert Museum founded

Literary	Historical	Cultural
1858 Arthur Clough, *Amours de Voyage* George Macdonald, *Phantastes*	**January** Princess Royal marries Prince Frederick of Prussia **March** Irish Republican Army (IRA) established **July** 'The Great Stink' pollution crisis in London; proclamation of peace in India, the formal end of the Mutiny; Jewish Disabilities Act enables Jews to become MPs **August** Property Qualification Act ends the requirement of financial level for MPs; India Act, East India Company transferred to the Crown, Governor General becomes a Viceroy; trade treaty opens, Japan to British commerce	William Powell Frith, 'Derby Day'; Darwin and Wallace papers presented to the Linnaean Society; Opera House Covent Garden opens; Brunel's *Great Eastern* launched
1859 Charles Darwin, *On the Origin of Species* J. S. Mill, *On Liberty* Charles Dickens, *A Tale of Two Cities* George Eliot, *Adam Bede* Edward Fitzgerald, *The Rubaiyat of Omar Khayyam* Alfred Tennyson, *Idylls of the King* George Meredith, *The Ordeal of Richard Feverel* Isabella Beeton, *Book of Household Management* Samuel Smiles, *Self Help*	**February** Disraeli's Reform Bill defeated	National Portrait Gallery opens
1860 J. S. Mill, *Treatise on Representative Government* Wilkie Collins, *The Woman in White* George Eliot, *The Mill on the Floss* John Ruskin, *Unto This Last*	**January** Cobden's free trade treaty with France **March** First Food and Drugs Act to prevent adulteration of basic foodstuffs **October** Treaty of Peking opens 11 new Chinese ports to British trade	Garibaldi and Cavour make possible the proclamation of united Italy

Literary	Historical	Cultural
1861 Charles Dickens, *Great Expectations* Anthony Trollope, *Framley Parsonage* George Eliot, *Silas Marner* Mrs Henry Wood, *East Lynne* Palgrave's *Golden Treasury*	**March** Pacification of the Maoris in New Zealand **April** Outbreak of American Civil War **May** Government announces neutrality in American Civil War **September** Post Office Savings Bank opens **December** Death of Prince Albert from typhoid fever	Morris and Co. design company founded; Thomas Cook's first continental tour; first iron warship; emancipation of serfs in Russia
1862 George Meredith, *Modern Love* Elizabeth Braddon, *Lady Audley's Secret* E. B. Browning, *Last Poems* Lord Kelvin, *On the Age of the Sun's Heat* Christina Rossetti, *Goblin Market and Other Poems*	Victoria unwell; Bazalgette begins Thames Embankment	International Exhibition of Science and Industry opens; Bismarck becomes chief minister of Prussia; first English cricket tour to Australia
1863 J. S. Mill, *Utilitarianism* Charles Kingsley, *The Water Babies* George Eliot, *Romola*	**January** First underground railway opened, Paddington to Farringdon **February** Greeks offer throne to Victoria's second son, government insists on refusal **March** Prince of Wales marries Princess Alexandra of Denmark **May** Second Maori war begins	Whistler, 'Symphony in White'; Football Association established; Whiteley's department store opened
1864 Robert Browning, *Dramatis Personae* Herbert Spencer, *Principles of Biology* John Henry Newman, *Apologia Pro Vita Sua* Charles Dickens, *Our Mutual Friend*	**April** London conference of European powers fails to resolve Schleswig-Holstein problem **May** Gladstone speech supporting universal suffrage and parliamentary reform **September** Navy bombards Kagoshima after Japan close ports to foreign trade, reopened in October	Trollope begins series of Palliser novels; Prussia and Austria invade Schleswig-Holstein; Louis Pasteur gives his name to his new invention, 'pasteurization'; first County Cricket Championship; Oxford public debate on Darwinian theory

	Literary	Historical	Cultural
1865	Lewis Carroll, *Alice's Adventures in Wonderland* Matthew Arnold, *Essays in Criticism* John Ruskin, *Sesame and Lilies*		Lister introduces antiseptic into surgical practice; the assassination of President Abraham Lincoln; Elizabeth Garrett qualifies as first woman doctor
1866	George Eliot, *Felix Holt* Elizabeth Gaskell, *Wives and Daughters* Charles Algernon Swinburne, *Poems and Ballads*		Alfred Nobel discovers dynamite; Gregor Mendel discovers the laws of heredity; petition for women's suffrage
1867	Karl Marx, *Das Kapital* Matthew Arnold, *New Poems*	**March** Second Reform Act	Invention of the typewriter
1868	Wilkie Collins, *The Moonstone* Robert Browning, *The Ring and the Book*	**May** Public hanging abolished	Founding of the British Trades Union Congress; telegraph network nationalized
1869	Matthew Arnold, *Culture and Anarchy* Francis Galton, *Hereditary Genius* J. S. Mill, *On the Subjection of Women*	**November** Opening of the Suez Canal	Mendeleev publishes his periodic table of elements; first issue of *Nature* published
1870	John Lubbock, *Origin of Civilization* D. G. Rossetti, *Poems*	**May** Foundation of Home Government Association, constitutional association for Irish Home Rule **June** Reform of the Civil service, examinations for entry; death of Dickens, leaving unfinished *The Mystery of Edwin Drood* **August** Irish Land Act, loans to peasants for land purchase, compensation for eviction; Married Women's Property Act, wives allowed property of their own; Forster's Education Act, accepts that provision of basic schooling is government responsibility	London and Australia linked by telegraph; Stanley sent to look for Livingstone; declaration of Papal Infallibility; France declares war on Prussia; Third French Republic proclaimed after capture of Napoleon III at Sudan; Italian army enters Rome, Italy's capital after 2 October

Literary	Historical	Cultural
1871 Charles Darwin, *The Descent of Man* Edward Bulwer-Lytton, *The Coming Race* Lewis Carroll, *Through the Looking Glass*	**January** Kaiser Wilhelm of Prussia proclaimed Emperor of Germany **March** Paris Commune begins (ends in May) **June** University Test Act removes religious tests for students entering Oxford and Cambridge **July** Abolition of the purchase of army commissions; British Columbia becomes a province of Canada **August** First Bank Holiday, after the Act providing three Bank Holidays a year	Whistler, 'The Artist's Mother'; first women's hall of residence opened in Cambridge; Cambridge establishes chair in experimental physics; Stanley finds Livingstone; opening of the Royal Albert Hall
1872 Samuel Butler, *Erewhon* George Eliot, *Middlemarch* Thomas Hardy, *Under the Greenwood Tree*	**February** Foundation of the Agricultural Labourer's union; Holland sells Gold Coast forts to Britain **June** Disraeli speech advocates building up a larger colonial empire **July** First secret ballot; Licensing Act limits times and places at which alcohol may be consumed	First FA Cup final
1873 Walter Pater, *Studies in the History of the Renaissance* J. S. Mill, *Autobiography* Herbert Spencer, *The Study of Sociology* James Clerk-Maxwell, *Treatise on Electricity and Magnetism*	**January** Napoleon III dies in exile in England **March** Gladstone resigns, Disraeli refuses to form government, Gladstone remains in office; court structure reformed, Court of Appeal established **April** Ashanti War begins when British attacked on Gold Coast	Natural History Museum completed; Custody of Infants Act allows greater rights to mothers after divorce or separation

Literary	Historical	Cultural
1874 Thomas Hardy, *Far From the Madding Crowd* James Thomson, *The City of Dreadful Night*	**January** Ashanti defeated **February** Rioting in Midlands towns; General Election; Gladstone resigns, Disraeli returns as Prime Minister; first organized strike of agricultural labourers **August** Factory Act establishes 56-hour working week, further safeguards against children working as chimney sweeps	First Impressionist exhibition, Paris
1875	**January** Gladstone resigns Liberal leadership **July** Public Health Act produces national code of sanitation **August** Artisans' Dwellings Act allows compulsory purchase and demolition of unfit buildings **September** Main sewage system for London completed **November** Prince of Wales makes first state visit to India; Disraeli buys 40% share of Suez Canal	Matthew Webb swims the Channel; London Medical School for Women founded; Rising in Bosnia-Herzegovina against Turkish rule initiates the Eastern Crisis
1876 George Eliot, *Daniel Deronda*	**April** Royal Titles Act enables Queen Victoria to become Empress of India **May** Disraeli refuses to cooperate with Germany, Austria-Hungary and Russia in pressing Turkey to reform in the Balkans **June** Newspaper reports of Turkish atrocities in Bulgaria, Disraeli downplays them; Serbia declares war on Turkey	Alexander Graham Bell invents the telephone; Thomas Edison invents the phonograph

Literary	Historical	Cultural
	August Disraeli made Lord Beaconsfield, remains Prime Minister **September** Gladstone publishes pamphlet *The Bulgarian Horrors and the Question of the East,* sells widely, after speech on Bulgaria he returns to active politics **October** Britain and France take control of Egypt's finances after it is declared bankrupt **November** Disraeli proposes cooperation with Russia and sets up conference on Constantinople	
1877	**January** Victoria proclaimed Empress of India at Delhi **March** European powers demand reforms within the Turkish Empire **April** Transvaal annexed Russia declares war on Turkey **July** Irish Home Rule MPs begin campaign of obstruction of parliamentary business, Charles Stewart Parnell MP becomes President of the Home Rule Confederation	Grosvenor Gallery opens; Wagner festival at Albert Hall
1878 Thomas Hardy, *The Return of the Native* Charles Swinburne, *Poems and Ballads*	**January** Cleopatra's Needle reaches London **March** Walvis Bay in SW Africa annexed **June** Turkey hands administration of Cyprus to Britain, defensive treaty with Turkey to protect Asiatic provinces from Russia; Berlin Congress on the Eastern Question **October** British troops enter Afghanistan	Ruskin/Whistler libel suit; Gilbert and Sullivan, *HMS Pinafore;* William Booth founds the Salvation Army; London University admits women to degrees

Literary	Historical	Cultural
1879 Charles Meredith, *The Egoist*	**January** Britain occupies Kandahar in Afghan War; British invade Zululand, battles of Isandhlwana and Rorke's Drift **May** British purchase right to occupy Khyber Pass in Afghanistan **September** Zulu War ends **October** Troops enter Kabul; Foundation of Irish National Land League	First women students at Oxford; electric street lighting in London on Embankment and Waterloo Bridge; agricultural depression
1880 Thomas Hardy, *The Trumpet Major*	**April** General Election returns Liberals, Gladstone is Prime Minister **May** Parnell elected Chairman of Irish Party in the Commons **October** First Boer War between Britain and Transvaal Republic begins	Gilbert and Sullivan, *The Pirates of Penzance*; first Ibsen production in Britain of an abridged version of *The Pillars of Society*; first cricket Test Match; refrigerated and frozen meat first comes from Australia and New Zealand
1881 D. G. Rossetti, *Ballads and Sonnets* Oscar Wilde, *Poems*	**January** First issue of postal orders; Irish Party MPs obstruct Parliamentary business for 41 hours **February** Boers defeat British at Majuba **March** Habeas Corpus suspended in Ireland after agrarian unrest, Peace Preservation Act authorizes coercive measures in Ireland; assassination of Tsar Alexander II **April** British recognize independent Boer republic of Transvaal under President Kruger; troops withdrawn from Afghanistan **June** League of the three Emperors Alliance between Germany, Austria-Hungary and Russia	Gilbert and Sullivan, *Patience*

Literary	Historical	Cultural
	July First London evening paper, *Evening News* **August** Irish Land Act **October** Parnell arrested for defying Irish Land Courts, Irish Land League declared illegal	
1882 R. L. Stevenson, *New Arabian Nights*	**May** Phoenix Park murders of Chief Secretary for Ireland and his deputy by Fenians; Italy joins Austria and Germany to form the Triple Alliance **June** Riots against the British and French in Alexandria, British Navy bombards in July **July** Irish Crime prevention Act abolishes trial by jury and extends police powers of arrest **August** Married Women's Property Act **September** Cairo occupied by British	Leslie Stephen begins *Dictionary of National Biography;* Gilbert and Sullivan, *Iolanthe;* Polytech- nic movement begins with opening of Regent Street Polytechnic; Society for Psychical Research founded; Pitt Rivers becomes first Inspector of Ancient Monuments; electric trams in London; Married Women's Property Act
1883 George Sims, *How the Poor Live* Andrew Mearns, *The Bitter Cry of Outcast London* R. L. Stevenson, *Treasure Island*	Risings in Egypt and Sudan **April** Britain warns German colonist in SW Africa to respect existing claims	Royal College of Music founded; Boy's Brigade founded; electric railway at Brighton; Thomson's paper on the atom
1884 G. A. Henty, *With Clive in India*	**January** Fabian Society established **February** Royal Commission on the Housing of the Working Classes; Britain– Portugal treaty attempts to check German colonial expansion **April** Earthquake in East Anglia, four people killed **July** India Office establishes protectorate on Somali coast	Work begins on the *Oxford English Dictionary;* first petrol-driven vehicle (a tricycle)

Literary	Historical	Cultural
	December Third Reform Act: uniform male suffrage in towns and rural areas enfranchises farm workers	
1885 Walter Pater, *Marius the Epicurean* Richard Burton, *Arabian Nights* W. T. Stead, *The Maiden Tribute of Modern Babylon*	**January** Westminster Hall and Tower of London damaged by Irish dynamiters; General Gordon killed at Khartoum, British forces arrive too late **March** Protectorate over Bechuanaland established **June** Protectorate over Niger River basin established **August** Irish Land Purchase Act: loans to help tenants buy land; Criminal Law Amendment Act: age of consent raised to 16, child prostitution outlawed, offence of gross indecency between men created **November** Campaign in Burma, British occupy Mandalay	Gilbert and Sullivan, *The Mikado*
1886 H. Rider Haggard, *King Solomon's Mines* R. L. Stevenson, *Kidnapped* and *The Strange Case of Dr Jekyll and Mr Hyde* Thomas Hardy, *The Mayor of Casterbridge*	**January** Upper Burma annexed **February** Salisbury resigns, Gladstone forms his third government; demonstrations by the unemployed lead to window-smashing in the West End, army on standby **May** British, French and Russian ships blockade Greece to discourage invasion of Turkish held territory **June** Gladstone's Home Rule Bill defeated **July** General Election, Conservatives returned, Salisbury is Prime Minister **November** Treaty with Germany over areas of East Africa	Repeal of the Contagious Diseases Act; Colonial and Indian exhibition opens in London to foster imperial pride; Mersey Railway completed; Severn Tunnel, the longest railway tunnel, opened

Literary	Historical	Cultural
1887 H. Rider Haggard, *She* Thomas Hardy, *The Woodlanders*	**June** Celebrations of Victoria's Golden Jubilee; Britain annexes Zululand **November** Bloody Sunday in Trafalgar Square, clashes between demonstrators and police, further unrest a week later, demonstrator killed	Gilbert and Sullivan, *Ruddigore* People's Palace opened in East End
1888 Rudyard Kipling, *Plain Tales from the Hills*	**February** Cecil Rhodes encourages Matabeleland to accept British protection; all mining rights conceded to him in October; first issue of the *Financial Times* **March** Protectorate established in Sarawak **May** Protectorates established in Borneo and Brunei **June** Accession of Kaiser Wilhelm II in Germany **July** Match Girls' Strike **August** Local Government Act: single women gain equal voting rights in local elections	Whitechapel Murders; pneumatic tyre invented by John Boyd Dunlop, after fitting to bicycles in 1891 cycling craze begins; *Orient Express*, Paris to Constantinople first runs
1889 George Bernard Shaw, *Fabian Essays in Socialism* Thomas Huxley, *Agnosticism* Jerome K. Jerome, *Three Men in a Boat* Tennyson's last poem, 'Crossing the Bar' R. L. Stevenson, *The Master of Ballantrae* Arthur Conan Doyle, *The Sign of Four* W. B. Yeats, *The Wanderings of Oisin*	**February** London County Council, first London-wide administration **August** Start of the London Dock Strike, widespread sympathy for the 'docker's tanner', return to work in September **October** Rhodes' British South Africa Company receives Royal Charter, expands into Mashonaland (Zimbabwe)	Barnum and Bailey circus

Literary	Historical	Cultural
1890 James Frazer, *The Golden Bough (Volume 1)* Henry Stanley, *In Darkest Africa* Charles Booth, *In Darkest England and the Way Out*	**January** First British picture paper, *The Daily Graphic* **March** Forth Railway Bridge opens **May** King Leopold of Belgium cedes land near Lake Tanganyika **June** Britain cedes Heligoland to Germany in return for Zanzibar and Pemba **September** Cecil Rhodes founds city of Salisbury (Harare) in Basutoland **November** O'Shea divorce case ends Parnell's political career **December** British authority established in Uganda	Morris founds the Kelmscott Press
1891 *Strand Magazine* (including Arthur Conan Doyle's 'A Study in Scarlet' serialized in its first editions) George Gissing, *New Grub Street* William Morris, *News from Nowhere* Thomas Hardy, *Tess of the D'Urbervilles* Oscar Wilde, *The Picture of Dorian Gray*	**March** Prince of Wales gives evidence in libel case based on cheating at cards **June** Jameson appointed administrator of South Africa company **August** Irish Land Act: Congested Districts Board set up to deal with housing problems **October** Gladstone approves the 'Newcastle Programme' containing Home Rule for Ireland, reform of the House of Lords, triennial parliaments	Ibsen, *Ghosts* performed and widely attacked in the press; Education Act abolishes fees for elementary schooling in England and Wales; public telephone links London and Paris
1892 Rudyard Kipling, *Barrack Room Ballads* Oscar Wilde, *Lady Windermere's Fan* George Bernard Shaw, *Widowers' Houses*	**March** India Councils Act: nominated Indian members to be allowed into administrations in India **July** General Election fought by Liberals on Newcastle programme, and Conservatives against Home Rule and for imperialism. Narrow win for	

Literary	Historical	Cultural
	Conservatives, but at first vote in August Irish Party votes with Liberals and Salisbury resigns. Gladstone becomes Prime Minister for fourth time, aged 82	
1893 T. H. Huxley, *Evolution and Ethics* George Gissing, *The Odd Women* Sarah Grand, *The Heavenly Twins* Oscar Wilde, *A Woman of No Importance*	**January** Foundation of the Independent Labour Party **March** Colonial Office takes over Uganda from East Africa Company **July** Rising in Matabeleland against South Africa Company **September** Lords reject Gladstone's Home Rule Bill	
1894 Aubrey Beardsley, *The Yellow Book* Sidney and Beatrice Webb, *History of Trade Unionism* Arthur Conan Doyle, *Memoirs of Sherlock Holmes* Anthony Hope, *The Prisoner of Zenda* George Du Maurier, *Trilby* Rudyard Kipling, *The Jungle Book* George Bernard Shaw, *Arms and the Man*	**January** Opening of Manchester Ship Canal **March** Local Government Act establishes parish councils and gives women the vote and candidacy **April** British protectorate established over Uganda **July** Britain recognizes Japan's national sovereignty **October** Dreyfus Affair begins with arrest of Alfred Dreyfus in Paris	
1895 Grant Allen, *The Woman Who Did* Thomas Hardy, *Jude the Obscure* Rudyard Kipling, *The Second Jungle Book* Arthur Morrison, *A Child of the Jago* H. G. Wells, *The Time Machine* Oscar Wilde, *An Ideal Husband* and *The Importance of Being Earnest*	**July** Responsibility for British East Africa transferred to the Foreign Office from the Company **May** Conviction and imprisonment of Oscar Wilde **August** General Election, Conservatives returned **December** Jameson Raid, invasion of Transvaal	National Trust founded

Literary	Historical	Cultural
1896 A. E. Housman, *A Shropshire Lad* H. G. Wells, *The Island of Dr Moreau*	**January** Jameson and raiders surrender to Boers; Kaiser congratulates Boers; anti-German demonstrations in Britain; new campaign to suppress unrest in Gold Coast **March** Campaign to re-occupy the Sudan begins, Protectorate over Ashanti established in August	Opening of the National Portrait Gallery; *Daily Mail* first published
1897 Rudyard Kipling, 'Recessional' H. G. Wells, *The Invisible Man* Henry Havelock Ellis, *Studies in the Psychology of Sex* Bram Stoker, *Dracula*	**June** Celebrations of Victoria's Diamond Jubilee **August** Beginning of campaign against Afghans on India's NW border	Opening of the Tate Gallery
1898 H. G. Wells, *The War of the Worlds*	**April** Kitchener's army defeats Khalifa's forces **May** Salisbury Albert Hall speech divides the world into 'living and dying nations' and emphasizes Britain's imperial character; Chamberlain urges better Anglo–American relations **June** Britain leases Chinese territory north of Kowloon **September** Kitchener enters Khartoum	First submarine for the Navy
1899 H. G. Wells, *When the Sleeper Wakes*	**March** Agreement between Britain and France over borders in Sudan **October** After various threats and provocations, Transvaal declares war on Britain, Boer War begins	Elgar, 'Enigma Variations'; first motor bus; founding of the Board of Education for England and Wales

Literary	Historical	Cultural
1900 George Bernard Shaw, *Three Plays for Puritans* Joseph Conrad, *Lord Jim*	**February** Labour Representation Committee (forerunner of Labour Party) set up **May** Relief of siege of Mafeking, national celebrations; Mines Act: no children under 13 to work in the pits; British occupation of Johannesburg **June** British occupation of Pretoria; British forces help suppress the Boxer Rebellion in China **July** Australia federated **October** 'Khaki election' won by Conservatives, two Labour MPs also elected; Transvaal annexed	Arthur Evans excavations at Knossos in Crete; Elgar, 'The Dream of Gerontius'
1901 Rudyard Kipling, *Kim* H. G. Wells, *The First Men in the Moon* Beatrix Potter, *Peter Rabbit*	**January** Death of Queen Victoria, accession of Edward VII; Commonwealth of Australia established **February** Funeral of Queen Victoria **September** Assassination of President McKinley	British Academy founded; Elgar, 'Pomp and Circumstance'; electric tramways in several British cities; petrol-driven submarine; Marconi wireless message from Cornwall to Newfoundland; Scott's first Antarctic expedition

2 The Historical Context of Victorian Literature

Alexandra Warwick

In order to be able to examine the relations between Victorian literature and the contexts in which it was produced, this section will give a series of accounts of aspects of contemporary social, political and economic circumstances. The relationship between literature and context is not one of passive reflection in which literature simply mirrors the world, but a more dynamic one of influence in both directions. For example, there are direct attempts by writers like Dickens to affect public perception and even political policy through his work. Then there are the material conditions of print culture, where the changing technology altered not only the ways in which work was published and distributed, but the form of writing too, as in the serial publication of novels. The content of literature did not just depict existing social roles and expectations, such as gender, but actively developed, reinforced or challenged those ideas. Thus the use of historical context in the reading of literature is not only to look for depictions of events, but also to think about the ways in which the kinds of relationships between text and context function. Throughout this chapter there are cross-references to other sections of the book where more details of particular aspects are given and relevant writers are suggested.

The Victorian Period

Victoria's reign, from 1837 to 1901, encompassed enormous changes, seeing a country that was essentially still rural and governed by systems that were centuries old, transformed to what is recognizably our modern world, with powered flight, telephones, cinema, tanks and machine guns. Over the course of the nineteenth century Britain was transformed from an agricultural base dominated by a small landowning interest to an industrial economy with a broader political class.

Machinery came to be driven by power other than that of the human or animal, and the work that people did was very different from what it had been in 1800. Over the century the population tripled, and for the first time in Britain's history a greater proportion lived in the urban areas rather than in the countryside. Society became increasingly stratified by the creation of a large industrial working class and the considerable expansion of the middle class. The situation of women changed, most obviously in the middle class, and although the right to vote was not granted until 1918, by 1900 women had gained other significant legal and social rights. The wider world too had changed, politically and in the balances of national power, but also in the way it was viewed. Work in the sciences, especially in geology, biology and physics, had altered the idea of the earth as a single creation with only 6,000 years of history to a view of it as a planet with continuously evolving living creatures and a past of hundreds of thousands of years.

Despite these great changes, it is important not simply to think of the nineteenth century as demonstrating a smooth upward curve of progress; the idea of progress was one with which the Victorians themselves struggled, uncertain of what it meant and how it might be measured. Within the period too, there are many shorter cycles of change that produce both continuities and discontinuities.

Before Victoria: The Early Nineteenth Century

At Victoria's accession in 1837 the nation was already quite different from the Britain of 50 years earlier. Most importantly it was a new state: the United Kingdom of Great Britain and Ireland, declared by the Act of Union of 1800. This was not a simple accomplishment of unity, however, and remained a subject of debate and sometime violent protest throughout the century. The

Europe in which this new state existed had also changed. France had been in turmoil since the revolution of 1789, and from 1793 to 1815, with only the brief exception of 1801 to 1803, Britain had been preparing for or at war with France. Britain maintained a distanced relationship with Europe, regarding itself as fundamentally different: free, with a system of common law that guaranteed that freedom, and contrasted with the governing systems of the rest of the continent. After the end of the Napoleonic Wars in 1815 the borders of European nations were re-drawn by the Congress of Vienna but, although the war was over, the nineteenth century was by no means an age of peace. There continued to be revolutions, smaller wars and military campaigns on the continent and, as the imperial ambitions of the great powers expanded, essentially European conflicts also took place much further away in Africa and the Middle East and Near East. Britain had lost part of its empire with the revolutionary wars and the subsequent declaration of independence of the American colonies in 1776, but during the nineteenth century it gradually acquired formal or informal authority over very widespread areas of the globe. Indeed by the end of the century issues of imperialism were the dominant aspect of British politics, and the identity of the nation was deeply influenced by a sense of itself as an imperial power.

(*See Chapter 3: Conrad, Kipling; Chapter 4:* Jane Eyre; *Chapter 5: Brantlinger; Chapter 6: Imperialism*)

Although such changes are more difficult to locate precisely than the dates of wars or treaties, the moral climate of Britain also shifted in the early part of the century. Part of the reason for this was the evangelical movement. Beginning in the 1780s, it presented a challenge to the existing religious establishment, which it saw as lazy and corrupt and as having drifted far from the simple principles of faith and good works. The movement began in rural areas, but soon gained strength in the towns and cities. It was not simply a system of private and personal religious belief: it also had greater implications for moral conduct in society and stricter codes of 'proper' behaviour. The influence of evangelicalism spread widely in all strata of society, and 'High Church' Anglicanism became increasingly associated with the establishment elite, and with the forces of reaction and conservatism.

The religious revival was not solely responsible for the general shift in moral tone, but it was nevertheless important to it. Whatever the detailed theological disagreements of the different evangelical groups, they emphasized values of temperance, sexual morality focused on family life and the demonstration of faith in the performance of good work in the community. The late eighteenth century and the very early years of the nineteenth century came to be seen as the 'old corruption', where drinking, gambling and sexual laxity were acceptable in public life. Although this was something of a caricature, it does show the self-conscious concern of the Victorians to construct a new age, distinct in character from what had preceded it. More visibly obvious than any of these changes, however, was the progress of the Industrial Revolution.

(See Chapter 3: Eliot, Thackeray, Condition of England Novels, Religion and the Church, The Rural, Self-Help)

The Industrial Revolution

The Industrial Revolution had a profound impact on every person in the country, although it was not really until the 1830s that the general population really became aware of the widespread and permanent nature of the changes taking place. The innovations that contributed to industrial transformation actually began in agriculture with mechanical planting and threshing. The landscape on which the new machinery operated was also changing. Land that had previously been used for farming in small lots, or open land used for grazing by smallholders was taken into large fields. The larger fields were more easily worked by mechanized processes, and in turn they yielded greater volumes of crops. As a result of enclosure, many previously independent rural people were now landless. Some became dependent agricultural labourers but many moved to towns, beginning the great migration from the countryside that was such a significant element of the industrial revolution. One effect of these changes was that British agriculture became highly efficient, meaning that a much smaller agricultural labour force could still feed the increasing urban population.

Ancillary to agriculture was textile production, and many of the early inventions of the industrial revolution were in this area. Devices that mechanized the processes of spinning and weaving previously carried out by hand greatly increased the quantities that could be produced. As with agriculture, the new machinery also required larger premises and where textile production had previously been carried out in small workshops it moved to mills and factories, which themselves became larger and larger, dominating the landscapes in which they sat and producing whole new towns around them, especially in the north of England.

The new machinery was driven by steam power. The steam engine was gradually improved as the manufacture of its components became more precise, and other innovations were added that increased its efficiency and ability to power different types of industrial machinery. Central to these developments was coal. The new engines depended on coal as it provided a steadier and hotter fuel source than wood. The increased demand for coal was in turn met by improvements in mining technology, and mines were themselves dependent on engines to pump water out of the excavations and to draw the coal and miners to and from the surface. British coal production vastly exceeded that of other European countries: between 1820 and 1824 production was 18 million tons, compared to 2 million in France, Belgium, Russia and Germany combined.

The rapid increases, not just in coal production but in other industries as well, meant that the technology and structure of transport needed expansion and improvement, both to supply raw materials and to transport the finished products. Early nineteenth-century roads were poor and, although there were improvements, road transport remained difficult and expensive. Therefore it was the waterways of Britain that provided the first mass transport of freight. Rivers had always been used to move people and goods, but in their natural form they were not ideal for transport on a larger scale. This led to the construction of the canal system, which was extensive in the late eighteenth century and, like so much of the Industrial Revolution, driven by private enterprise and not by government planning. The canal system contributed to the changing of the landscape, but also very significantly to the geography of power and prosperity. The growing industrial towns were now linked to each other and to the sea ports, and some areas without major rivers, like Derbyshire, were able to develop their manufacturing centres through the ability to transport raw materials and finished products.

Crucial though the canals were to early industrialization, it is another form of transport that dominates the Victorian period and our later symbolic recollection of it: the railway. There had been small-scale use of rail before 1800, but it was the development of locomotive engines from stationary ones that provided the technology for the railways. George Stephenson opened the Hetton railway in 1822, the Stockton and Darlington in 1825 and the Manchester and Liverpool in 1830. The death of the prominent politician William Huskisson in an accident at the opening of the Manchester–Liverpool line proved to be no deterrent: in the 1830s railway development underwent a speculative boom and hundreds more miles of track were laid. Some lines prospered, others did not, and a few companies came to control the majority of the system. Initially railways made more money from passengers than from freight, but gradually railway companies also gained control of their competitors, the canal companies, and by the 1850s much of the commercial traffic had been transferred to rail. The railways were more than just part of the industrial developments: for the mass of the population they were one of the most obvious symbols of the changes taking place. The great railway stations were among the most impressive buildings in the new cities and towns, but the lines also cut through urban and rural areas, further changing the face of the landscape.

(See Chapter 3: Dickens, Eliot, Gaskell, Condition of England Novel, The Rural; Chapter 5: Poovey; Chapter 6: Industrialism)

Beginnings of Reform

The French Revolution and its aftermath, particularly the violence of the Terror (1793–4), had a great impact on British political life, producing a lingering anxiety that a revolution could happen at home. Although the fear of revolution evoked a strong conservatism in some quarters, it also produced recognition of the necessity of reform in order to neutralize the threat of more sudden and violent change. Despite this recognition, the First Reform Act of 1832 was only passed after intense debate and disagreement, both in parliament and more widely. The Act extended the franchise, increasing the electorate by about 50 per cent. Some 20 per cent of all adult men were now entitled to vote, but women remained entirely excluded.

More significantly the Act also created new electoral districts. Because of the changes in population distribution that had taken place over the preceding 30 years, there was serious inequality in the distribution of political power, with disproportionately high representation of some areas that had been central to the economy of pre-industrialization, and almost nothing from new industrial towns. Tiny towns with as few as 30 voters were entitled to elect two members of parliament, while Manchester (population 200,000) returned no MPs at all. Many other seats were not contested, often being passed on from father to son. Money and patronage were necessary to get elected, and the ballot was public, so it was difficult to vote against the local powerful interest or landowner. Religious requirements also meant that anyone not belonging to the Church of England was excluded from becoming an MP, so effectively only the tiniest minority of men stood any chance of election, and a very small section of the population were able to vote. Although the Reform Act meant that the large new industrial towns such as Manchester, Bradford and Birmingham were able to elect MPs for the first time, it produced relatively limited reform, and inequalities still remained.

(See Chapter 3: Eliot, Condition of England Novel, Politics; Chapter 4: Middlemarch; Chapter 5: Poovey; Chapter 6: Industrialism)

Other reforms followed the Act of 1832. The Factory and Mines Acts, for example, introduced some controls and restrictions of conditions in the new workplaces. Women and children worked in factories and mines as well as men and, even after the parliamentary commissions of inquiry into working conditions and the regulations of the Factory Acts, children were still employed in them. The 1833 Factory Act prohibited children under nine from work, and limited those aged nine to 13 to nine hours a day. The 1842 Mines Act stopped women and young children working underground (though many still continued in jobs on the surface, such as sorting coal) and in 1844 a further Factory Act introduced a 12-hour day for women workers, and reduced the child's day to six hours. The limitation of women and children's working hours was not entirely welcome as many households relied on the income of all family members and could not afford to lose part of it.

The Poor Law Amendment Act (1834) was intended to deal with the increasingly visible problem of poverty. The Act allowed for the creation of the work houses that came to symbolize its harshness and provided the focus for the opposition to it. It was the only systematic provision of benefits for the poor, but was an extremely austere, and at times corrupt, system.

(See Chapter 3: Dickens, Gaskell, Condition of England Novel, Utilitarianism; Chapter 4: Class, Industrialism; Chapter 5: Poovey)

1837–50: The Early Victorian Period

This was the nation of which Victoria became Queen in 1837: already advanced in its industrial transformation and beginning to adjust socially and politically to the new conditions. The rapid rate of expansion meant a very unstable economy, and the 1840s were especially difficult with many short cycles of boom and bust. The rate of industrial change was also not uniform across different industries, and it varied in different areas of the country. By the late 1840s, industry appeared to have reached the limit of productivity. By this time changes in banking law and practice had regularized some of the fluctuations in the economy, but there were still many across the social spectrum who were vulnerable: enterprising investors and businessmen who lost their money, and workers – particularly the unskilled – who lost their livelihoods. Wages increased very little in real terms and were not sufficient to support the new conditions of urban existence where working people had to pay rent and buy all the goods and food that they needed, instead of being able to grow their own food and engage in barter. Employment fluctuated, and unemployment could mean starvation. There was resentment against employers, as well as tensions between those prepared to work for lower wages and those attempting to organize labour into forms of trade unions.

By this time it was clear that the changes that had taken place were permanent. Industrialization had been largely unplanned and undirected by government, but increasingly parliament was conducting commissions of inquiry into the conditions of the population and producing legislation. However, such measures to ameliorate the worst of conditions were reactive and often quickly outpaced by the speed and scale of development. The dominant belief in laissez-faire economics also trusted that certain resolutions of the problems would emerge naturally.

(See Chapter 3: Dickens, Gaskell, Condition of England Novel, Politics, Utilitarianism, Self-Help; Chapter 5: Poovey; Chapter 6: Class, Industrialism)

It was a mixed period: marked by a growing confidence in progress but also politically anxious. One of the largest popular movements for political change was Chartism. The People's Charter at the centre of the movement's activity had six points: universal male suffrage, the secret ballot, annual elections, equally sized electoral district, abolition of the property qualification for MPs and the introduction of wages for MPs. Three mass petitions demanding the enactment of the charter were presented to parliament in 1839, 1842 and 1848. There was sometimes violence at Chartist demonstrations: in Wales in 1839 soldiers opened fire on a large group and several demonstrators were killed. All over Britain protest and demonstration continued. Chartism was always strongest in industrial areas, and the economic boom of 1843 to 1844 drained away some of its support, but the presentation of the last great petition in 1848 caused the government to make large-scale preparations against possible insurrection, with 10,000 special constables sworn in for duty on the streets of London.

1848 was a year of particular anxiety about popular uprisings. Dubbed the 'year of revolutions' there were revolts, for different reasons, across Europe. There was serious concern that Britain would experience violent insurrection, and the government responded with great force, as can be seen by the preparations for the Chartist demonstration. Although revolution never materialized, the fear of the mob remained.

(See Chapter 3: Chartism, Politics; Chapter 6: Class; Marxism)

Sometimes the interests of the manufacturers coincided with those of the workers, and changes produced incidental benefits for working people. One of these was the agitation against the Corn Laws. Manufacturers, concerned at falling profits, wished to lower wages but saw the price of basic food as an obstacle. Bread was the staple diet of the working class but its price was dependent on the cost of wheat. The price of wheat (and the farmers that produced it) was protected by the 1815 Corn Law that prevented the import of cereal. The principal figures in the movement to repeal the Law were Richard Cobden, a cotton merchant; John Bright, a Quaker carpet manufacturer and James Wilson, a journalist and founder of *The Economist*. The first mass meeting was held in Manchester in 1838, and both the location and the professions of the founders are significant – typical of the commercial, provincial middle class whose power was growing. The repeal movement also mobilized nonconformists (and utilized the new penny post) against the land-owning agricultural aristocracy and the Prime Minister Sir Robert Peel who was associated with them. The eventual repeal of the Corn Laws in 1846 split the Tory Party and they lost the next six general elections.

It is not easy to understand nineteenth-century politics by relating them to twenty-first century political conditions. Party organizations did not really exist at this time, nor is it possible to identify parliamentary politics or politicians with the broad categories of left and right that become more familiar in the twentieth century. Politics consisted of broad groups representing quite diverse interests and positions, and with a great deal of shifting allegiances on specific issues.

In early nineteenth-century Britain there were two main groups: Whigs and Tories. The Whigs were characterized by a commitment to reform through major legislation, for example the abolition of slavery (1833), the Factory Act (1833) and the Poor Law Amendment Act (1834), but proved to be unable to hold the factions of the group together, and their governments through the 1840s disintegrated. In the early part of the century the Tories were identified by strong commitments to tradition in the maintenance of order, the established Church and the interests of property owners. This position became harder to maintain against the kinds of changes taking place, and the Tory election victory of 1841 was the last until 1874.

(See Chapter 3: Trollope, Politics; Chapter 6: Class)

After the fluctuations and uncertainties of the 1830s and 1840s there seemed to come a turning point of stabilization, and there is a surge in confidence and prosperity that marks the next 20 years. The rise in confidence is often identified with the Great Exhibition of 1851 and although the Exhibition is not the reason for the change, it is an important symbol of what Britain had become by the middle of the century.

1850–70: The Mid-Victorian Years

The Great Exhibition was conceived as a demonstration of the achievements of British industry and manufacturing, as well as an assertion of the nation's place as the world-leading force of civilization and progress. Despite early difficulties in launching the project, it was an enormous success. There had been widespread scepticism about the practicality of constructing such an exhibition as well as fears about the attraction of large crowds to London that could possibly include undesirable elements such as foreign revolutionaries.

(See Chapter 3: The Great Exhibition)

Among the thousands of items at the Great Exhibition was a huge block of coal. It weighed 24 tons and stood at the entrance: a very obvious symbol of the powerful industrial nation that Britain had become. Between 1850 and 1870 Britain was established as the 'workshop of the world'. Its production of coal and iron increased, not only to supply its own industries, but also to export to countries that were undergoing industrialization, such as Germany and America. The statistics of Britain's production and consumption at this

Figure 1: Detail from H. C. Selous's painting of Queen Victoria opening the
Great Exhibition, May 1851. From a photograph in the collection of the Editors.

time are startling. Among the many examples, raw cotton consumption in
1850 was 267,000 tons, while the rest of Europe combined only reached 162,000
tons. The manufacturing sector produced an enormous and diverse range of
goods, from ships and trains to the smallest decorative items, which were
exported all over the world. Goods, particularly 'exotic' luxuries, were also
imported in huge quantities, and the expansion of the shipping trade created a
need for larger, more modern docks and warehouses. As well as the physical
structures associated with trade, there were also great profits in the banking
and insurance companies that financed and supported the businesses.

By 1851 the population of Britain was almost 21 million, double what it had
been in 1801 when the first census took place. The census of 1851 also showed
that for the first time in Britain's history more people lived in towns and cities
than in the countryside. The size and rate of growth of the population is
important because it provided both the workforce and the consumers in the
cycle of expanding markets, increasing demand and enabling higher production. Also crucial is the distribution of the population. New cities like Glasgow,
Birmingham, Liverpool and Manchester grew rapidly and assumed a greater
importance, eclipsing the old centres like Exeter. In 1801 nowhere in Britain,
apart from London, had more than 100,000 inhabitants, but by the end of the
century 80 per cent of the population was urbanized, with 74 towns having

over 50,000 inhabitants. There were several cities of over a million people and London had a population of almost 4 million.

(See Chapter 3: Dickens, Gaskell, The City; Chapter 5: Poovey)

Politics

The pattern of mid-Victorian governments was a coalition of different interest groups from the Whig/Liberal side, bargaining and dealing over measures to be passed, until they could no longer reach compromise. The government would then go out of office, usually without dissolving parliament, the Tories would form a minority government, during which time the other groups would again reach a compromise, defeat the Tories, force a General Election and resume power. In this way the Tories were effectively excluded from political power for over 20 years between 1846 and 1868. Despite this apparent instability in politics, the 1850s and 1860s saw the establishment of a series of liberal reforms that consolidated the gains of the Industrial Revolution. Banking, insurance and other service industries expanded, driving the security and prosperity of the new middle class. William Gladstone (Chancellor, 1853–5 and 1859–65) was instrumental in this, producing a series of budgets that established Free Trade. Free Trade came to mean more than simply the abolition of protective tariffs, but stood for a whole philosophy that valued enterprise, individualism and self-reliance. Although the Chartists had not succeeded as a movement, many who had been part of it made their way in mainstream politics, and by the late 1850s versions of their demands for constitutional reform were being enacted. The political position that dominated the 1850s and 1860s was a new coalition that shared beliefs in the importance of free trade, the moderate modernization of institutions, greater religious pluralism and a sense of 'progress'. As such it echoed the values of the urban industrial and commercial middle class that had emerged, and progress was the keynote. In wider social terms these ideas gained impetus from interpretations of Darwin's work in biology, and a concept of gradual evolution tied to an idea of progress permeated every area of Victorian political and social life.

(See Chapter 3: Dickens, Trollope, Politics; Chapter 6: Class, Darwinism)

The Victorian City

The Victorian city was a site of contrasts, and one that shows the double-edged nature of 'progress'. On one hand it was a place of wealth and achievement, even of great beauty, and certainly of great spectacle; on the other it was the scene of the some of the most desperate human experience. The density of habitation in the industrial towns was appalling. It was common for several families to live in one house, even in one room, and there were many lodging houses for young male migrant workers. Liverpool is just one example where the population density was very high: when the average for the country was 275 persons per square mile, Liverpool saw something like 138,000. The death rate was correspondingly high; the average age of death was 17 (compared to 20 in Manchester and 26 in London). Because of the mortality rate, the populations of these cities were not self-sustaining, and only a constant influx of migrants from other areas of Britain and Ireland maintained the numbers. The new cities also spread outwards into large urban conurbations where the areas of habitation linked up, as in Greater London, Merseyside, Tyneside, Clydeside, South-east Lancashire, West Midlands and West Yorkshire. Between them these areas contained more than a third of the whole population of Britain.

There was a great deal of new building, but much of it was back-to-back housing and, while it could be an improvement on the use of older houses, the terraces were often poorly built and only exacerbated existing problems of drainage and sanitation. The slums were highly vulnerable and there were frequent outbreaks of disease. Edwin Chadwick's *Inquiry into the Sanitary Condition of the Labouring Population* (1842) recommended the establishment of local boards of health and national public health commissioners, and gradually there were local projects of work in clearance of slums, the construction of better housing and control and regulation of building and drainage.

Even after such improvements slum conditions persisted in parts of the cities, most notoriously in the East End of London. Philanthropists, as well as profit-making companies, built blocks of housing in many of the worst areas and the rules of occupation of such tenements are evidence of the larger concerns about the health, cleanliness and social conformity of the poorest people. Residents were all to be vaccinated, all communal areas had to be cleaned every week and swept every morning by 10 a.m., washing was only to be done in the laundry and tenants were obliged to report any illness to the superintendent.

The growth of the railways was crucial in the expansion of the cities. Although they were primarily regarded as a means of travelling or transporting across the country rather than within the cities themselves, the shorter routes enabled the growth of the suburbs. The better-off citizens, including those on relatively modest incomes, were able to escape living in the dirt, pollution and overcrowding of the centres by travelling into their workplaces on the commuter routes, and new areas of habitation grew by radiation out from the stations. Whole towns also came into being as a result of those travelling out of the cities on day trips and excursions: the seaside town of Blackpool for example was connected by rail in 1846 and became a popular destination for the people of the Lancashire towns.

(See Chapter 3: Dickens, Trollope, Crime; Chapter 6: Darwinism, Degeneration)

The Place of Women

Mid-century liberalism also produced women's movements, and the 'Woman Question' became a topic of public and parliamentary debate. Campaigners like Barbara Leigh Smith worked on a range of social and moral issues, but there was not concerted agitation for the vote at this stage. This comes after the second reform crisis of 1866 to 1867, when J. S. Mill raised the question in parliament. The National Society for Women's Suffrage was formed: in 1869 some women property owners got the vote in local elections, and in county council elections in 1888. Education for women was expanding too, and the first women began attending university in the 1870s with the foundation of Girton College (Cambridge). Initially they were allowed to attend university, but not to gain degrees, with the first admissions to degrees being in London University in 1878.

It is important to remember that the situation of women varied enormously according to a variety of a factors, class and geographical location perhaps being the most obvious but also age and marital status. It is not true to say that women were excluded from the world of work because millions of women did work, and their earnings were crucial to low-income households. Rates of pay for women were always lower and their employment more precarious, and in working-class households the labour of the wife was huge, even if she was not engaging in paid work outside the home.

Domestic service was a large category of work for women: in 1841, 55 per cent of working women were servants and even at the turn of the century the figure was 40 per cent. Domestic service was not confined to very wealthy households – relatively modest middle-class homes often employed cooks and maids of all work. The textile industry was the next largest category of employment and at the end of the century there were nearly twice as many women as men in the industry. Women worked less in heavy industry and mining: these tended to be better-paid occupations and the non-working wife was a sign of pride in these communities.

As for all groups in Victorian society, the situation of women over the century underwent considerable change. There were shifts in the legal status and rights of women, for example after 1857 divorces could be obtained, though it remained a costly procedure. Divorce was further reformed in 1878 when the Matrimonial Causes Act recognized violence against women and allowed abused wives to seek separation and maintenance payments from husbands. One of the most important legal changes was the Married Women's Property Act 1882, which gave married women the right to retain their own money and assets after marriage. Very gradually a view of women as having the right to self-determination in matters of money and their own person was developing. Women began marrying later in their lives, and smaller families became normal in the middle class. Although the New Woman was something of a media invention, in reality greater access to education and work was beginning to alter the opportunities available to the young women of the late century.

(See Chapter 3: Brontës, Elizabeth Browning, Eliot, Hardy, Rossetti, Tennyson, Wilde, Education, Marriage, New Woman, Sensation; Chapter 5: Gilbert and Gubar, Flint; Chapter 6: Gender, Sexuality)

1870–1900: The End of the Century

If the future for some women appeared more optimistic in the last decades of the Victorian period, this was not the case for society at large. In thinking about the latter part of the nineteenth century it remains important not to regard it simply as a period of depression, decline and anxiety, even though these are distinct elements of it. In the mid-Victorian decades, Britain was the richest and most powerful country in Europe, and its culture and influence were being spread throughout the world. Although this prosperity and expansion was already intercut with political tensions and international difficulties, from 1870 onwards the dominance of Britain in international trade and politics is seriously challenged, and domestically the liberal middle-class consensus also comes under threat.

Britain's advantage had been its early industrialization, but other countries were undergoing similar developments, often taking advantage of British machinery and processes. As countries like Germany and America expanded their manufacturing and production, Britain's dominance of world trade was challenged. Other countries were also able to adopt improved processes, where Britain in some areas continued with older practices and equipment, thus reducing competitiveness. British manufacturing was hard-pressed from the 1880s onwards and there were closures of major works, such as ironworks in the north-east in the late 1880s and 1890s. Britain was still a significant force however: in the 1880s coal production was greater than that of France, Germany, Russia and Belgium put together. In 1890, 90 per cent of the world's ships were built in Britain, and it was also the centre of finance, meaning that such influential aspects of world economy as commodity prices and insurance premiums were all set in London. Although Britain remained among the three leading powers in the world in 1914, a sense of decline persisted throughout the last decades of the nineteenth century.

(See Chapter 3: Arnold, Conrad, Hardy, Kipling, Shaw, Swinburne, Wells, Wilde, Aestheticism, Decadence, Evolution, Gothic, Sensation; Chapter 6: Degeneration, Darwinism, Race, Sexuality)

It was not just in trade and manufacturing that difficulties were experienced. The nature of Britain's colonial possessions had changed during the course of the century; in the colonies of white settlement, like Australia and New Zealand, authority was gradually devolved, but at the same time as loosening that direct control Britain was adding huge areas of land in Africa, the Far East and the Pacific to its Empire. In Africa the expansion of British interest is most striking. Until the 1860s there were only a few small possessions on the west coast, but in the 40 years until the end of the century almost 3 million square miles and 40 million people were taken over by the British. All major European powers were part of the 'Scramble for Africa' and Britain was drawn into conflicts with them, as well as with settlers like the Dutch Boers and with indigenous peoples. Throughout the century there had been challenges to British domination, the Indian Mutiny of 1857, for example; conflicts caused by protecting trade like the Opium Wars with China and clashes with other European powers, such as the Crimean War (1854–6). In the last decades though, such conflicts multiplied and intensified, and importantly British forces were sometimes defeated, undermining confidence in the imperial project.

(See Chapter 3: Conrad, Kipling, War; Chapter 6: Imperialism, Race)

It was an imperial possession much closer to home that also had a crucial effect on British politics: Ireland. Ireland's experience of the Industrial Revolution was almost opposite to that of the other countries of the Union: its population declined drastically and it remained overwhelmingly rural, with only a very few industrial centres. Land was mainly owned by Protestants, whereas a significant proportion of the people were Catholic. The country lacked capital investment and its economy could not sustain its population: large numbers continued to emigrate, further depressing economic and social conditions. Even before the famine emigration was high, but the devastating potato blights of 1845, 1846 and 1848 caused terrible suffering, and in that decade approximately 1.5 million people died and at least another million emigrated.

There had been Irish movements attempting to repeal the Act of Union in the 1830s and 1840s, and the widespread perception that the British government had failed to offer any assistance during the famine combined with the existing resentment of absentee Protestant landlords to produce the Irish Republican Brotherhood (the Fenians) which in the 1860s attempted several risings and conducted a bombing campaign in England. Alongside the Fenians' more violent presence, the constitutional movement for home rule developed, led after 1877 by Charles Stewart Parnell. Initially Parnell worked successfully within British politics, with his group of Irish MPs representing a powerful faction in the closely balanced parliaments. The shocking murders of the Irish Home Secretary and his secretary in Dublin in 1882 also gave impetus to what seemed to be Parnell's more moderate solution. However, Gladstone's adoption of Home Rule as the position of the Liberal Party weakened both

Parnell and ultimately Gladstone and the Liberals. The moderate Home Rule Bill of 1886 was defeated and split the Liberal Party, and Parnell was disgraced by a divorce scandal in 1890. Further attempts to introduce Home Rule were unsuccessful and the problems in Ireland festered violently throughout the twentieth century.

After the late 1870s government was pre-occupied with foreign and colonial issues, but there were also domestic changes. One of the effects of 1867 Reform Act was that Tory government again became possible, and the Party under Disraeli had a decisive electoral victory in 1874. The Tories did not attempt to reverse the Liberal reforms of the preceding 30 years, and their dominance of the last decades of the century was accomplished largely by linking the old aristocratic Anglican tone with the aspirations of the middle and lower middle classes in the suburbs of the cities, defining themselves as the party of property and patriotism. Their legislation in 1874 to 1880 was directed at social reform in areas such as licensing, public health, pollution, food and drugs control and education, intended to show that they could govern the urban areas. However, the problem with their link to patriotism and its appeal to middle-class values was that imperialism was increasingly costly, and becoming associated with some disastrous military actions, such as those in the second Boer War (1899–1902).

(See Chapter 3: Conrad, Kipling, Shaw, Trollope, Wells, Politics, War)

When Queen Victoria died in 1901, Britain had changed profoundly. She died an empress, when she had come to a throne that ruled a collection of colonial possessions. The Empire was enormous and very powerful, yet it was clear that such a large and far-flung network, while generating many millions of pounds in trade, was difficult to maintain, and was bringing Britain into conflict with other European states. Having started the century at war with France, Britain now considered France, along with Russia, a tentative ally against Austria-Hungary and Germany: an alliance that would be tragically tested in little more than a decade.

The physical appearance of the nation had transformed, it was now characterized by large urban areas and spreading suburbs. The countryside, despite terrible conditions of poverty, had become romanticized in the popular imagination as embodying a real, traditional England. Movements to record and revive folk customs, music and dance indicate the nostalgia for what was imagined to be slower, shared and ordered social life contrasting with the speed and materialism of atomized modern society. It was a divided society, where class divisions had hardened, and the education and better conditions of the working classes had produced a distinct separation between high and low culture. The working class had become more politically active and in 1900 the forerunner of modern Labour Party, the Labour

Representation Committee was formed, and was to become a critical force in twentieth-century politics.

Science and technology had altered everyday life. The scientific world-view was embedded in popular consciousness, and even though the Church remained strong there were many more varieties of religious (and non-religious) belief. The scientific disciplines that had emerged during the course of the century were to continue to have profound effects on society, very obviously in the physical sciences, but increasingly too in the social sciences like psychology, which some have argued is *the* science of the twentieth century. Technology was no longer most obvious in the world of industry, but in people's homes where some already had electric light and telephones.

The flags that lowered to half-mast in January 1901 marked the end of Victoria's life and the end of a tumultuous century, but certainly not the end of its legacy in the modern world.

3 Literary and Cultural Contexts

Kirsty Bunting and Rhian Williams (eds)

Chapter Overview

Figures

Matthew Arnold (1822–88)
Major works: *The Strayed Reveller and Other Poems* (1849), *Empedocles on Etna, and Other Poems* (1852), 'The Scholar Gipsy' (1853), 'Stanzas from the Grande Chartreuse' (1855), 'Dover Beach'(1867), *Essays in Criticism* (first series 1865, second series 1888), *Culture and Anarchy* (1869).

Son of Thomas Arnold, the reforming headmaster of Rugby School, Matthew Arnold also spent many years in education, serving for 35 years as an inspector of schools and later as Professor of Poetry at Oxford. He believed strongly in the need for educational reform, and these beliefs, although detectable in his poetry, are most strongly evident in his later critical writing. His poetry received relatively little attention and mixed reviews during his lifetime, although now poems like 'Dover Beach' are much better regarded and frequently studied. Arnold is better known for his works of literary and social criticism, which are seen as having had a profound influence on the development of English studies in the twentieth century. He argued that the study of poetry should consist of objective close reading, and that the arbitration of its worth should rest on its ability to express 'high truth' and 'high seriousness'. Seriousness is the keynote of his thought; he was an agnostic but respected any committed engagement with religious questions. *Culture and Anarchy* is the major expression of his belief in the crucial importance of culture, which he defined as 'the best that has been thought and said'. He believed its role to be the provision of common standards of moral value in the dangerous vacuum left by the decline of religious belief, a vacuum that he saw increasingly occupied by the 'Philistine' and 'Barbaric' low culture of the middle and working classes.

Alexandra Warwick

Elizabeth Barrett Browning (1806–61)
Major works: *Poems* (1844), *Sonnets from the Portuguese* (1850), *Casa Guidi Windows* (1851), *Aurora Leigh* (1856).
See also: *Robert Browning.*

Viewing the extant literary tradition, Elizabeth Barrett Browning (EBB) bemoaned 'I look everywhere for Grandmothers and find none', yet her poetry is in constant engagement with tradition as it is forged by both inspirational men and innovative women. Invalided for much of her life, books were a life-line. Especially celebrated for her pioneering 'discourse of the feminine', EBB worked to extend the influence of the 'Poetess' (a figure explicitly drawn in response to Madame de Staël's Corinne) into the social and political sphere: 'The Cry of the Children' (*Poems*, 1844) is an impassioned and emotional form of political radicalism. Later, writing from her Florentine home (having eloped with Robert Browning in 1846), EBB's intense personal identification with Italy informed her experiments with poetic reportage: *Casa Guidi Windows* provides an eyewitness account of political upheaval during the Italian Risorgimento. Her most ambitious project was *Aurora Leigh*, a narrative poem of monumental length. Somewhere between autobiographical epic and social-realist novel, it stages literary revolution through daring generic experiment (disrupting patriarchal rhetoric would be to disrupt patriarchal politics). As it charts the development of the woman-as-poet, it forms the culmination of EBB's tireless desire to establish an aesthetic in which women are producers of meaning, rather than mirrors for male reflections. Claiming this as a passionate aesthetic, her poetry moves between melancholic lament and burning feeling; EBB wrote startlingly and erotically of married love. Refuting her famous statement, EBB's legacy has been the recovery of women's writing more broadly; indeed, stirring feminist debate continues in her name, perhaps fulfilling her ambition to 'rush into drawing rooms . . . and speak the truth as I conceive of it'.

Rhian Williams

The Brontës
Charlotte (1816–55), Emily (1818–48), Anne (1820–49)
Major works
All: *Poems* (1846); Charlotte: *Jane Eyre* (1847), *Shirley* (1849), *Villette* (1853), *The Professor* (1857); Emily: *Wuthering Heights* (1847); Anne: *Agnes Grey* (1847), *The Tenant of Wildfell Hall* (1848).
See also: Gothic, Education, Religion and the Church.

Despite a relatively small literary output, the impact of the Brontës' work has been phenomenal. *Jane Eyre* and *Wuthering Heights* were included in the canon long before the explosion of critical interest in women's writing, and since the emergence of feminist criticism in the 1970s, the entire Brontë output has been subject to close scrutiny. Particularly notable for their portrayals of human passions and desires and their evocation of landscape, the extent of the Brontës' influence is indicated by the number of rewritings and film and stage adaptations which continue to appear. Three very different writers, Emily's work is marked by its emotional intensity and Anne's, particularly in *The Tenant of Wildfell Hall*, by a feminism that seems almost radical for its time, while Charlotte's engagement with the woman question is significantly more conservative. However, it is not just for their exploration of the role of women that the Brontës continue to attract immense interest: the psychological nature of their work, and their portrayals of complex, three-dimensional characters – both male and female – persist in fascinating critics. Their male leads (Rochester and Heathcliff in particular) have become ingrained in the public imagination as the epitome of the romantic hero, yet they are multifaceted, often villainous, characters. Over 150 years after their deaths, the impact of these three women from the small village of Haworth in West Yorkshire continues to resonate.

Jessica Cox

Robert Browning (1812–89)
Major works: *Sordello* (1840), *Men and Women* (1855), *Dramatis Personae* (1864), *The Ring and the Book* (1868–9), *Asolando* (1889).
See also: Elizabeth Barrett Browning.

Critics attempting to capture the essence of Robert Browning's poetry have often reached for the word 'grotesque' to describe it. He has a fascination with the extreme and the sordid – what his own Bishop Blougram calls 'the dangerous edge of things' – and expresses this fascination in argumentative, angular and syntactically complex verse. Although he produced work in a variety of genres, from stage plays to the notoriously impenetrable medieval epic *Sordello* (1840), he is best known for the dramatic monologue, a form of poetry in which a fictionalized speaker addresses a (usually silent) interlocutor within a clearly defined dramatic context. Monologues like 'My Last Duchess' (1842) and 'Andrea del Sarto' (1855) blend psychological insight, narrative drive and lyric intensity to produce memorable studies of individuals at decisive moments of their lives. In *The Ring and the Book* (1868–9) – based, typically, on the records of a squalid and long-forgotten Roman murder story – a series of interlocking dramatic monologues is used to study the event in question from competing social, psychological and moral points of view. This 12-book epic was regarded by Browning's contemporaries as his masterpiece, and helped to secure his reputation as one of the greatest poets of his age.

Joseph Phelan

Joseph Conrad (1857–1924)
Major works: *Heart of Darkness* (1899), *Lord Jim* (1899–1900), *Nostromo* (1904), *The Secret Agent* (1907), *Under Western Eyes* (1911).

When Józef Teodor Konrad Korzeniowski began writing fiction in the 1890s under the pen name 'Joseph Conrad', he served notice of a new cosmopolitan sensibility in late Victorian literature. Conditioned by childhood exile in northern Russia and spells in the French and British merchant services (the son of Polish patriots, he was born a Russian subject in a Ukranian province of Tsarist-ruled Poland), Conrad's artistic vision is both more expansively global and more fiercely introspective than the provincial realism that dominated nineteenth-century fiction. Key early works such as *Almayer's Folly*, *Heart of Darkness* and *Lord Jim* chart the disastrous misadventures of European expatriates in 'exotic' outposts of empire, providing ironic revisions of the adventure tradition of Haggard and Stevenson. Foreshadowing the modernism of Joyce and Woolf, Conrad also gets the reader on unsettlingly intimate terms with the fragile mental worlds of his protagonists: these angst-ridden voyagers, deluded underachievers and self-destructive megalomaniacs are the focus of a series of devastating case studies of masculine subjectivity in extremis. The violent collision between tradition and modernity is also registered in his fictional techniques, especially when narrative authority is delegated to an ingratiatingly talkative raconteur (most famously Marlow in *Heart of Darkness*, and *Lord Jim*), an old-fashioned storyteller who personifies Conrad's characteristically modernist obsession with the spellbinding power and suspiciously tantalizing limitations of language.

Michael Greaney

Charles Dickens (1812–70)
Major works: novels (including *David Copperfield* (1849–50), *Bleak House* (1852–3) and *Great Expectations* (1860–1)); short fiction and sketches; children's literature; journalism; letters; travel writing; editorial.
See also: Sensation Fiction, The Periodical Press, The Great Exhibition, Education, The City.

Best known for 14 (and a half) much-adapted novels, Dickens was also a master of shorter fiction and journalism as well as a skilled editor of his periodicals *Household Words* (1850–9) and *All the Year Round* (1859–93), projects through which he invigorated serial publication. Though broadly considered a realist novelist, he expressed his enthusiasm for social reform (of, for example, the New Poor Law in *Oliver Twist* (1837–8)) in hybrid form, through often experimental genres including historical fiction, gothic, melodrama, sensation and the ghost story. A pioneer also of the literary detective (Nadgett in *Martin Chuzzlewit* (1843–4) and Bucket in *Bleak House* (1852–3)), Dickens adapted the Newgate novel to explore the more widespread horrors of poverty, dire sanitation and overcrowding in his contemporary London. Now a lucrative Dickens heritage industry (set in motion by the man himself, with his public readings, energetic control of literary copyright and masterly management of his celebrity image) positions Dickens as a figurehead of English cultural identity, balancing the 'darker' Dickens with the apparent conviviality of his Christmas books and domestic scenes.

The nationalizing of Dickens and overstatement of his domestic idealism (in spite of his own chequered family life) has resulted in a somewhat conservative critical heritage that broadly positions him as bourgeois, heterosexist, patriarchal and, above all, respectable. New recognition of the extent of Dickens's political radicalism is complemented by recent attention to the nuances of gender and sexuality in a corpus as wide-ranging in character and theme as in form. This has complicated the orthodoxy of Dickens as mouthpiece for exclusively middle-class values, displaced the unhelpful angel/ shrew model of Dickens's women, recognized the spaces available for more multiple masculinities and erotics and begun to explore the surprising plethora of alternative 'family' groupings. Such re-visions continue to dismantle the false synonymy of Dickens/Victorian/old-fashioned, demonstrating the continuing importance of Dickens to an understanding of both his society and our own.

Holly Furneaux

George Eliot (Mary Anne, later Marion, Evans) (1819–80)
Major works: *Translation of Feuerbach's Essence of Christianity* (1854), *Scenes of Clerical Life* (1858), *Adam Bede* (1859), *The Mill on the Floss* (1860), *Silas Marner* (1861), *Romola* (1863), *Felix Holt the Radical* (1866), *Middlemarch* (1871–2), *Daniel Deronda* (1876), *The Impressions of Theophrastus Such* (1874).
See also: *Education, The Rural, The Periodical Press.*

In an age in which many gifted female novelists came to prominence, George Eliot's significant achievements mark her out as particularly pre-eminent. The author of many of the key works of Victorian fiction, Eliot is rightly seen as one of the great English novelists. Her brother–sister novel *The Mill on the Floss* still divides critics into those who see its rural setting as skilful portrayal and others who feel the novel's end is too arbitrary. *Silas Marner* likewise has a rural location and contains moments of rustic humour beneath its exploration of solitariness and individual contentment versus the dominant modes and expectations of society. The great realist novel *Middlemarch*, concerned with 'provincial life' in its religious, economic and social forms between 1829 and 1832, allowed Eliot to explore the 'web of society' and its relationship to the fulfilment or stifling of the individual's potential (although evangelical in her youth, Eliot later described herself as agnostic). Her quasi-scientific approach in the text, examining her characters through the utilization of metaphors of a new biological discourse, means that her portrayal of the lives and choices of Dorothea, Casaubon, Lydgate and Ladislaw is fair and even-handed. Eliot's final novel, *Daniel Deronda*, marked a move away from the near historical into the contemporary while maintaining similar themes to her previous works, such as scholarship and reality, the individual and society and the morality of the Victorian age.

Mark Llewellyn

Elizabeth Gaskell (1810–65)
Key works: *Mary Barton* (1848), *Cranford* (1853), *Ruth* (1853), *North and South* (1855), *The Life of Charlotte Brontë* (1857), *Sylvia's Lovers* (1863), *Cousin Phyllis* (1864), *Wives and Daughters* (1866).
See also: *Charlotte Brontë, Charles Dickens, The Condition of England Novel, Religion and the Church.*

Elizabeth Gaskell first came to prominence with the early instalments, published in Dickens's journal *Household Words*, of her Manchester-based industrial novel *Mary Barton: A Tale of Manchester Life*. Although criticized in Tory-leaning reviews for her sympathetic portrayal of the industrial, urban working classes, Gaskell's powerful depiction of urban life among Manchester's varied population brought her many admirers. Her reputation as a leading commentator on the Victorian social world was enhanced by the publication of *North and South,* perhaps the greatest condition of England novel of the mid-Victorian period. Once again set in Manchester, *North and South* sets a female protagonist from the rural and genteel south against (and alongside) two very different men: a self-improving, northern middle-class mill-owner and a politically active, poverty-stricken factory worker. While Gaskell handles very well the complexities of class difference within the chaotic and ever-changing world of urban Manchester, modern critical opinion views her own middle-class position as ultimately dominant over the novel's structure and plot. Equally Gaskell's faith – she was a practising Christian and was married to a Unitarian minister – played a part in her fictional representation of the responsible role of the middle-class woman faced by urban poverty. Besides her novels of Manchester life, Gaskell also wrote of the lives of women, particularly rural women. After *Mary Barton* she did so in *Cranford* and similarly, after *North and South,* she returned to the countryside in her last novel, *Wives and Daughters.* Gaskell's other great achievement was her biography of Charlotte Brontë. Regarded on publication as a masterful portrayal of a life, it still receives the same critical acclaim today.

Martin Willis

Thomas Hardy (1840–1928)
Major works: *Far From the Madding Crowd* (1874), *The Return of the Native* (1878), *The Mayor of Casterbridge* (1886), *Tess of the D'Urbervilles* (1891), *Jude the Obscure* (1895), *Wessex Poems* (1898), *Time's Laughingstocks* (1909), *Late Lyrics and Earlier* (1912), *Human Shows, Far Phantasies, Songs and Trifles* (1925), *Winter Words* (1928).
See also: *The Rural, Wars and Conflicts.*

A prolific writer and profound thinker, Hardy produced 15 novels, a number of collections of short stories and over a thousand poems during his life. A biography, published posthumously under his second wife's name, is now also recognized as being his own work. The ideas and attitudes displayed in Hardy's work are the results of a mind constantly striving towards a better understanding of human relations and the human condition. Contradictions and volte-faces therefore form an intrinsic part of his work. During his career as a writer he experimented with plot, character, genre and style. Themes that recur throughout his work include beautiful and detailed descriptions of the natural world and a consideration of the tension between the 'natural' and the 'civilized' worlds. Not a religious man, he also considered the role of fate or chance in human existence, often leaving the reader with a bleak view of the fate of the individual. He was an astute social commentator; several of his novels deal with issues such as sex outside marriage and the injustices of the class system, most notably *Tess of the D'Urbervilles* and *Jude the Obscure*, which excited public debate and derision. His first wife Emma died suddenly in 1912, inspiring Hardy to write what are generally considered to be some of his finest poems. Hardy's influence on literature is significant and ongoing; he broke new ground in terms of form, style and content and his treatment of both humanity and nature inspired many modernist writers of the early twentieth century.

Jessica Pearce

Gerard Manley Hopkins (1844–89)
Major works: 'The Wreck of the Deutschland' (1875), 'St Beuno' sonnets (1877), 'The Sonnets of Desolation' (1885–6), *Poems of Gerard Manley Hopkins* (1918). *See also: Religion and the Church.*

Hopkins's poems appeared only posthumously, edited by his friend, Robert Bridges. Hopkins's was an extraordinary talent; his idiosyncratic approach to rhythm, rhyme and syntax (influenced by his passion for Welsh poetry) shaped his proficiency at 'sprung rhythm' (described in his self-penned 'Author's Preface'). Raised a High Anglican, association with Cardinal John Henry Newman eventually directed his conversion to Rome: he became a Jesuit priest and his poetry is celebrated for its complex enunciation of faithful devotion. Sonnets written at St Beuno's express thrill and awe in apprehending God's majesty in nature, realizing notions of inscape and instress (respectively Hopkins's word for the unique quality of a thing, and for the sensation of energy which sustains it) as each element 'finds tongue to fling out broad its name'. His attraction to male beauty is also considered to inform his Christian aesthetics. His most ambitious piece 'The Wreck' – written in response to the drowning of five Franciscan nuns – is a daring synthesis of tested faith and radical poetics. A difficult period in 1885 (while Professor of Greek literature in Dublin) nevertheless gave rise to a brilliant collection of sonnets that confront the very depths of despair. Hopkins's voice resonates with the complexities of Victorian faith and expresses them with startling poetic experimentalism.

Rhian Williams

Rudyard Kipling (1865–1936)
Major works: *Plain Tales from the Hills* (1888), *The Light That Failed* (1890), *Life's Handicap* (1891), *Barrack-Room Ballads* (1892), *The Jungle Book* (1894), *Kim* (1901), *Just So Stories* (1902), *Puck of Pook's Hill* (1906).

Born in India, Kipling returned to Britain for his education, then spent three years in India working as a journalist before living for a while in the USA. When he returned to live in Britain again, he still made regular and extended visits to South Africa. His connections with the two most important sites of

British imperialism mark both his writing and his reputation, and make him a difficult figure in British literary history. He was a very prolific writer in a range of forms including non-fiction, poetry, short stories and children's fiction. In the Victorian period he was extremely popular: his poem 'Recessional' written for the Queen's Diamond Jubilee in 1897 exemplifies his position and attitude as the poet of Empire. His use of simple and striking versification, ballad forms and colloquial speech made him especially popular with ordinary readers, but the literary elite, many of whom (like Henry James) were personal friends, did not regard his work highly. Increasingly in the twentieth century he came to be regarded as the representative of a conservative and jingoistic imperialism that was no longer the dominant tone, and the development of postcolonial critical perspectives in the later twentieth century meant that, although his work continued to be studied, it was often the subject of negative readings. Although this view can certainly be sustained in reading some of his work, he remains an important figure in the consideration of the representations of Empire, and there has also been a more appreciative re-evaluation of Kipling's technique as a writer, particularly in his short stories.

Alexandra Warwick

Christina Rossetti (1830–94)
Major works: *Goblin Market and Other Poems* (1862), *A Pageant and other Poems* (1881), *The Face of the Deep* (1892).
See also: Religion and the Church, Children's Literature.

Rossetti's first volume of poetry, *Goblin Market*, like *The Prince's Progress and Other Poems* (1874) and *A Pageant*, includes a section of secular poetry followed by a section of devotional poetry (Rossetti was a High Anglican). In all three volumes, Rossetti experiments with the sonnet form, lyric verse and long narrative poetry. Thematically, she tackles controversial issues such as illegitimacy and fallen women. Her two other volumes of poetry include *Sing Song: A Nursery Rhyme Book* (1872) and *Verses* (1893), both of which are equally innovative and diverse in their poetics and subject matter. Although Rossetti derived inspiration from Dante, Herbert, Milton and Spenser, her engagement with contemporary concerns indicates that her poetry was unquestionably a product of its time.

Later in life, after suffering from profound ill-health, Rossetti published six books of devotional prose and a number of short stories. Despite being immensely popular towards the end of the nineteenth century, her devotional prose books have been largely neglected by critical scholarship following the rise of modernism. Their literary and theological significance and their central place in the literature of the Oxford Movement is only now beginning to be recognized. Underlying each book is an emphasis on the importance of focusing on God in order to find meaning in a cold and indifferent universe consumed by 'vanities'.

Elizabeth Ludlow

George Bernard Shaw (1856–1950)

Major works: *Widowers' Houses* (1892), *Arms and the Man* (1894), *Mrs Warren's Profession* (1898), *Man and Superman* (1903), *Major Barbara* (1905), *Pygmalion* (1913), *Saint Joan* (1923).

Shaw was born in Dublin, where he lived for 20 years before moving to London and beginning his literary career. He retained a strong sense of his Irishness, a quality he shared with his contemporary and fellow Dubliner Oscar Wilde. Both men were playwrights, socialists and supporters of women's rights, and their outsider status in English literary life arguably contributes to their ability to write comically and satirically on the society of which they were not quite a part. Shaw was an incredibly prolific author, writing over 60 plays, millions of words of journalism, essays and reviews and more than 250,000 letters. Throughout his long life he was also an energetic public speaker and campaigner for a number of radical causes. He was an early champion of Henrik Ibsen, whose work he saw as the kind of dramatic engagement with social and moral issues that nineteenth-century British theatre lacked. He emulated such engagement in his own plays, taking on topics such as slum landlords in *Widowers' Houses*, prostitution, the New Woman and male hypocrisy in *Mrs Warren's Profession* and military profiteering in *Arms and the Man*. His treatment of these issues was often controversial: *Mrs Warren's Profession* was banned from public performance, leading Shaw to engage in a passionate campaign against censorship. His output was uneven in quality and, although its wit has always been applauded, his political commitment and use of his plays as vehicles for the exploration of political issues has sometimes been seen as detrimental to their literary and dramatic effects.

Alexandra Warwick

Algernon Charles Swinburne (1837–1909)

Major Works: *Atalanta in Calydon* (1865), *Poems and Ballads* (1866), *William Blake* (1868), *Songs before Sunrise* (1871), *Essays and Studies* (1875), *Poems and Ballads, Second Series* (1878), *William Shakespeare* (1880), *Tristram of Lyonnesse and Other Poems* (1882), *Songs of the Springtides* (1880), *Victor Hugo* (1886), *Ben Jonson* (1889), *Poems* (1904), *Tragedies* (1905).
See also: Aestheticism, Decadence, Oscar Wilde.

Aristocratic by class, Swinburne nevertheless rebelled against Victorian proprieties (originally a High Anglican, he turned to anti-theism and was a free thinker). He lived in the 1860s a life sodden with dissipation, his poetry fiercely anti-theistic and provocative in alternate sexualities and, in *Songs before Sunrise*, politics. Among the avant-garde in admiring Walt Whitman, Percy Bysshe Shelley and Charles Baudelaire (he wrote the first *English Review*, 1862), he championed literature, including ballads, outside the canon. In his later criticism he celebrated not only Shakespeare but the lesser Elizabethan and the Jacobean dramatists. His elegy on Baudelaire, 'Ave atque Vale', is a sobering antidote to Tennyson's *In Memoriam*. His study of Blake was seminal in articulating the grounds of 'art for art's sake', preparing the way for Walter Pater, Oscar Wilde, aestheticism, decadence and modernism. His radicalism moderated with time, but his early exuberant sympathies and the intoxication of his complexly musical poetry attracted the young and repelled the establishment. Tennyson thought Swinburne's works would ignite 'the fiercest battle the world has yet known between good and evil, faith and unfaith'; Swinburne was famously denounced for being, with D. G. Rossetti, of 'the Fleshly School of Poetry'. Immersed in classical and continental literature, Swinburne expanded both the subject matter and verse forms of English poetry.

Terry L. Meyers

Alfred (Lord) Tennyson (1809–92)

Major works: *Poems, Chiefly Lyrical* (1830), *Poems* (1832), *Poems* (1842), *In Memoriam* (1850), 'Ode on the Death of the Duke of Wellington' (1851), 'The Charge of the Light Brigade' (1854), *Maud, and Other Poems* (1855), *Idylls of the King* (1859, expanded periodically until 1874).
See also: Wars and Conflicts.

Tennyson's domination of Victorian poetry was secured by his appointment as Poet Laureate in 1850. This appointment produced a reputation for entrenched conservatism, yet his poetry is arrestingly ambivalent. Variously angry, melancholic, despairing, jingoistic, erotic, sensuous or sensational, and (contra-twentieth-century accusations of sentimentalism) complexly political, Tennyson and his poetry are now examined as a dynamic interface between the public and private self, where an energetic and unsettling critique of the supposed monolith of 'Victorian culture' is found. His greatest (and the century's greatest) commercial poetic success was, paradoxically, the often seemingly private, and deeply loving, *In Memoriam* – an elegy in memory of his young friend and early champion, Arthur Hallam. Its success was mainly due to the work's preoccupation with providence, purpose, journey and consolation, which intimated a broader social, cultural and religious sense of loss underpinning Victorian progress. Early lyrics (often named for women – 'Mariana', 'The Lady of Shalott' – indicating a complex perspective on gender that persists in his work) set a personal tone, but individual voice comes under pressured scrutiny in Tennyson's oeuvre, which moved energetically between expressive and performative genres. Indeed, even the potential nostalgia of his celebrated medieval revivalism (see the Idylls), proves a framework for interrogating the cultural tenets that hold up the Victorian present. Rightly recognized for technical prowess and beguiling cadence, Tennyson's poetry may suggest that sound is more important than sense, yet, with an ear sharply tuned to the nuances of rhetoric and accent, Tennyson's poetry is both overtly (see his late poems on Irish Home Rule) and covertly engaged by the politics of aesthetics, which characterizes the most energetic Victorian writing.

Rhian Williams

William Makepeace Thackeray (1811–63)
Major works: *Vanity Fair* (1848), *The History of Pendennis* (1850), *The History of Henry Esmond* (1852), *The Newcomes* (1855), *The Virginians* (1862).
See also: Charles Dickens.

Born in India and educated (partially) in England, Thackeray enjoyed a dissolute lifestyle in his early adult years, working his way through a sizeable inheritance in the process. He turned to writing in an attempt to regain the financial position he had lost by the 1840s. His first novel, *Vanity Fair*, published serially in 20 parts from January 1847 to July 1848, remains his most critically acclaimed work. Its focus is the manifold vanities of his contemporaries; the novel's satire is directed at the selfishness and corruption borne out of the Victorians' pride in the superior moral and social circumstances they had created for themselves. Above all else, the novel gives us one of the most enduring female characters in Victorian fiction, Becky Sharp. Born without the advantages of wealth or social position, Becky Sharp's active and keen intelligence, as well as her flexible morality, allows her to gain access to the upper echelons of society. For readers and critics alike Becky Sharp represents both the attractive anti-hero (like *Wuthering Heights'* Heathcliff) and the stereotypical Victorian villainess (comparable to Mary Elizabeth Braddon's Lady Audley). *Vanity Fair* was lauded by critics, including Thackeray's fellow novelists, but was also condemned for its vicious and uncompromising portrayal of the perceived failings of Victorian society. The novel made Thackeray one of the most popular of the mid-Victorian novelists and throughout the late 1840s and 1850s he rivalled Dickens in critical, if not quite in general, popularity. The most important of his novels that followed *Vanity Fair* are more clearly autobiographical in origin. *The History of Pendennis*, which ran alongside *David Copperfield* from 1849 to 1850 is, like Dickens's novel, a semi-autobiographical fiction of the title character. Likewise, *The History of Henry Esmond* draws on moments from Thackeray's own experience but is a greater historical tour de force than any of his previous works.

Martin Willis

Anthony Trollope (1815–82)
Major works: 'The Barsetshire Chronicles' including *The Warden* (1855), *Barchester Towers* (1857), *The Small House at Allington* (1864), *The Last Chronicle of Barset* (1867), the 'Palliser' novels including *Can You Forgive Her?* (1864), *The Eustace Diamonds* (1873), *The Prime Minister* (1876). Also: *The Way We Live Now* (1875).

Trollope began writing while employed at the Post Office, where he rose to become a senior civil servant and numbered the introduction of the red pillar box among his achievements. He had already completed his first series of novels, 'The Barsetshire Chronicles' before he left the Post Office in 1867, at which time he stood unsuccessfully as a Liberal candidate for parliament. His involvement in the business of politics and the civil service is used to fictional effect in his novels, which are often set directly in the Westminster political world or in the shifting contests of power in provincial society and institutions. His work is concerned with the human element of political and social life, and concentrates on the presentation and exploration of character: indeed he wrote in his autobiography that the author should live completely with his characters, that they should be with him 'as he lies down to sleep, and as he wakes from dreams'. This intense involvement with character and his interest in developing them over long periods of fictional time led to his establishment of the novel sequence in the Barsetshire and Palliser series, where figures appear and reappear throughout. It also contributed to his immense popularity in the 1860s and 1870s: readers admired his depictions of social life. At the same time, it was a reason for his relatively low critical esteem: his regular writing schedule was seen as mundane and mechanical rather than truly creative. It still remains interesting, however, in its extensive detailing of personal and political interaction and the minutiae of class and social distinction.

Alexandra Warwick

Herbert George Wells (1866–1946)
Major works: *The Time Machine* (1895), *The Island of Doctor Moreau* (1896), *The Invisible Man* (1897), *The War of the Worlds* (1898), *When The Sleeper Wakes* (1899), *Love and Mr. Lewisham* (1900), *The First Men in the Moon* (1901).
See also: Evolution; Science and Science Fiction.

Only a proportion of H. G. Wells's novels are strictly Victorian: the self-styled 'Scientific Romances' (comprising his first four novels) that he completed between 1895 and 1898, his novel of the future, *When The Sleeper Wakes*, his realist novel, *Love and Mr Lewisham* and another science fiction narrative, *The First Men in the Moon*. Unsurprisingly, it is for his science fiction that Wells is

57

best known; indeed Wells is often regarded as one of the originators of the genre of science fiction, and while this can be contested when we consider him as a Victorian writer, it is certainly the case that Wells was innovative within the genre and enormously influential on science fiction writers in the twentieth century. In his scientific romances Wells is predominantly concerned with explorations of biology, physics and scientific technologies. Unlike George Eliot, for example, who draws implicitly on emerging scientific theory in realizing an entire fictional world, Wells explicitly engages with science in its various forms. *The Time Machine* investigates the social implications of Darwin's evolutionary theory, as well as the new physical examinations of the solar system of James Clerk Maxwell. In *The Island of Doctor Moreau* (which immediately followed *The Time Machine*) Wells continues to develop his imaginative understanding of evolution, while also considering the moral and philosophical implications of animal experimentation. *The War of the Worlds*, the concluding scientific romance, once again engages with the human costs of evolution, this time on a universal scale and with an alien civilization, the Martians. Although *When The Sleeper Wakes* and *The First Men in the Moon* can, to some extent, be regarded as a continuation of Wells's science fiction these two novels are also late Victorian examples of the utopian novel, a genre made popular by Edward Bulwer-Lytton's *The Coming Race* (1871) and further developed by William Morris's *News from Nowhere* (1890).

Martin Willis

Oscar Wilde (1854–1900)
Major works: *Poems* (1881, 1892), *The Picture of Dorian Gray* (1890–1), *The Importance of Being Earnest* (1895, 1899), *The Ballad of Reading Gaol* (1898), *De Profundis* (1905).
See also: Aestheticism, Decadence, Gothic, The Victorian Stage, Algernon Charles Swinburne.

Wilde's work is characterized by a witty epigrammatic style (at its best in the dazzling dialogue of *The Importance of Being Earnest*), unresolved paradoxes and generic diversity. His oeuvre, which includes journalism, criticism, short stories, plays, poetry and a novel, demonstrates the aesthetic influence of Walter Pater (Wilde was a prominent exponent of the theory of 'art for art's sake'), an interest in socialism and individualism and a sympathy with the notion of an idealized love between men. Although his work was criticized by his contemporaries for immorality and frivolity, Wilde often explores complex moral issues, most notably in *The Picture of Dorian Gray*, and his society comedies combine flippant humour with serious social comment. A number of his texts are highly topical, demonstrating an awareness of current affairs and the interests of his reading public, yet the proliferation of coded references and the small, expensive print runs of, for example, *Poems* (1892), suggest that much of his writing was produced for a coterie. Wilde's work challenges conventions, exploring social boundaries and exposing hypocrisy and vice, while simultaneously celebrating the appeal of the social transgressor. His voice, which is often one of defiance in the face of Victorian conventionality, has become almost synonymous with the decadence and aestheticism of the 1890s.

Lizzie White

Genres, Movements and Contexts

Aestheticism

Representative figures: James McNeil Whister, Oscar Wilde, John Ruskin, Walter Pater, Matthew Arnold, Vernon Lee (pseud. Violet Paget).
See also: Decadence, Religion and the Church, Oscar Wilde, Algernon Charles Swinburne.

Aestheticism was a literary and artistic movement flourishing in England in the 1880s and 1890s associated in particular with figures such as artist James McNeil Whistler, Oscar Wilde, John Ruskin and Walter Pater. Aestheticism falls into two camps: those who believed in 'art for art's sake' (closely associated with decadence), and those who believe in art's moral or social purpose, such as Matthew Arnold. Both groups' chief concern, however, was the appreciation of beauty. Ruskin, English art and social critic, interrogated the relation of science to beauty particularly in his *Modern Painters* series (five volumes, 1843–60). Ruskin claimed that appreciating beauty and reaching an understanding of the essence of the world which surrounds us was only possible when the observer suppressed the ego and assumed an 'innocent', unanalytical and unscientific gaze. In doing so the observer can apprehend not only the physical beauty and perfection of form (what he terms Vital Beauty) in the art work or natural world, but is also able to feel the moralizing and improving effect of making the connection between God's presence within that object (the object's Typical Beauty) with the perception of the beautiful. Pater, countering Ruskin's aesthetic theories, wrote in his *Studies in the History of the Renaissance* (1873) that only persons of a sensitive and receptive nature can hope to perceive beauty fully and accurately, and therefore art cannot have a moralizing effect upon the masses. Pater's main concern is capturing and maintaining the fleeting moments of pleasure that the perception of the beautiful affords; God is absent from his theories, in line with much aesthetic thinking. His novel *Marius the Epicurean* (1885) explores the aesthetic theories of his earlier career, before he attempted to distance himself from accusation of incitement of his young disciples to hedonism.

Vernon Lee is recognized as the principal female aesthete of the nineteenth century. A disciple of Pater, she developed his notion of the vivifying nature of art appreciation, in line with European physiological aesthetics, to include the vitalizing effect upon the body and mind under the influence of visual stimuli. For Lee, positive and involuntary physical responses to art were necessary in order to recognize the beauty of the subject of the gaze. Lee attacked the morally degenerate and more decadent aspects of aestheticism in her novel *Miss Brown* (1884). Pater, Lee, Wilde and many other aesthetes' works looked to the Italian Renaissance as the first moment in European culture in which art, imagination and the beautiful were free from the restrictions of religion and moralizing didacticism.

Kirsty Bunting

Chartism

Representative figures: Feargus O'Connor, owner of the *Northern Star* newspaper and Chartism's most influential leader from 1838 to 1848; George Julian Harney, founder of the East London Democratic Association (1837), editor of the *Northern Star* (1844–50) and *Democratic Review* (1849/50) and *Red Republican* (1850); Bronterre O'Brien, radical journalist and political theorist, William Lovett, secretary of the London Working Men's Association; John Frost, leader (with Zephaniah Williams and William Jones) of the failed Newport rising; Thomas Cooper, author of 1842 poem, *The Purgatory of Suicides* (1845); Ernest Jones, Chartist poet, Gerald Massey, Chartist poet.
See also: Politics, The Periodical Press, The Rural, The City.

From 1848 onwards, Chartism became increasingly influenced by European republican and socialist ideas, many of which were formally incorporated into a new Chartist programme in 1851. Chartism embodies the working-class response to the economic and social changes wrought by industrial capitalism. It harnessed and synthesized the organizational and ideological forces created by the 'factory movement', the campaign against the New Poor Law and the 'great betrayal' of the 1832 Reform Act. Although Chartism never achieved its political aims, its social and cultural impact was immense. Between 1838 and 1852 its political and ideological presence prevented the consolidation of bourgeois hegemony. The three main Chartist mobilizations (1839, 1842, 1848) were sufficiently alarming to the government to be met by forcible repression. Chartism also haunted the middle-class imagination as evidenced by the 'condition of England' novels of the 1840s and 1850s. In addition to causing consternation among the ruling classes, Chartism also gave hope to many for whom it represented an entire culture (encompassing cooperation, education and mutual improvement) as well as a programme and an organization.

Chartism was an extremely literate movement. At local, regional and national level its leaders were frequently poets, some of whom (most notably

Thomas Cooper, Ernest Jones and Gerald Massey) enjoyed a literary reputation beyond the Chartist movement. Chartism's leading newspaper, the *Northern Star* (peak circulation was 50,000 copies), contained a regular poetry column which published over 1,400 pieces between 1838 and 1852. A similar commitment to poetry is found in many other Chartist newspapers. While poetry was the dominant literary genre, fiction became an increasingly important aspect of Chartism's literary activities. T. M. Wheeler's Chartist novel, *Sunshine and Shadow* (1849/50), was serialized in the *Northern Star*. Jones also turned to fiction in the 1850s, most notably with *De Brassier* (1851) and *Woman's Wrongs* (1852). In addition, Chartism contributed to the development of radical and popular journalism.

Michael Sanders

Children's Literature
Representative figures: Edward Lear, Lewis Carroll, Christina Rossetti, Jean Ingelow, George MacDonald, Robert Louis Stevenson.
See also: Christina Rossetti.

Major distribution outlets for children's literature included The Religious Tract Society (RTS), The Society for Promoting Christian Knowledge (SPCK), Sunday schools, 'ragged schools', larger publishing houses, magazines and compendiums.

Of the many themes within children's literature, religious and moral instruction, fantasy and gender issues are three that recur throughout the era. The early years were dominated by religious and moral tracts made available through mass production.

Respected organizations like the RTS distributed books that emphasized strict religious observance for both rich and poor and promoted middle-class ideology. Writers like Sherwood were instrumental in achieving huge sales of religious tracts that were seen as the antidote to the questionable morality of popular literature. Yet there was also a mixed market where instructional texts sold alongside the newly translated and entertaining folk/fairy tales of the Grimms (1823) and Andersen (1846), exotic fantasies like *Tales of the Arabian Nights* (1839–41) and Edward Lear's *Book of Nonsense* (1846). After 1850 there was a noticeable change in the way literature was presented to children and social comment became a more prominent feature. Child characters now had a new, authoritative voice and the child reader was no longer considered inferior. When Lewis Carroll's *Alice's Adventures in Wonderland* (1865) appeared, it was seen as the turning point from dull to exciting. Charles Kingsley's *The Water Babies* (1863) highlighted the plight of boy chimney sweeps and Christina Rossetti, Jean Ingelow and George MacDonald continually challenged social injustice. The years after the 1870 Education Act saw an improvement in reading skills as well as the development of separate (gendered) stories for boys and girls. Robert Louis Stevenson's *Treasure Island* (1883) endorsed a world of manly adventure and the *Boys' Own Paper* (RTS 1879) reinforced public school values and healthy adventuring whereas the *Girls' Own Paper* (1880–1907) bridged the gap between traditional, domestic ideology and the ambitions of the New Girl/Woman.

Linda Claridge-Middup

The City
Representative figures: Friedrich Engels, Elizabeth Gaskell, Henry Mayhew, Charles Dickens, Joseph Chamberlain, Charles Booth, James Thomson, Amy Levy, Thomas Carlyle.
See also: The Rural, Charles Dickens, The New Woman, Chartism, Politics.

In 1851 the Census for England and Wales offered a statistical abstract of a social change that novelists and critics had been working through for the past two decades: the population was on the move and, for the first time, those dwelling in urban areas outnumbered the inhabitants of the countryside. The Municipal Corporations Act of 1835 had acknowledged the rapid growth and increasing influence of cities in the industrial era. Yet the election of councils with responsibility for ensuring the provision of water, lighting, paving and public order seems to have done little to regulate the growth of cities such as Manchester. In 1845 the young industrialist Friedrich Engels published *The Condition of the Working Class in England* (in German), an analysis grounded on his experience of working in Manchester. Like Elizabeth Gaskell's *Mary Barton* (1848) and, to a lesser extent *North and South* (1855), Engels's study maps the geographical separation of rich and poor in industrial cities that insulated the factory-owning classes from the living conditions of their workers. Accounts of the slums and fetid cellars that formed such homes drew on James Phillips Kay's *The Moral and Physical Condition of the Working Classes of Manchester* in 1832 and shaped responses to what Thomas Carlyle termed the 'Condition of England question' over the following decade. While the Artisans' Dwellings Acts of 1868 and 1875 (Torrens and Cross Acts) empowered local authorities to force improvements on owners of slum dwellings, these came too late to mitigate the mass displacements and overcrowding caused by railway construction; a phenomenon that forms a dominant theme in Charles Dickens's *Dombey and Son* (1847–8). Over the following decades many cities developed distinct civic identities and municipal cultural provision, best exemplified by the work of Joseph Chamberlain, elected Mayor of Birmingham in 1873. Increasingly, literary representations, such as Dickens's *Bleak House* (1852–3) and *Our Mutual Friend* (1864–5), imagined the city as a complex organism of interdependent parts, influenced, perhaps, by the taxonomy of resourceful recyclers evident in Henry Mayhew's *London Labour and the London Poor* (1851). From the 1860s in London the growth of department stores, the opening of the Metropolitan Underground Railway (1863) and the consolidation of omnibus companies offered increasing freedom and mobility to middle-class women in particular: aspects of 'modern' womanhood refracted Amy Levy's *A London Plane Tree* (1889) and the work of other contemporary women poets. For the poet James Thomson ('B.V.'), however, London remained a 'City of Dreadful Night' (1880): a vision given material substance by sensationalist exposes of East End poverty like George Sims's *How the Poor Live* (1889), campaign material such as William Booth's *In Darkest England and the Way Out* (1890) and 'scientific' social investigation in the form of Charles Booth's *Life and Labour* series (1889–1902). Such works informed and were informed by the writings of British novelists influenced by literary naturalism such as George Gissing, Arthur Morrison and Margaret Harkness.

Ruth Livesey

The Condition of England Novel
Representative figures: Thomas Carlyle, Charles Dickens, Benjamin Disraeli, Elizabeth Gaskell, Charles Kingsley.
See also: Charles Dickens, Elizabeth Gaskell, Chartism, The City, The Rural.

The condition of England novel is often categorized under a number of different thematic headings, including the social problem novel, the industrial novel or the novel with a purpose. From these interlinked headings it is clear that the condition of England novel was a fictional product of industrial Britain, dedicated to both highlighting the social problems associated with industrialization and seeking for them some form of action intended to bring remedy or relief. Although the condition of England continued to interest writers throughout Victoria's long reign, it is the late 1830s, 1840s and 1850s where this theme dominated the newly emerging realist novel.

Thomas Carlyle was one of the first social commentators to write extensively about the problems associated with the second impetus of the Industrial Revolution, which led to a dramatic rise in the urban population of Britain, increasingly mechanized, dangerous and low-paid work and numerous problems arising from an overcrowded and poor populace. In 'The Condition of England Question' (1839) Carlyle highlighted the 'ominous position' of the 'condition and disposition of the Working Classes' across Britain. It was not long before Carlyle's questions found literary expression. Indeed Charles Dickens had already exposed some of the problems of urban poverty in *Oliver Twist* (1837).

However, it was Benjamin Disraeli – a member of parliament since 1837 and Prime Minister in 1868 – who directly investigated the varied conditions of

England in his three political novels, *Coningsby*, *Sybil* and *Tancred* (all written in the mid-1840s). *Sybil* is the most celebrated of the three; in it he depicts the 'Two Nations' (the phrase is the novel's subtitle) of Victorian Britain – its working classes and aristocracy. Through the title character Disraeli examines the Chartist Movement's campaign for social and economic justice for Britain's working classes. Where Disraeli considers the problems of both the rural and urban population, Elizabeth Gaskell focuses on the plight of the urban poor. Her two novels, *Mary Barton* (1848) and *North and South* (1855) detail the suffocating conditions of urban life for those living on factory wages. Gaskell's fiction is effective in portraying the economic and political disenfranchisement of the working classes at mid-century. Like Dickens and Disraeli, Gaskell's fiction has as its purpose the revealing of the plight of the working classes to a middle-class audience as well as a desire to promote an active response to the 'real' problems she articulates. Just as Charles Dickens – especially in his portrayal of the destitute child Jo in *Bleak House* – hoped that the emotional response to his fiction would be turned into positive action in the real world, so too does Gaskell aim to persuade her readership that intervention in society was not only necessary but also one's responsibility.

Other writers and novels had also struggled with the question of resolving the increasing tensions between the working classes and the wealthy. Charlotte Brontë had attempted to do so in *Shirley* (1849), as had Charles Kingsley in *Alton Locke* (1850). Charles Dickens returned to the subject himself in *Hard Times* (1855). Certain political developments, most importantly the eventual (and partial) success of Chartism in the 1850s, led to a decline in condition of England novels. Nevertheless, these novels provide a fascinating account of the social problems of Britain in the 1840s and early 1850s; not just the problems of economic and political marginalization for the working classes but also the conditions of existence for women and children, the inequalities inherent in legislation and the manifold problems associated with life in the growing Victorian cities.

Martin Willis

Crime and Detective Fiction
Representative figures: Wilkie Collins, Charles Dickens, Arthur Conan Doyle.
See also: Charles Dickens, Sensation Fiction.

Critics generally agree that crime fiction or detective fiction (these terms are used interchangeably) originated with the nineteenth-century American writer Edgar Allan Poe, who wrote a series of short stories focused on the detection of amateur criminologist C. August Dupin in the 1840s. Victorian crime fiction was certainly indebted to Poe's work, but it was equally influenced by the late eighteenth- and early nineteenth-century fascination with real crime stories that were produced for public consumption in the *Newgate Calendar* (real life stories of infamous criminals), and various penny dreadfuls (cheap 'shock' literature of dubious quality and often with criminal themes). Charles Dickens's early novels, in particular *Oliver Twist* with its focus on London criminal life, drew inspiration from these popular publications, and it was Dickens who created one of the earliest Victorian detectives in his novel *Bleak House* in the early 1850s. Inspector Bucket, the pragmatic semi-official police detective differed substantially from the cerebral Dupin: Bucket worked tirelessly and drew on an extensive knowledge of his environment in seeking the evidence required to solve his crimes, while Dupin treated crimes as though they were intellectual puzzles, coming to solutions through a series of thought experiments.

For the majority of the Victorian period, fictional detectives followed Dickens's characterization. Wilkie Collins's *The Moonstone*, for example, was much more substantially a novel of detection than *Bleak House* yet his detectives, both professional and amateur, are in the Bucket tradition. Wilkie Collins was an influential figure in the development of crime fiction, although through the 1860s the genre had partly mutated into sensation fiction, of which he was a leading proponent, and which combined criminality and detection with the sensational discovery of domestic secrets. It was in the late 1880s and 1890s that crime fiction re-emerged and in this period the characteristics of the genre were solidified. Several crime novels, none of which form part of the present canon of Victorian literature, proved popular to the Victorian reading public, led by Fergus Hume's *The Mystery of a Hansom Cab* (1887).

It was, however, in the short story form that crime fiction flourished. Grant Allen was one of the first to publish crime fiction in the new monthly magazine *The Strand* in 1891, but it was the series of stories focused on the amateur consulting detective Sherlock Holmes that had the greatest impact. Arthur Conan Doyle's Sherlock Holmes stories began their run in *The Strand* in late 1891, reprieving the character whom he had first introduced in the short novella, *A Study in Scarlet*, in 1887. Sherlock Holmes combined the intellectual power of Dupin with the active knowledge of Bucket. It was this mixing of the characteristics of two different types of detective that proved so successful, especially when given the foil of Dr Watson as Holmes's partner and the ostensible narrator of the stories. Doyle continued to write short detective fiction in the early twentieth century, drawing the series of Holmes short stories to a close in 1927. The influence of these collected works on crime fiction in the twentieth and twenty-first centuries is pervasive.

Martin Willis

Decadence
Representative figures: Joris Karl Huysmans, Oscar Wilde, Ernest Dowson, Lionel Johnson, Arthur Symons, Richard Le Gaillienne, Aubrey Beardsley.
See also: Aestheticism, Oscar Wilde, Algernon Charles Swinburne, Religion and the Church.

British decadence stemmed directly from French decadent authors such as Paul Verlaine (1844–96), Charles Baudelaire (1821–67), and Theophile Gautier (1811–72), who in the preface to his novel *Mademoiselle de Maupin* (1835), first publicized the notion that '[n]othing is really beautiful unless it is useless'. Such thinking was embraced in the 1890s by decadent poets and artists who continued his cry of 'art for art's sake', in opposition to Victorian moral and spiritual didacticism in art. Arthur Symons in *The Decadent Movement in Literature* (1893) described it as literature's 'new and beautiful and interesting disease' characterized by hedonism, unwholesomeness and sexual perversity. Swinburne's *Poems and Ballads* (1866) can be read as the first British decadent book due to its satanism, paganism and fleshly libidinousness, which helped to widen the scope of decadent subject matter in Victorian literature. The movement only gained full momentum in Britain with Walter Pater's *Studies in the History of the Renaissance* (1873), and specifically its famous 'Conclusion', which appealed to young intellectuals to revel in the fleeting, pleasurable experiences afforded by art and life. Their purpose was '[t]o burn always with this hard, gem-like flame, to maintain this ecstasy, is success in life'. The Rhymers' Club, founded by W. B. Yeats, included Oscar Wilde, Ernest Dowson, Lionel Johnson, Arthur Symons and Richard Le Gallienne, and can be seen as the nodal decadent literary group which followed Paterian teaching, along with George Moore, John Gray and Lord Alfred Douglas. Altogether their writings explore the morbid, diseased, perverse and the shocking. *The Yellow Book* was the principal journal of the decadent movement. Aubrey Beardsley's illustrations further impress upon the reader its contents' louche excesses. Joris Karl Huysmans' novel *À rebours* (1884) centres on degenerate French aristocrat Des Essientes, the ultimate decadent, whose lifestyle eventually ruins his health and mind. Oscar Wilde's statement in the preface to *The Picture of Dorian Gray* (1891) that 'there is no such thing as amoral or an immoral book. Books are well written or badly written. That is all' was believed to be a kind of manifesto for amoral existence in which intensity and beauty were the sole standards.

The decadent's weariness and unwholesomeness (both of the literary characters and their authors) was a mark of his transcendence of the mundane and bourgeois and is the result of his self-destructive quest for new experiences. The cult of artifice arose from the French decadent concern with rising above the base, natural state of man, encapsulated by Baudelaire's preference for the music box over the nightingale's song. Libidinous, destructive *femmes fatales* recur throughout decadent writing, further emphasizing the passivity and enervation of the decadent male. The decadent interest in death and degeneration was heightened by a sense of foreboding at the impending century's end and the widespread belief in civilization's imminent downfall. On one hand the characteristic postures and interests of the aesthetes and decadents became comic targets of satire, for example in Gilbert and Sullivan's opera *Patience* and in *Punch*, but on the other they were seen as corrupting and dangerous influences, especially on young men.

The trial of Oscar Wilde in 1895 represented more than just the prosecution of one person: the whole philosophy and practice of decadence was on trial, and with Wilde's conviction it was dealt a heavy blow. *The Yellow Book* closed soon afterwards. Significantly, the final years of the century saw many writers turn to Roman Catholicism in search of confessional sanctuary while also attracted by its sumptuous imagery, Marian worship and visceral religiosity, all of which provided succour for the jaded decadent.

Kirsty Bunting

Education

Representative figures: Thomas Arnold, Matthew Arnold, Dorothea Beale, Mary Buss, Charles Dickens, Charlotte Brontë, Thomas Hughes, Charles Kingsley, John Ruskin, George Eliot, John Henry Newman.
See also: Charles Dickens, George Eliot, Religion and the Church, The Brontës.

The aims and objectives of Victorian educational reformers extended to widening of the educational franchise, development of an educated, modern, competitive workforce and the intellectual and moral growth of the individual. The expansion of educational opportunity in England during the century proved crucial to Britain's economic growth, and one of the first legal requirements for education derived from industry. The Factory Act (1833) made provision for at least two hours' schooling per day for working children. Teacher training was introduced for both men and women in the 1840s, and the significant improvement in standards was confirmed by the Newcastle Commission (1861). In the mid-century attention began to be focused on the reform of educational provision for girls, largely thanks to campaigners such as Mary Buss and Dorothea Beale. Both helped to secure access to the endowments used to support boys' schools during the Schools Inquiry Commission (1864–7), the results of which fed into the Endowed Schools Act (1869). The Education Act (1870) was the most significant educational document of the century because it asserted the principle of mass education on a previously unseen scale, made the state more active in education but still allowed voluntary activities at community level, and granted school boards the power to charge fees and enforce attendance of almost all children younger than 13. Over 5,000 new schools were founded by 1874. Towards the end of the century more consideration was given to the issue of the 'night schools' which had been established, together with Working Men's Colleges based on Christian socialist thought, in the 1850s. The Revised Code of 1862 limited their curriculum to elementary education, but by the 1890s a far wider range of subjects was available. At university level, the predominance of Oxford and Cambridge suffered attack in the 1850s and, although they maintained their independence, the Devonshire Commission Reports of the 1870s led to their adoption of science subjects in the curriculum. The century also saw the establishment and growth of the civic or 'red brick' universities. These changes had a profound impact on the way in which education was explored in literary texts, ranging from Charles Dickens's *Hard Times* (1854) and *Nicholas Nickleby* (1838), George Eliot's *Middlemarch* (1871–2), Charlotte Brontë's *Jane Eyre* (1847), to Thomas Hughes's *Tom Brown's Schooldays* (1857). Importantly, many of the leading social commentators (Kingsley, Ruskin, Newman and Matthew Arnold) were involved in educational progress and experimentation.

Mark Llewellyn

Evolution
Representative figures: Charles Darwin.
Major works: *On the Origin of Species by Means of Natural Selection* (1859), *The Variation of Animals and Plants under Domestication* (1868), *The Descent of Man and Selection in Relation to Sex* (1871), *The Expression of Emotions in Man and Animals* (1872).
See also: *H. G. Wells, Gothic, Science and Science Fiction.*

Darwin joined the HMS *Beagle* as a gentleman companion and naturalist from 1831 to 1836. After returning to England, he began recording his ideas about changeability of species in his 'Notebooks on the Transmutation of Species'. Darwin's belief that species gradually came into being by selective processes would prove crucial to the later establishment of his theory of natural selection, in *On the Origin of Species* (1859), as the simultaneous preservation of favourable individual differences and variations, and the destruction of injurious ones. In *The Descent of Man* (1871), Darwin vigorously pursued his theory of sexual selection, acknowledging the influence of female choice on the production of male ornamentation. Although it conformed to the principles of natural selection, by ensuring survival through reproductive success and aesthetic power, sexual selection could nevertheless exert a contrary force to the pure principle of successful survival, whenever aesthetic manifestations endangered the lives of their performers. Therefore, sexual selection deviated from natural selection in that it emphasized will, desire and pleasure for the individual.

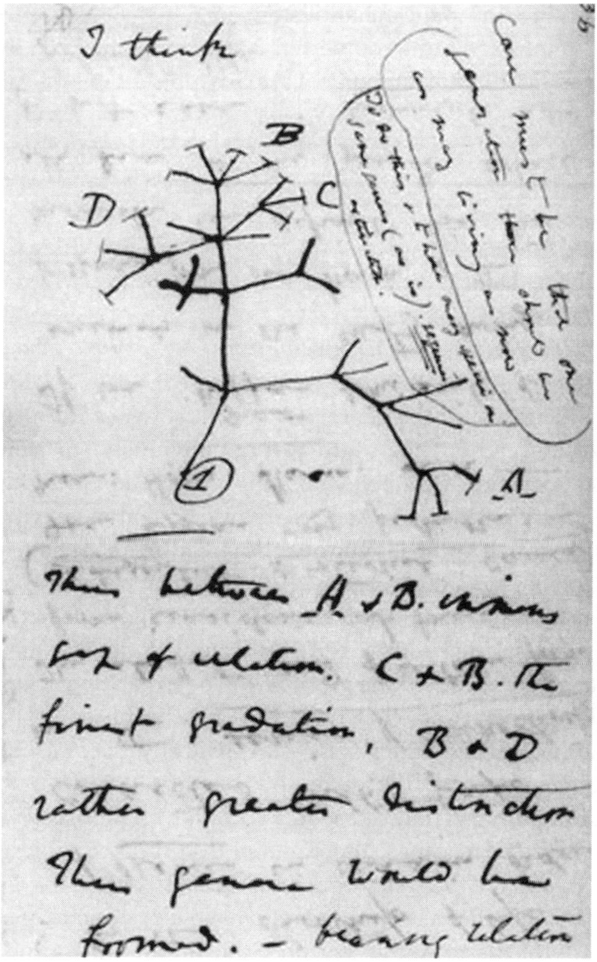

Figure 2: Darwin's 'Tree of Life' from his work for
On the Origin of Species (1859).
Reproduced courtesy of the British Library.

The work of Charles Darwin also reinforced the differences between men and women. For Darwin, evolutionary demands had made men physically and intellectually superior to women as a result of male competition for the possession of females. On the contrary, Darwin held that women were 'tenderer and less selfish, more emotional and less capable of reasonable thought'.

Although Darwin's work is often associated with atheism, he felt that 'the mystery of the beginning of all things is insoluble to us; and I for one must be content to remain an Agnostic'. Ultimately, Darwin's contribution needs to be understood within the patriarchal system in which it was formulated. His works both reinforced and subverted the prevailing gender ideologies, exposing the anxieties and ambiguities already present in social, historical and cultural arenas.

Sara Graça da Silva

Gothic

Representative figures: Mary Shelley, Charlotte Brontë, Wilkie Collins, Robert Louis Stevenson, Henry Rider Haggard, Oscar Wilde, H. G. Wells, Bram Stoker, Richard Marsh.
See also: Sensation Fiction, The City, Evolution, Oscar Wilde, The Brontës.

Victorian Gothic is a slippery genre; it is a diffuse set of ideas appearing in a range of texts throughout the century, most obviously surfacing in popular forms such as sensation, detective and adventure fiction bringing the 'Gothic' into contemporary settings. In recent years psychoanalytical critical theory has dominated discussion of the Gothic enabling readings that have given authority to the genre's psychological play. But historical critical approaches have given new meaning to some Gothic motifs in the light of Victorian scientific and anthropological discourses. Indeed, scientific developments gave Victorian Gothic a new villain in the guise of the overreaching scientist, irresponsibly meddling in practices that were beyond the human. However, while Victorian Gothic can sometimes be simplistically seen as anti-science, it actually engages with the intricacies of scientific discourse to explore the development of human 'civilization' in a complex relationship with the 'primitive'. Thus, in these readings, the eighteenth-century Gothic theme of past secrets that haunt the present becomes situated within the body, marking monstrous Gothic bodies as primitive returns to a prior state of evolution. The close proximity of the primitive within civilization – including the criminal, the insane and the sexual 'invert' – is a common motif in Victorian Gothic, which exploits fears of the breakdown of distinctions in images of monstrosity. Through contemporaneous discourses, the Victorian Gothic monster can be seen as the embodiment of un-differentiation, resisting categorization in terms of race, gender, class and species by utilizing the language and concerns of those very sciences that sought to name and classify. Subjects the Gothic addresses can include: the primitive, atavism, degeneration, fetishism, the superhuman, scientific experimentation, mutation, sexual 'perversion', insanity, criminality, the *doppelgänger*, the labyrinthine city and uncharted regions of the globe.

Sara Clayson

The Great Exhibition of the Works of Industry of all Nations, 1851
Representative figures: Prince Albert, Joseph Paxton.
See also: Charles Dickens, Politics.

Housed in Paxton's Crystal Palace (a pre-fabricated structure) in Hyde Park, the Great Exhibition ran from 1 May to 31 October 1851 and displayed over 100,000 exhibits of industry and manufacture from around the world, classified as either raw materials, machines, manufactures or fine arts and arranged by national status: United Kingdom, Colonies and Dependencies and Foreign States. It was conceived by The Royal Society of Arts and the Royal Commission led by Prince Albert, in response to a flagging economy following the 'hungry forties', and was intended to attract visitors and investors to London, raise funds for the Royal Society of Arts and kick-start an interest in technical education to fill Britain's industrial skills gap. Paid for by voluntary subscription, not taxes, it proved massively popular with its 6 million visitors, despite George Augustus Sala's parody by caricature in *Vanity Fair* of the Exhibition's internationalism and foreignness. It had several material and cultural effects: the building's expanse of iron and glass influenced the external architecture of the department store and its array of exhibits protected and seductively displayed developed the shopping culture within as a practice of looking at objects. Indeed, it propelled a modern and metropolitan relationship to the material world seen in the museum complex (funded by the Exhibition's profits) around Exhibition Road that institutionalized looking at objects as industrial education, while the classification system figured industrial capitalism as a national mission: it celebrated commoditization as a sign of progress, making differences in industrialization stand for stages of national development. Ruskin, Dickens and Morris detested the structure, yet it inspired a new economy of the visual, colouring the cultural valency of reflection and transparency, as can be detected in *Bleak House*, written immediately after the Exhibition. In Dostoyevsky's *Notes from Underground* (1864) the Palace figured the shock of the new, but in George Gissing's *The Nether World* of 1888 it is the now empty glass house's second site in Sydenham that is evoked, suggesting its glamour had long since faded. Finally, it coincided with the end of the old Whig–Tory political system and, since the Royal Commission brought together various persons and ideas which within a few years would be named Liberal, the Exhibition may be seen to have catalyzed the establishment of this political ideology and party.

Louise Purbrick and Kirsty Bunting

The Historical Novel
Representative figures: Walter Scott, Edward Bulwer-Lytton, Charles Dickens, George Eliot, W. H. Ainsworth, Robert Louis Stevenson.
See also: Gothic.

The historical novel is a genre which was most popular before the Victorian period, but which had significant influence upon it. There is a close connection between the historical novel and the Gothic, which in early texts like Horace Walpole's *The Castle of Otranto* (1760) is usually set in the past. The location and distance of that past varies in Gothic and in subsequent historical fiction, but the medieval period is frequently chosen in these early texts. Late eighteenth- and early nineteenth-century historical novels are also often concerned with issues of national identity, and this intensified after the Act of Union of 1800 with many texts coming from, or being set, in Scotland and Ireland. Significant episodes and stories from a nation's past were re-presented, serving to establish a mythical 'national character'.

The pre-eminent historical novelist is Walter Scott, whose 25 'Waverley' novels were published between 1814 and 1832, including *Rob Roy* (1818) and *Ivanhoe* (1820). Scott died before Victoria's accession, but the genre was firmly established and moreover was regarded as the most respectable of novel forms. It was seen as instructive and informative, and was further dignified by its association with factual works of history. Conventionally, the main characters of historical novels are invented, with real historical figures featuring only in passing. Likewise, major real events are often only the backdrop to the interactions of the characters and the dramatic (often romantic) action.

Scott was imitated by many minor writers, such as William Harrison Ainsworth, who produced a large number of highly popular historical novels including a group of works covering almost four centuries of Lancashire life. Scott's legacy was also felt by novelists more usually thought of as firmly engaging with contemporary life: Charles Dickens, for example, wrote *A Tale of Two Cities* (1859), set during the French Revolution, George Eliot's *Romola* (1863) takes place in Renaissance Italy, and Thomas Hardy's *The Trumpet Major* (1880) in the Napoleonic Wars. In Victorian historical fiction, the period varies more widely than in the eighteenth century: in fact there is a sense in which all of Eliot's novels are historical; *Middlemarch*, for example, is set 30 years earlier than the date of writing. This perhaps indicates a changing motivation for the use of historical setting. During the century the scholarly discipline of history developed and scientific theories changed ideas about time and the human relationship to it. As the question of progress became an important one, the past assumed a new importance as a measure of the advance or, as some feared, the backward movement of civilization. Historical fiction then offered a chance to explore change over time and to consider the relations of present and past. Not all historical fiction had such serious ambition however, and the end of the century saw an increase in adventure stories for boys, many of which exploited the past for tales of heroism and bravery.

Alexandra Warwick

Marriage

See also: Decadence, Aestheticism, The New Woman, Sensation Fiction, Religion and the Church, Theatre, Elizabeth Barrett Browning, Robert Browning, Henry James, Christina Rossetti, Algernon Charles Swinburne, Alfred Tennyson.

In a predominantly Christian culture, Victorian sexuality – at least officially – was defined and sanctioned through the framework of marriage. However, extending from broad discussion of the nature and practice of femininity and masculinity, the century saw the cultural depiction of a range of sexual identities and relationships.

Lisa Surridge points to the 1828 Offences Against the Person Act as a watershed in Victorian scrutiny of domestic conduct as it opened magistrates' courts to abused working-class wives. The reading public's appetite for tales of marital strife thus awakened, the Divorce Court, created by the Matrimonial Causes Act of 1857, continued to provide newspapers with reports of psychological cruelty previously ideologically naturalized through the institution of marriage. However, the novel's generic alignment of a wedding with symbolic culmination meant that marriage was already a question of aesthetics. Where Browning's 'My Last Duchess' used the dramatic monologue to uncover a discomforting objectification linking marriage with the art object, novelists such as the Brontës, Dickens, Gaskell and Eliot used the novel's social and psychological commentary to map together the public and private experience of marriage. In such novels, psychological reflection and development are often figured by a successful second marriage, succeeding a disastrous first one typically predicated on an imbalance of influence and power; apparent coincidences, such as inherited female wealth, work to endorse the novels' central realignment of marital relations. With an eye to the cultural patterns of marriage, however, post-1857 treatments register the unravelling of marriage as an ideological construct in their striking reconfiguration of form: so, for example, sensation novels' scenes of revealed horror and cruelty direct the reader's response to the frequent depiction (as in Wilkie Collins's novels) of divorce or unorthodox, clandestine, bigamous or falsified marriage. Notions of female ownership and status within marriage were widely debated in social commentary (see Frances Power Cobbe's 'Criminals, Idiots, Women, and Minors' (1868) and J. S. Mill's *The Subjection of Women* (1869)) and installed in law with the Married Women's Property Acts of 1870, 1882 and 1884. (Previously, the concept of 'coverture' effectively erased a woman's legal right to ownership and representation by dictating they be merged with those of her husband.) Such debate escalated in the century's final decades, partly instigated by Mona Caird's inflammatory essay, 'Marriage' (1888), whose discussion of the indignities suffered by married women sparked a war of words in the press and set the context for New Women writers such as Sarah Grand, whose *The Heavenly Twins* (1893) depicted the assault that sexual double standards could effect on married women's mental and emotional wellbeing. Further, marital breakdown implies family breakdown, and such paradigmatic collapse informs the epistemological questions in Henry James's novel of divorce-related custody battles, *What Maisie Knew* (1897). Debate was not restricted to the novel, however: the period's two significant sonnet sequences, *Sonnets from the Portuguese* (E. B. Browning) and *Modern Love* (George Meredith, 1862), expressed heterosexual coupling as loving salvation (the former was celebrated as marital) and jadedly bitter respectively. Late nineteenth-century poets such as Amy Levy (in *Xantippe* (1881)) used Classical reference to debate the contemporary issue of intellectual bondage within marriage, a theme also treated in E. Nesbit's poetry. Meanwhile, Ibsen's dramas raised the curtain on marital relations and family dynamics on the Victorian realist stage.

Rhian Williams

The New Woman

Representative figures: Olive Schreiner, George Egerton (pseud. Mary Chavelita Dunne, Mona Caird), Sarah Grand (pseud. Frances Elizabeth McFall).
See also: The City.

New Women writers aimed to explore sexual difference and reconfigure female subjectivities in their fiction, as well as advance debate on widening women's access to employment, education, politics and other public offices. As they engaged with aesthetic theories, some New Woman writers addressed stylistic considerations polemically, others more obliquely. Formal and aesthetic techniques range from fragmentary, psychological short stories, through social realism and the naturalistic, to the didacticism of novels with a purpose. The subjects of social purity feminist campaigns – women's status in marriage, the conditions of prostitution, opposition to the Contagious Diseases Acts – are important for some of these writers. The moral implications of maternity for women and 'the race' are considered; female agency was remodelled in romance plots to promote eugenicist aims as well as to address marital discontent. Contemporary conceptions of femininity are challenged in the various and multiple identities – writers, artists, 'platform women', mothers, *femmes fatales* – of the New Woman protagonists. Concepts of ambiguous and modern sexuality and gender are explored through the themes of androgyny and cross dressing, 'free love' and seduction. The emergence of the New Woman followed the century-long engagement with the 'woman question'; she became an icon in the debates on sexual politics of the 1890s. As a discursive figure she was successfully mobilized by her supporters to generate discussion on social change in relation to women's political and cultural status. In fact and in fiction she was largely a middle-class phenomenon. While some feminist intellectuals and activists were interested in ameliorating the sufferings of the working class, the New Woman's demands mostly centred around middle-class interests and ideals; her ideas had little impact on the lives of most women. New Woman fiction shocked, challenged and outraged its readers with its frank treatment of 'unwomanly' subjects. The candour with which these writers addressed the sexual double standard, venereal disease and other aspects of the marriage question shook the culture of the censorial circulating libraries. As well as infamy, this fiction enjoyed success in the literary market and was among the best sellers of the 1890s: Egerton's *Keynotes* was printed in eight editions and seven languages in two years, Grand's *The Heavenly Twins* sold over 20,000 copies in Britain, 100,000 in the USA. With new subject matter many New Woman writers also made innovations to the short story. Elements of the prose of Egerton, Grand, Schreiner and other New Woman writers are arguably proto-modernist, but have largely been ignored or disavowed by subsequent literary movements.

Lyssa Randolph

The Periodical Press
Representative figures: W. M. Thackeray founded *The Cornhill Magazine* (1860); William Blackwood founded *Blackwood's Edinburgh Magazine* (1817), major contributors include Walter Scott; Thomas Hood founded *Punch* (1841); Jeremy Bentham and James Mill founded *Westminster Review* (1823), assistant editor George Eliot from 1851–54, major contributors include Thomas Carlyle. *See also: Chartism, Charles Dickens, George Eliot, The Rural.*

Increasing industrialization in the nineteenth century permitted the flourishing of the periodical as a popular literary form. Mechanization entered the printing process at all levels, meaning that printed matter could be produced more rapidly and easily than ever before. London, Edinburgh and Manchester were significant centres of periodical production. These periodicals found an eager, expanding readership as they were distributed to the newly industrialized and urbanized population, into whose limited leisure time they neatly fitted. The growth of the periodical opened up new fields of potential authorship. The writing process was swifter and more reliably remunerative than novel writing, while widespread anonymous publication encouraged literary experimentation and socio-political outspokenness. Women were increasingly involved, both as writers and as editors, Mary Elizabeth Braddon and George Eliot being particularly prominent. This burgeoning opportunity contrasted with anxieties about the dangerous nature of the cheap press, which some saw as fostering either political radicalism (for example, Henry Hetherington's Chartist *Poor Man's Guardian*) or moral decay (for example, Edward Lloyd's *Calendar of Horrors* and other penny bloods). Gradually, though, cheap periodicals such as Charles Dickens's *Household Words* and *All the Year Round* created the new genres of sensation and detective fiction, the latter mode enduring through Arthur Conan Doyle's Sherlock Holmes stories for the *Strand*. Dickens, along with writers like G. A. Sala, was also instrumental in the development of investigative reporting, while the *Illustrated London News* anticipated modern photo-journalism. Late in the century the New Journalism, typified by George Newnes's *Tit-Bits*, purveyed digested news items to a busy readership and set the precedent for present-day popular journalism. The scope and content of Victorian periodicals were inevitably varied, but included political campaigning, social reform, public education, popular entertainment, religious proselytizing, literary and cultural theorizing. Periodicals fostered a sense of community between social groups, forged new social and intellectual links and provided a democratic outlet for artistic creation and critical response.

Lorna Huett

Politics
Representative figures: Robert Peel (1788–1850), William Gladstone (1809–98), Benjamin Disraeli (1804–81), Samuel Smiles (1812–1904), Anthony Trollope (1815–82).
See also: Chartism, Wars and Conflicts, The City.

The story of politics in the Victorian era is one of containment and change. The political system was renewed: reform acts of 1832, 1867 and 1884 greatly extended voting rights so that by the end of the century, around two thirds of the adult male population could vote; there was a major redistribution of seats to secure the representation of the new industrial centres; the secret ballot was introduced in 1872 eliminating the power of influence and intimidation on polling day; seats were contested more regularly and legislation effectively tackling corruption and bribery at elections was passed. Yet there was no fundamental revision of the constitution, in contrast to more tumultuous events in the rest of Europe, and votes were still regarded as privileges rather than rights, ones which women had not yet earned. The radical demands of the Chartists were determinedly resisted.

The political structures of the nation proved remarkably resistant to change. The upper classes continued to provide a majority of MPs in the House of Commons until the 1870s, and a majority of cabinet members until 1905. Both major political parties, though undergoing transformations (the Whigs becoming the Liberal Party and the Tories becoming the Conservative Party), continued to stand for the protection of property, privilege and empire. The middle classes perhaps made their influence felt more directly at the local level, with the Municipal Corporations Act of 1835 creating elected councils in the new towns, providing new political opportunities for businessmen and professionals. The civil service, traditionally staffed by the aristocracy and riddled with corruption, only slowly adopted the principle of recruitment on merit and, despite the gradual introduction after 1853 of competitive examinations, nepotism remained rife.

Nor did the role of the state undergo a revolution in these years, despite the myriad problems thrown up by industrialization. Conditions of work in the factories of the Midlands and the north, the squalor of the new urban conurbations and life in the workhouse were central themes of the condition of England novels of the 1830s and 1840s. Popular concern prompted some significant reforms, including the Public Health Act of 1848, which established local boards of health and the Factory Act of 1850, which fixed a maximum ten-hour working day in textile factories. Yet such legislation was piecemeal, limited in its scope, and was hedged around with exceptions and exemptions.

Indeed, retrenchment, not expansion, was the principal aim of Victorian politicians, who were eager to reduce government spending and defend themselves against charges of 'extravagance' and 'corruption' which had been the bread and butter of radical rhetoric since Georgian times. The aims of retrenchment were carried out most successfully by Sir Robert Peel, whose second Conservative ministry (1841–6) presided over the repeal of many contentious taxes, culminating in the repeal of the Corn Laws of 1846, which had been seen as an unfair prop to the landowning classes. The project was continued in the 1850s and 1860s in a series of 'free trade budgets' by Chancellor William Gladstone, later Prime Minister. Although civil government expenditure as a percentage of total expenditure rose in the later years of the century, it did so hesitantly: from 10 per cent in 1846 to 1850 to 22 per cent in 1876 to 1880. Military spending and interest payments on the national debt still swallowed the bulk of the state's money.

With the forbidding institution of the workhouse being the closest the state came to providing a safety net for the less fortunate, people were left to fend for themselves. The defining political dogma of the mid-Victorian years was 'self-help', most closely associated with the Scottish author Samuel Smiles who wrote biographies celebrating the lives of self-made entrepreneurs and engineers. The belief that hard work, determination and self-improvement would lead to eventual success was a message reinforced in the pages of countless Victorian novels.

The 1860s and 1870s saw the premiership passed back and forth between the Conservative Benjamin Disraeli (a prolific writer who claimed novels as the best channel for influencing public opinion) and the Liberal Gladstone, who eventually took charge four times, finally in 1894. Anthony Trollope's contemporaneous series of *Palliser Novels* (1864–79) – featuring plots set around parliament – debate the political machinations surrounding fragile governments and often register reservations about adjustments in Victorian political and cultural life. Politics in late Victorian Britain shifted away from consensus and became increasingly polarized. The Conservatives enjoyed considerable electoral success from the 1880s with a reactionary agenda of limited state intervention, defence of the Union with Ireland, preservation of the monarchy and the Church of England and, most importantly, imperial expansion. However, these years also saw the emergence of a 'New Liberalism' which advocated higher taxation and more social legislation, and the first stirrings of what was to become the Labour Party, events which paved the way for the dramatic political clashes of the Edwardian years.

James Taylor

Religion and the Church
Representative figures: James Martineau, John Wesley, John Keble, John Henry Newman, Isaac Williams, Edward Bouverie Pusey, Elizabeth Gaskell, Gerard Manley Hopkins.
See also: Gerard Manley Hopkins, Christina Rossetti, Decadence, Aestheticism, Education, The Brontës.

Victorian Britain was primarily Protestant, the English Anglican Church having merged with the Church of Wales (1536) and the Church of Ireland (1801) and retaining a status that identified them with government and crown. Anglicanism's monopoly in Britain had been undermined by the Act of Toleration (1689), legalizing dissenting congregations and (eventually) encouraging an acceptance of Roman Catholicism, dominant in Ireland, and nonconformism, popular in Wales. Any crisis Enlightenment ideology posed to Christianity as a whole, however, was largely defeated by the eighteenth-century Protestant Revival, which sought to instil enthusiasm in believers and awaken them from the assumed inertia and corruption of the Church of England. Even the rationalist Unitarian movement remained associated with the emotive, mysterious and revelatory elements of faith through the efforts of preachers like James Martineau. The Revival's most popular branch, Methodism, attracted half a million converts between 1740 and 1840. Its founder, John Wesley, insisted that Methodism never left the boundaries of the Church and duly inspired a series of Victorian Anglicans, including the initially evangelical theologian, John Henry Newman.

Many evangelicals, however, became disillusioned by Anglicanism's departure from Church tradition and sought to reinstate a 'Catholic' Protestantism rooted in Laudian tradition. In 1833, John Keble outlined these goals in his 'national apostasy' sermon in Oxford, inspiring a group of men including Newman, Isaac Williams and Edward Pusey to form a new religious movement. The 'Oxford Movement' or Tractarianism (named after 90 *Tracts for the Times* written to define their beliefs) was led by figures religious and literary alike, invested as they were in questions of reserve, the Eucharist, confession, the incarnation and analogy and valuing poetry as the best way to explore such ideas (see Keble's 1832–41 *Lectures on Poetry*). As the movement dispersed in the mid-nineteenth century, its aesthetic impact was channelled into Anglo-Catholicism, notably 'Ritualism' which stressed the symbolic and visual value of worship and was attractive to the religious (G. M. Hopkins) and secular (Walter Pater) alike. Many Tractarians, however, eventually converted to Roman Catholicism, disillusioned by a Church that seemed equivocal on key issues (the famous 'Gorham Judgement,' for example, supported the clergyman G. C. Gorham's decision not to teach the doctrine of baptismal regeneration, suggesting that a secular court had the power to uphold heresy). Roman Catholicism also proved attractive to many whose sexual preference or aesthetic outlook saw them relegated to the margins of society. Accordingly, Anglo-Catholicism in all its varieties was continually accused of 'Romanism' by evangelicals who remained loyal to an emotional experience of conversion free of ritual, belief in original sin, a focus on prayer and communion and the idea that the Bible was the central source of revelation. Crossing denominational boundaries between the established Church and dissent, evangelicalism emphasized the salvation of individuals in return for their contribution to promoting equality in society continuing the previous era's philanthropic practices of voluntary charity and moral reform that had promoted abolitionism, national welfare, education (through Robert Raikes's formation of Sunday schools in 1780) and rights for women.

The early nineteenth century also saw the progression of Unitarianism (a radical Protestantism), which functioned as a feminist religion in the work of women such as the Brontës and Elizabeth Gaskell. Evangelicalism's stress on material change through faith also produced groups such as William Booth's Salvation Army (1865) and stood against spiritualist and mystical religions that were in vogue towards the end of the period. While critics used to argue that this watering down of Christianity into related forms of worship reflected a process of secularization, current scholarship shows that Christianity remained ideologically dominant well into the twentieth century, inculcated into public and private life through the continued importance of the Bible,

prayer and hymns. Moreover, the bestselling books of this period were cate-
gorically Christian, Keble's *The Christian Year* (1827), Henry Thornton's *Family
Prayers* (1834) and countless conversion narratives remaining popular with
readers from all social classes. Many writers did nevertheless struggle with
religious faith, and some of them very publicly (Tennyson's *In Memoriam*, for
example), and it is telling that the term agnostic is coined (Thomas Huxley in
1869) to describe a position between acceptance and denial of the existence of
God. The term signals the seriousness with which religious belief was taken,
and for some agnosticism did give way to acceptance or denial, while for
others the struggle was lifelong.

Emma Mason

The Rural

Representative figures: Joseph Arch, James Caird, (Samuel) Luke Fildes,
Charles Kingsley, John Clare, Richard Jeffries, H. R. Haggard, Thomas Hardy,
Helen Allingham, George Clausen.
*See also: The City, Chartism, Religion and the Church, The Periodical Press,
George Eliot, Thomas Hardy.*

The countryside was subject to considerable change during the Victorian
period. 'Improving' farmers used new technologies to maximize output and
profits. For these, the period from 1837 to 1870 was one of growth. However,
the profits of the 'High Farming' period from 1850 to 1870 (advocated by
James Caird) dwindled in the last quarter of the century as arable farmers
faced poor harvests in the south and pastoral farmers tackled disease, while
competition from abroad increased and prices fell. As farming was put on a
capital footing, so agricultural labourers, dispossessed by the ongoing enclosure of common land, became increasingly dependent on cash wages. Living
and working conditions were poor. Women and children's work was investigated and legislation passed to regulate their employment in agricultural
gangs. At the end of the century the National Agricultural Labourers' Union,
led by Joseph Arch, hoped to reduce working hours and establish a bread-
winning wage.

In terms of cultural representation, the classically educated literate elite
would have been familiar with texts such as Virgil's *Eclogues*, in which a rural
golden age was contrasted with change. Victorian Anglicanism also invested
heavily in pastoral imagery. In consequence, though the more comic elements
of rural life to be found in Shakespeare were also widely known and played
upon by journals like *All the Year Round* and *Punch*, the idyllic model of
simplicity versus complexity dominated representations of the rural.

Many depictions of the country set it automatically against the city; where
the country was associated with nature, the city was associated with culture.

The rapid processes of industrialization and urbanization reinforced this division, with the countryside being treated nostalgically as representative of a lost way of life. However, it was recognized that, like the city, the country had its problems, as suggested in Gaskell's *North and South* (1855). The official reports that set out the pitiable living and working conditions experienced by the rural poor were taken up by authors like Charles Kingsley in *Yeast: A Problem* (1848–50). Yet the expectation that country people lived in an idyllic world contributed to a sense of shock for many Victorian readers. George Eliot wrote an impassioned essay bringing literary culture to task for pastoral misrepresentation (a criticism that artist Helen Allingham has also attracted). John Clare, labourer and poet, although largely unknown to Victorians, is celebrated for authentic depiction of rural life. Demonstrating changing notions of the rural, artist (Samuel) Luke Fildes moved between appealing to the Victorian conscience in depicting social hardship and using pastoral motifs in his portraiture. George Clausen used rural scenes to execute a careful naturalism; novelists H. Rider Haggard and Richard Jeffries were also noted commentators on rural life. Later in the century, Thomas Hardy used the poverty of rural life as a screen on which to project wider social ills. Alongside this however, the rural idyll came to be associated with the native culture of the nation, and Englishness in particular.

Karen A. Sayer

Science and Science Fiction
Representative figures: Charles Darwin, T. H. Huxley, James Clerk Maxwell, Edwin Abbott, Samuel Butler, H. G. Wells.
See also: H. G. Wells, Evolution, The Supernatural.

Science across the Victorian period was dominated by evolutionary theories, the most significant of which was set down by Charles Darwin in *The Origin of Species* in 1859. Yet Victorian science is about much more than evolution, despite its pre-eminence. Science changed substantially during Victoria's reign, so much so that the state of science in 1837 looked very much like the science of the previous century, while science in 1901 is recognizably the science still in operation today. In the 1830s science was still the amateur pursuit that it had been since the Scientific Revolution of the seventeenth century. There were few, if any, professional scientific positions within the universities or the limited number of specialist scientific institutions that existed. Science was undertaken by those wealthy enough, or dedicated enough, to go without either state-sanctioned or remunerated recognition. Through the mid-nineteenth century, however, and in response to the enormous economic and intellectual achievements of science and its practical twin, technology, the sciences began to receive greater attention, and an increasing number of

81

recognizable positions within the burgeoning number of newly created scientific institutions. By the end of the Victorian period, science was at the centre of Victorian social, economic and political life. It was almost entirely professionalized, and institutionalized within universities, societies and the workplace.

Science was also much more specialized than it had been in the early Victorian period. In the 1830s, and indeed through to the 1860s, scientific writing was, at least to some extent, readily understood by the educated layman. Many works of science were read by a large audience, the same audience in fact that would read novels or poetry. With increasing knowledge, however, science became increasingly specialist. It developed its own vocabulary and began to presuppose existing knowledge in its readership. By the end of Victoria's reign very little scientific writing was accessible to the educated population.

What constituted a science was also very much open for debate throughout the Victorian period. While certain sciences were, and remained, central to science in Britain – biology, geology, physics, for example, kept at the centre by influential scientists like T. H. Huxley and later, James Clerk Maxwell – other scientific inquiries were more marginal, and some were condemned as pseudo-sciences. In the mid-nineteenth century mesmerism was arguably a science with specific medical application, but by the end of the century it had been relegated to a pseudo-science and overtaken by hypnotism, with its applications in the emerging science of psychology. Later in the century spiritualism was also investigated scientifically and championed as a science by several leading Victorian scientists, but it largely remained marginal to the orthodox sciences.

The relation between science and literature is a complex one across the Victorian period. Many writers drew on developments in the sciences in their work; Tennyson did so in his long poem *In Memoriam*, and George Eliot and the Brontës continually had recourse to science in their novels. At the same time, scientific writing was influenced by the narrative structures and tropes of imaginative fiction. Science fiction, defined very strictly, was a product of the later nineteenth century and is dominated by the work of H. G. Wells. There were, however, a number of earlier science fictions, following in the footsteps of Mary Shelley's pre-Victorian novel, *Frankenstein* (1818). Samuel Butler's utopian novel *Erewhon* (1872) dealt with intelligent machines, and Edwin Abbot's *Flatland* (1884), inspired by Euclidean geometry, imagined a world devoid of a second or third dimension. The majority of science fiction in the Victorian period, however, comes from outside Britain. Edgar Allan Poe and Jules Verne are the most canonically recognizable of its proponents from the 1840s to the 1870s. Defined more broadly, however, Victorian science fiction can arguably include a great many works that have science as their foundation; of these, George Eliot's 'The Lifted Veil' (mesmerism and clairvoyance) and Rider Haggard's *She* (archaeology) are but two of the finest examples.

Martin Willis

Self-Help
Representative figures: Samuel Smiles, Adam Smith, Charles Dickens.
See also: Utilitarianism, Religion and the Church.

Samuel Smiles's book *Self-Help*, published in 1859, is a distillation of the ideas of individual responsibility that dominated social and political thought. It was an immensely popular book, selling 50,000 copies in the year of publication. Smiles's work is a series of accounts of the achievements of great men, stressing their ordinary origins and the progress of their careers through their own individual efforts. The idea of self-help was closely linked to the economic doctrine of laissez-faire, most well known from Adam Smith's *Inquiry into the Nature and Causes of the Wealth of Nations* (1776), which argued that state intervention and regulation had a damaging effect on the naturally enterprising nature of individuals. Such intervention was thought to create a culture of dependency in which a person would look to others, or to institutions, to support him, rather than utilizing his own energy and ingenuity to take care of himself and his family, and to contribute to the greater good of society as a whole. This belief was at the heart of social and political thought, and of legislation such as the Poor Law Amendment Act of 1834. The Act, which led to the construction of the notorious workhouses, embodied the view that poverty was an individual's own responsibility, as was the impetus to raise himself out of it through dedication to work.

Smiles also wrote a three-volume work, *Lives of the Engineers* (1862) which took figures like George Stephenson as exemplary of the virtues of self-help. His later books, *Character*, *Thrift* and *Duty* have self-explanatory titles. Despite Smiles frequently being taken as the voice of Victorian values, writers of the period have a more complex relationship with his ideas. Dickens, for example, is well known for his opposition to the Poor Law as is seen in *Oliver Twist*, but a work like *Great Expectations* appears firmly to espouse the virtues of self-help, illustrating perhaps the tensions between philosophical positions and lived reality.

Alexandra Warwick

Sensation Fiction
Representative figures: Wilkie Collins, Mary Elizabeth Braddon, Mrs Henry (Ellen) Wood, Charles Reade, Florence Marryat, Rhoda Broughton.
See also: The Periodical Press, Gothic, The Supernatural.

Notable for the challenges it posed to class and gender boundaries, the sensation novel is traditionally associated with the 1860s. Recent work, however, has shown that its popularity and influence extends from the 1850s to the 1890s. Characterized by its portrayals of marriage, adultery, divorce, bigamy, fraud and murder and by its contemporary setting, the genre's roots lie in the Gothic fiction of earlier writers such as Anne Radcliffe, in Victorian melodrama and in the Newgate novel. Sensation writers frequently drew upon newspaper reports of shocking and sensational crimes in their work, such as the Madeleine Smith murder trial and the Yelverton bigamy case. The female villain became a stock character in the sensation novel. Associated particularly with the Victorian woman writer and reader, the popularity of the genre provoked an anxiety that mirrored that arising from the Women's Rights movement. Many sensation novels were also novels with a purpose and highlighted various injustices in the Victorian legal system, such as the marriage and lunacy laws. Since the 1980s, sensation fiction has been the focus of increasing critical attention, with scholars particularly interested in the genre's social commentary, its representations of the role of women and the way in which sensation breaches class boundaries, not only through its depiction of cross-class marriages, but also through its unification of the working-class and middle-class reader.

Jessica Cox

The Supernatural
Representative figures: Sheridan Le Fanu, Vernon Lee, Charles Dickens, Mary Elizabeth Braddon, Algernon Blackwood, M. R. James, Daniel Dunglas Home, Florence Crookes, Henry Sidgwick.
See also: Gothic, The Periodical Press, Sensation Fiction.

Varieties of the supernatural play an important part in Victorian culture and society and are manifested in many different ways. In the novel, the legacy of eighteenth-century Gothic is strong and appears in texts by Dickens and the Brontës, among many others. It is quite difficult to disentangle the plethora of practices under the broad heading of the supernatural, but in the most general terms all are characterized by the belief in forces or presences that are beyond the earthly, the power or effects of which can be observed, however fleetingly, on the terrestrial plane. This is further complicated by the development of science in the Victorian period, where such 'unseen' forces as electricity and magnetism occupy a place in both 'proper' scientific theories and those often described as pseudo-science.

Mesmerism, palmistry, clairvoyance and telepathy are only among the best known of the many fashions in Victorian society, and again they are complex phenomena in that some people were true believers, while others were more cynical exploiters of such beliefs. Writers too had different relations to movements of this kind; some were using supernatural phenomena in their work simply for entertainment, while others engaged more seriously. George Eliot's short story 'The Lifted Veil', for example, can be seen as a piece of Victorian Gothic, but it also comes out of her interest in phrenology, animal magnetism and clairvoyance, and at the same time deals with narrative and authorial voice as aspects of 'special knowledge'.

One of the most powerful currents of Victorian supernaturalism was Spiritualism, a movement which began in America in 1848 with the experience of the Fox sisters receiving audible communication from the 'other world'. Seances, in which mediums would contact spirits who would them speak through them, became very popular in Britain, with the manifestations growing ever more spectacular. Although almost every medium was eventually exposed, the movement did not really weaken, and enjoyed another revival at the end of the century. Critics have argued that there are many reasons for the continued popularity of spiritualism, for example that it was a democratic movement open to all, and that it provided a significant space for women's self-expression. At the end of the century people as diverse as the scientist Alfred Russel Wallace, socialist thinker Robert Owen and novelist Arthur Conan Doyle were all spiritualists. In response to the movement, as well as to other claims of supernatural events like haunting or telepathy, the Society for Psychical Research was formed in 1882 to apply scientific investigation to the phenomena. Ruskin, Tennyson and Gladstone are among those associated with it. Other writers, including Arthur Machen, Algernon Blackwood and W. B. Yeats belonged to the Order of the Golden Dawn, an elitist and secretive group that practiced ritual magic. The Order was later to become more notorious under the leadership of Aleister Crowley, but some of their practices, such as intense mediation designed to project the magician into a visionary world are evident in literature, particularly the poetry of Yeats.

Machen and Blackwood are better known for their mastery of that other Victorian genre: the ghost story. This flourished in the works of writers like Sheridan Le Fanu and in those of women authors such as Vernon Lee and Mary Braddon. It was given particular impetus by the periodical press, to which the short story is particularly appropriate, and through which Dickens has become closely associated with the development of the tradition of the Christmas ghost tale. The last decades of the century see some of the best examples of the form, in the work of Henry James and M. R. James.

Alexandra Warwick

Theatre
Representative figures: Herbert Beerbohm, Augustus Harris, Wilson Barrett, Henry Irving, Henrik Ibsen.
See also: Oscar Wilde, George Bernard Shaw.

Theatre was central to Victorian culture. In the absence of cinema and television theatre was not only immensely popular but also truly universal. Theatre in late Victorian Britain was characterized by three main factors:

centralization, commercialization and increased social acceptance. Chiefly due to improved transport links, many of the independent regional circuits collapsed in the course of the nineteenth century and theatrical life increasingly concentrated in London, particularly in the West End. The established theatres at Covent Garden, Drury Lane and the Haymarket were joined by new playhouses, such as Henry Irving's Lyceum and Herbert Beerbohm Tree's Her Majesty's, as well as a rising number of variety theatres and music halls especially in the East End. This centralization also meant that the provincial stock companies were replaced by touring versions of West End successes, which created a national theatrical taste. Audiences enjoyed a wide variety of performances. Tragedy, melodrama, comedy, farce, burlesque, extravaganza, musical comedy, operetta, opera and adaptations of German and particularly French plays – or a mix of all – were available. Augustus Harris's sumptuous Drury Lane pantomimes sum up the theatrical spirit of the late Victorian stage. They were spectacular, expensive, colourful, effective, fast and loud, and they unashamedly used the traditional pantomime to include music hall turns and borrowed from other theatrical formats too.

In the absence of subsidies, Victorian theatre was driven by supply and demand. A new breed of actor-managers such as George Alexander, Wilson Barrett, Irving and Tree used their celebrity status as actors to turn their theatres into viable businesses and created sensational popular melodramas such as *The Sign of the Cross* or *The Silver King*. The profit-driven character of the Victorian stage is generally illustrated by attempts to play safe regarding the choice of plays, especially in comparison to subsidized continental theatres which staged avant-garde drama by Ibsen, Strindberg and Hauptmann when in Britain they were still largely unknown. From the 1890s onwards, however, the 'new drama' by Shaw, Wilde and Pinero – literary, sophisticated and examining a wide range of social issues – found its way onto the London stage but was fiercely contested and rejected by many. Actors, managers and directors at the end of the nineteenth century were at pains to disassociate themselves from the rough image and low regard the stage was held in during previous decades. They wanted to be taken seriously and to attract bourgeois audiences to their playhouses. Many theatres were extensively renovated during the era and turned into 'temples of art', places of aesthetic delights, of 'dignified things to be done', as Shaw put it.

Managers were also quick to put to good use the new technologies, especially electricity, which allowed for sophisticated stage lighting, sensational effects as well as eye-catching advertisements. The lavish, elaborate and historically 'correct' production of Shakespearean plays in particular not only proved to be a way of achieving respectability for the theatres but also for their managers. Irving became the first actor to be knighted in 1895, others followed soon after.

At the same time the increasing social acceptance – indeed 'gentrification' – of the theatre also resulted to some extent in a division. On the one hand there was the working-class, often rowdy, enormously creative and witty world of the music hall, and on the other the bourgeois, progressive and sophisticated 'new drama', which, as many commentators have claimed, deliberately alienated less 'refined' audiences with its increasing elitism. At the same time, however, one could argue that Irving's magnificent Lyceum productions still united audiences from different quarters and truly played to a national audience.

Heinrich Anselm

Utilitarianism
Representative figure: John Stuart Mill.
See also: Politics, Self-Help.

Utilitarianism was an important and influential philosophy in the Victorian period. It is a moral theory according to which the rightness of an action is judged according to its conformity with the principle of utility. An action is right if it will produce more pleasure or happiness, or prevent more pain or unhappiness, than any alternative. This is not simply happiness for the individual however, but for everyone affected by it. In its most simplified form it is sometimes stated as the 'the greatest happiness of the greatest number'.

Although the earlier work of Jeremy Bentham (1748–1832) is also important, the figure most closely associated with Victorian Utilitarianism is Bentham's disciple John Stuart Mill. Benthamite principles were the basis of the Philosophical Radical party, which was influential on a number of early nineteenth-century democratic reforms. Notoriously however, one of these, the Poor Law Amendment Act (1834) seemed to reveal the inhumanity of such a statistical philosophy, and Dickens's *Oliver Twist* is only one of the many public reactions to its perceived harshness.

The range of Mill's writing on all major areas of philosophy and his influence on social and political culture is remarkable. Mill's *On Liberty* remains one of the best known and widely read writings of liberalism, in which he argues for liberal freedom, in particular freedom of expression and individuality. His essay *Utilitarianism* argues for a theory of morality founded on the promotion of happiness as the good, but with a distinctively Aristotelian flavour. Mill served as Liberal member of parliament for Westminster from 1865 to 1868. He was a leading light in many radical political causes including the abolition of slavery and the campaign for women's suffrage. The *Subjection of Women* graphically portrays the horrors of domestic violence and is considered a classic feminist text, provocatively radical in its day and enduring in its influence. He argued for a form of representative democracy that some regard as elitist and others as

87

radically egalitarian. He fought for workers' rights and advocated a system of producers' and consumers' workers cooperatives.

Wendy Donner

Wars and Conflicts
Significant conflicts: Crimean War (1854–6); Indian Mutiny (1857–8); 'Scramble for Africa' (1880s); Boer War (1899–1902).
Representative figures: W. M. Thackeray, Alfred (Lord) Tennyson, Charles Kingsley, H. R. Haggard, Rudyard Kipling, Thomas Hardy, Wilfred Scawen Blunt, Hilaire Belloc, Thomas Buchanan Read.
See also: Politics, The Historical Novel, Alfred (Lord) Tennyson, Thomas Hardy.

In every year of Victoria's reign British troops were fighting somewhere in the Empire. However, after the Napoleonic Wars ended in 1815 Britain no longer felt threatened on home territory. A middle-class, liberal, contractual, non-military culture developed, of which the dominant literary form was the domestic, realist novel. Relative to other centuries, war was little depicted in the most enduring literature. Exceptions include Thackeray's *Vanity Fair* (1848), which shows otherwise ineffectual men rising to their duty at Waterloo. Whereas Tennyson's 'The Charge of the Light Brigade' (1854) is typical of patriotic Crimean War poetry, his *Maud* (1855) – in which the unbalanced, ambivalently heroic narrator enlists in the army – is not. Kingsley's *Westward Ho!* (1855) reveals the economic basis of imperialism, and ambivalently depicts martial masculinity. The 1880s saw the rise of new imperialism and jingoism. The ideology of Christian militarism, which was meant to reconcile domestic, democratic, Christian culture with imperial aggression, informed such boys' adventure stories as those of Henry Rider Haggard. Kipling, however, both criticized and defended military culture. The Boer War unsettled previous attitudes, since neither romance nor realistic modes of fiction seemed adequate to describe its guerilla warfare with new weapons against fellow Europeans. Consequently, there was a revival of interest in Napoleonic Wars (Hardy's *The Trumpet Major* (1880)), and a turn to lyric poetry. Hardy's war poems express delicate sympathy with the civilian experience of loss. A civilian anti-war movement was represented by such poets as Blunt, Belloc and Buchanan Read.

Catherine Brown

4 Case Studies in Reading Literary Texts

Kirstie Blair, Michael Helfand, Priti Joshi, Grace Moore and Tamara Wagner

---

Chapter Overview

The following five case studies deal in turn with five key Victorian literary texts, the five most often taught on undergraduate courses focused on Victorian literature. The texts are *Jane Eyre, In Memoriam, Bleak House, Middlemarch* and *The Importance of Being Earnest*. Each of the case studies should be read as first-class examples of short critical essays dealing with a novel, sequence of poems or play. By turn, each case study reveals the best methods for dealing with an author's own biography, or the wider contexts of the period in which they were writing. They highlight the necessity of combining thematic analysis with a close reading of language and narrative structure. Of course, each case study is both very broad in approach (of the kind of breadth that takes a work of book length to deal with appropriately) and also the product of the interests of the individual critic. This is to say that none of the case studies is exhaustive, nor do they attempt to be. They should be read, therefore, along-side the other criticism listed in the Further Reading section at the end of this book. Suggestions for that reading can be found at the end of each case study.

Charlotte Brontë, *Jane Eyre* (1847)

Edition cited: *Jane Eyre*, Oxford University Press, 2000.

Critical Views

When *Jane Eyre* appeared in 1847, readers were taken – some shaken – by its force and unconventionality. Variously hailed as original, passionate and coarse, the novel was a runaway success. Today's readers may no longer be shocked by – or even notice – the novel's unorthodoxy, but *Jane Eyre*'s power to captivate abides. This was not always so: after its auspicious beginnings and half a century of acclaim, *Jane Eyre*'s reputation declined, prompted partially by Virginia Woolf's declaration that to write in anger, as she argued Charlotte Brontë did, was to renounce artistry. For much of the twentieth century, Brontë's novel stood in the shadows of her sister Emily's *Wuthering Heights*. Not until the 1970s and second wave Anglo-American academic feminism did *Jane Eyre* return to the forefront of critical discussion and consumption. (At least 20 major film and TV adaptations of it exist, and US college students report that they are assigned the novel anywhere from three to five times in their undergraduate years.) The very factors that earned the novel criticism early in the twentieth century – its anger, its 'messiness' – appealed to feminist and poststructurally trained scholars who read them as evidence of the difficulties of writing as a woman or articulating 'women's experience'. This brief history of the novel's fortunes reminds us that our appreciation and understanding of a text is never entirely neutral, but always shaped by our critical and social locations and concerns.

Jane Eyre was published under the androgynous pseudonym Currer Bell. When Victorians learned that the author was an unmarried woman, the daughter of a parson in a 'remote' Yorkshire town, the novel's sensation value soared and London-based critics emphasized its anomalies and break with tradition. The impulse to view Charlotte and Emily Brontë as 'lonely geniuses', 'isolated' from society, sprung whole from rough-hewn and unpropitious materials is a powerful but mistaken vein in Brontë studies. While the Brontë sisters were certainly brilliant and innovative writers, it is a mistake to view them as outside their historical moment, marginal and removed from the clamour of society. The 1840s were a turbulent period in Britain; the Reform Bill (1832) and Abolition (1833) seemed to settle the charged issues of the franchise and slavery, but food shortages and the famine in Ireland, revelations of brutal working condition in factories and mills, the mushrooming of unplanned cities and the increasing gap between rich and poor stirred unrest among the poor, creating what Disraeli was to call a society of 'two nations'.

This was the context in which Brontë wrote her tale of a disenfranchised, lower-middle-class, orphan girl who rises up the social ladder by individual bravery. In its pages the novel captures, refracts and offers resolutions – some fantastic – to many of the pressing issues of the day. The opening pages establish its contemporaneity when an angry Jane cries out to John Reed, 'You are like a murderer – you are like a slave driver – you are like the Roman emperors!' (11). The retrospective narrator pauses to explain 'I had read Goldsmith's History of Rome' (11), but the attempt at distance by placing the allusion in ancient Rome is promptly undercut when the analogy is pursued and Jane tells us that she 'resisted all the way', that she was 'rather *out* of [her]self, as the French would say', that 'a moment's mutiny had rendered [her] liable to strange penalties' and that 'like any other rebel slave' she was prepared to go to 'all lengths' (12). The language evokes two momentous and anxious events for Britons: the French Revolution of 1789 and the slave rebellions in the colonies that partly mobilized Abolition. Both uprisings resulted in liberty for some, but also unleashed considerable violence and bloodshed. While reactions in Britain to the revolution and Abolition were by no means homogenous, most Britons were relieved and proud that their nation had avoided the violent conflagrations of revolution and had used the law to abolish the moral scourge that was slavery. Drawing on the language of slavery, slave rebellions, mutiny and revolution, Brontë presents Jane, a native Briton, as akin to a slave, lacking the freedoms and liberty they were struggling for. The suggestion is radical because, contrary to the self-congratulation of having averted revolution, it revealed that within Britain were those as oppressed as slaves or French peasants. Furthermore, it hinted that the disenfranchised were on the brink of revolution.

Female Rebellion
The novel reverberates with such 'languages of rebellion'. Throughout, in moments of crisis, Jane deploys this language to speak of her plight and plead her case. The most famous moment is in Chapter 12, the scene in which a housed, clothed and employed Jane nevertheless 'restlessly' paces 'backwards and forwards' on the roof of Thornfield (109). In a dangerously revolutionary manifesto, she announces that 'millions are in silent revolt against their lot. Nobody knows how many rebellions besides political rebellions ferment in the masses of life'. If the spectre of widespread unrest beyond the political were not enough, Jane then speaks of women, insisting that they 'need exercise for their faculties . . . as much as their brothers do . . . and it is narrow-minded in their more privileged fellow-creatures to say that they ought to confine themselves to making puddings and knitting stockings' (125–6). Simultaneously an appeal to the sympathetic and an attack on those who might resist, the passage frames sexual emancipation as a political question. More words have been written about this scene than perhaps any other in the novel. From Brontë's

contemporary Lady Eastlake who recoiled against the passage's 'murmuring against the comforts of the rich' (Allott, 110) to Virginia Woolf who cited the passage as *the* instance of Brontë's flaw of writing in 'rage where she should write calmly' (72–3) to those who celebrate the passage as Brontë's most explicitly 'feminist' statement, Jane's rooftop musings, trenchantly interrupted by Grace Poole's laugh, have spurred readers to debate Brontë's politics and art.

The awkward laugh that arrests Jane's manifesto has also been the source of controversy. For some it indicates Brontë's awareness that thoughts of women's equality were akin to madness (Rich, 469), for others that Jane's rage finds voice in Bertha (Gilbert and Gubar, 348–9). Like Jane's turn to languages of rebellion during moments of crisis, this gesture of self-interruption too is one that is frequently repeated. The most striking instance comes early: having challenged John Reed, the 'rebel' Jane is incarcerated in the red room. John Reed's brutality and Aunt Reed's pusillanimity has roused her blood and ours as well; we cannot but wholeheartedly agree with Jane that the situation is 'Unjust! – Unjust!' (15). At this point, however, the text veers off and Jane announces, 'I was a discord at Gateshead Hall . . . They were not bound to regard with affection a thing that could not sympathize with one amongst them; a heterogeneous thing, . . . a useless thing, . . . a noxious thing' (15–16). The remark is unsettling; we have been sympathizing with the wronged Jane, but suddenly that very Jane interrupts to tell us that the Reeds were justified in their treatment. Of course it is not 'that very Jane' who interrupts and speaks these words, but an older Jane, the narrator who is telling this tale from a distance of some years. Why would Brontë rouse us to sympathy and righteousness on behalf of Jane, and almost simultaneously undercut that fellow feeling?

Part of the answer lies in the dangerous game Brontë was playing in deploying the languages of rebellion on behalf of Jane. The analogy with slaves and the oppressed French elevated the lower-middle-class English girl's plight to a political issue not only of injustice but also of rights and emancipation. But it also raised the spectre of the Terror and the violence of slave uprisings. This was dangerous territory. For Jane to be associated with violence and rebellion was for Jane to lose readers' sympathies. Consequently, Jane draws on languages of rebellion when in crisis, but also distances herself from them as advancement beckons.

Nowhere is this more apparent than when, having accepted Rochester's proposal and in danger of losing herself in his fantasy of a wife clothed in silks and jewels, Jane counters furiously – little knowing how close she is to the truth – that she will not be a part of his 'seraglio' but will 'go out as a missionary to preach liberty to them that are enslaved – your Harem inmates amongst the rest. I'll get admitted there, and I'll stir up mutiny' (269). The language of rebellion surfaces again, but this time Jane's rhetoric is tested. She learns shortly that Rochester *does* in fact already have a wife, and that to marry him *would* be to join his harem. While no sensible reader would expect Jane to commit bigamy, her own rhetoric suggests that she should be concerned with the liberation of those 'enslaved' by Rochester. Instead, as she surveys her situation, she chooses herself, stirringly declaring '*I* care of myself' (317). We cannot but admire Jane's spirit. But we must not forget her abandonment, of her ideals and, of course, of Bertha Mason. (Tellingly, staying or leaving are the only two options Jane considers; to Bertha she gives no thought.) While we may ask what a woman in Jane's situation could do to 'liberate' Bertha (many historically plausible options come to mind, but we will allow that Brontë did not wish to pursue them), it is also fair to recall that when given the opportunity to be a missionary by St. John Rivers, Jane refuses it on the flimsiest of excuses.

Colonial Politics

Jane's refusal to accompany St John keeps her from realizing her ideals, but it also keeps her from actively participating in Britain's colonial project. Yet that does not mean that she – and Brontë – do not tacitly endorse Britain's expansionist vision. Not only does St John get the final word in this narrative of a young girl who has struggled to speak in her own voice rather than be spoken for, but he is praised for his energy and zeal in 'labour[ing] for his race' and 'hew[ing] down like a giant the prejudices of creed and caste' (452). More subtly, as Susan Meyer has argued, St John and Jane neatly divide the task of labouring for their race: he improves 'heathens' overseas, while she remains at home, cleansing it – literally and metaphorically – 're-humanizing' and 'ministering' to the heathenish Rochester (436, 445). Furthermore, Jane's ascent up the socio-economic ladder is accomplished on the backs of the colonized: it is worth remembering that the source of Jane's generously shared inheritance is goods produced by slavery and Jane's marital happiness can only come at the cost of Bertha's. Rochester's demonized, vilified and unjustly incarcerated first wife must die in a violent conflagration in order for 'this one little English girl' (269) to realize her story.

For postcolonially inclined readers, Bertha remains the thorn in the side that exposes the limits of the novel's liberalism or politics of inclusion. Second-wave feminists read Bertha as Jane's double, the one who expressed and enacted Jane's rage. But as critic Gayatri Spivak points out, to view Bertha merely as an expression of Jane's psyche is to repeat the error of second-wave feminism that spoke of 'women' as a unified entity when they actually only referred to the concerns of certain women (metropolitan, white, middle class) at the expense of the differing and possibly antithetical interests of 'subaltern' women (women of colour, third-world women, working-class women). To view Bertha as simply Jane's *alter ego* is to render her invisible – precisely what Rochester sought. It is also to ignore that she is a very real person who is violently erased for Jane's story to achieve its successful conclusion. Bertha, the Creole woman who, it is hinted, has 'tainted' blood *is* the reason Jane must distance herself from those languages of rebellion: the rebellious slave, the angry woman has no place in Brontë's exclusionist and simultaneously expansionist Britain.

Priti Joshi

Further Reading
See the critical work by Beer and Gilbert and Gubar in **Gender and Sexuality**, by Meyer and Spivak in **Colonialism, Imperialism and Race**, and Shuttleworth in **Psychology and the Mind**.

Alfred (Lord) Tennyson, *In Memoriam* (1850)

Edition cited: *In Memoriam*, in *The Poems of Tennyson*, 3 vols, ed. Christopher Ricks, Harlow; Longman, 1987.

Publication Contexts
Tennyson's *In Memoriam* was one of the best-known and best-loved poems of its period, and could indeed be read as the quintessential Victorian poem in its combination of personal, heartfelt expression and reflection upon wider social concerns. Consisting of 133 separate short poems, usually divided into 131 sections plus prologue and epilogue, it is an odd hybrid of the epic, book-length poem and the individual lyric. Critics have sought various ways to define the structural principles at work, but Tennyson himself claimed that none existed: 'The general way of its being written was so queer that if there were a blank space I would put in a poem' (*Memoir* I: 304–5). The poem as published, however, is clearly organized around cyclical processes of decay and rebirth. There are three Christmas Eves described in *In Memoriam*, and each one brings a new shift in the poet's feelings. Sunrise and sunset are mentioned repeatedly; spring turns to winter and back to spring again; the poet stands outside his dead friend's door twice, once in despair and once in acceptance (7, 119), and in the epilogue, a marriage thwarted by death is re-visited in a wedding celebration for Tennyson's sister Cecilia. Rather than consisting of a linear narrative, *In Memoriam* is a series of circling meditations, constantly returning to its starting point and revisiting ideas, images and even individual words, but each time with subtle differences of tone and context.

The full title of Tennyson's 1850 poem, on its anonymous publication, was *In Memoriam A. H. H.*, a title which immediately draws attention to the fact that this is a poem primarily about one person: Arthur Henry Hallam, Tennyson's closest friend and the fiancé of his sister Emily. Hallam's sudden death in 1833 at the age of 22 was the defining event of Tennyson's life and, although poems published in the 1830s and 1840s (such as the dramatic monologue 'Ulysses') reflect some of Tennyson's shattering grief at Hallam's death, it was to be 17 years before the private poems Tennyson had been writing about his loss found shape as *In Memoriam*. First and foremost, then, *In Memoriam* is an elegy, and as such it fits into an important literary tradition including such poems as Milton's 'Lycidas', Shelley's 'Adonais' and, from the Victorian period, Matthew Arnold's 'Thyrsis'. Like the men commemorated by Shelley and Arnold (John Keats and Arthur Hugh Clough), Hallam was himself a poet and a promising writer. As Christopher Ricks and others have shown, *In Memoriam* contains a network of allusions to his unpublished writings and those of other Cambridge friends, constituting in some sense a continued conversation between Tennyson and the dead.

In a culture familiar with death and fascinated by the rituals of mourning, the intensity of the grief expressed in *In Memoriam* touched a chord, and Victorian readers quickly adopted the poem. Although some contemporary critics felt uneasy about the poem's representation of love between men (twentieth- and twenty-first-century critics, such as Alan Sinfield, Jeff Nunokawa and Christopher Craft, have expanded on these potentially homoerotic readings), *In Memoriam* nonetheless became a vital cultural expression of the transitions of grief, a book read by many deathbeds and used as consolatory literature. Seen in this light as an affective text, one which created and then soothed emotions in its readers, the highly personal narrative of Tennyson's friendship with Hallam became broadened to encompass the experience of all those who had lost someone. Most famously, Queen Victoria found the poem deeply helpful after the death of Prince Albert, altering lines so that they would be more applicable to her own situation.

Public and Private Poetry

Such intense engagement from Victorian readers immediately raises the first of many paradoxes associated with *In Memoriam*: it is an acutely private poem which not only became a celebrated public work, but also ensured that its author was appointed to the post of Poet Laureate. The poem itself reflects anxiously on this paradox, as Tennyson, as speaker, asks whether the publication of his intimate feelings can ever be justified. In section 21, for instance, the speaker imagines three antagonistic voices which scorn him for producing poetry about 'private sorrow's barren song' (21: 14) in an age of civil disturbance and scientific advancement; surely, this section asks, good poetry should deal with more than one man's feelings for another? One of the earliest and most important sections, section 5, takes this further by suggesting that even the attempt to represent these feelings in poetry is doomed, because of the nature of language itself:

> I sometimes hold it half a sin
>   To put in words the grief I feel;
>   For words, like Nature, half reveal
> And half conceal the Soul within.
>
> But, for the unquiet heart and brain,
>   A use in measured language lies;
>   The sad mechanic exercise,
> Like dull narcotics, numbing pain. (5: 1–8)

Language here is the faulty external representation of an inner truth that can never fully be expressed. In this sense, for Tennyson to describe his emotions of grief is automatically to betray them, since no linguistic expression can do them justice. This is a recurring fear throughout the poem, making *In Memoriam* a vital text in critical debates on the disjunction between language and 'reality'. Moreover, the anxiety here is that Tennyson's motive for writing *In Memoriam* is not to produce a fitting memorial to Hallam but selfishly to cure his own distressed heart and mind through the process of writing.

Section 5 additionally self-consciously highlights one of the most remarkable aspects of *In Memoriam*: the steady beat of the iambic tetrameter. In 'But, for the unquiet heart and brain' the comma after 'But', introducing a potentially awkward pause and the fact that 'unquiet' can be pronounced with either two or three syllables, means that the line itself is 'unquiet', in sharp contrast to the regularity of 'The sad mechanic exercise', which mechanically falls into a set metrical pattern. These conjunctions of form and content and variations on an underlying metrical form are crucial in *In Memoriam* precisely because, unlike other long Victorian poems such as Tennyson's *Maud* or Arnold's *Empedocles on Etna*, it is premised on rhythmic continuity. In section 5, Tennyson worries that this continuity might be weary and numbing, but elsewhere he suggests that it is the relentless beat of the rhythm that holds the poem – and the speaker – together, and that makes *In Memoriam* memorable. The poem itself, as noted most intelligently by Eric Griffiths (*The Printed Voice of Victorian Poetry*), makes repeated comparisons between rhythm and breath or heartbeat, suggesting that the reassuring rhythm underlying the fluctuations in the speaker's thought might be comparable to the unwilled organic processes that keep him going, despite the ravages of grief.

If rhythm is crucial in *In Memoriam*, so is rhyme. Tennyson did not invent the *abba* stanza, but he deployed it with such mastery that it is now commonly known as the '*In Memoriam* stanza'. Using a rhyme scheme in which the central couplet is enclosed within the first and last line creates another circular pattern and a sense of containment: note how lines 1 to 4 in section 5 again reflect upon this in their discussion of concealment and what lies within. The *abba* pattern also contributes strongly to the 'one step forward, two steps back' feel of the poem, since it requires the reader to look back to the first line of each stanza to find a rhyme. Every individual stanza thus operates both as a separate unit and as a microcosm of the whole poem and its methods.

Religion and Science

Besides including vital considerations of personal emotion and its function in poetry, not to mention reflections on the function of poetry itself in this period, *In Memoriam* is a public, socially committed poem in that it engages directly with perhaps the two most important and conflicted discourses in Victorian culture at this time: religion and science. *In Memoriam* is frequently referred to and taught as a central text of 'Victorian doubt'. While it is important to recognize that the poem concludes with a definite assertion of faith, it is undeniable that it takes on central problems in nineteenth-century Christianity, whether directly in the case of scientific developments that called biblical accounts into question, or indirectly in general reflections on the difficulties of interpretation and belief. Tennyson was well read in contemporary science and *In Memoriam* is particularly affected by his knowledge of Charles Lyell's work on geology, which along with other similar works had demonstrated conclusively that biblical accounts of the formation of the earth could not be historically or literally true. In *In Memoriam*, geology contributes to a sense of impermanence and instability:

> There rolls the deep where grew the tree.
>   O earth, what changes hast thou seen!
>   There where the long street roars, hath been
> The stillness of the central sea.
>
> The hills are shadows, and they flow
>   From form to form, and nothing stands;
>   They melt like mist, the solid lands,
> Like clouds they shape themselves and go. (123: 1–8)

Nothing in the external world is solid or fixed; everything is in flux. At the start of the poem, this sense of 'Eternal process moving on' (82: 5) is profoundly unsettling, but by section 123 Tennyson has come to view his own and Hallam's incorporation into such vast natural processes as reassuring. Geological changes in nature are paralleled by evolutionary changes in men and animals. Tennyson's poem substantially predates Darwin (*On the Origin of*

Species was not published until 1859), but was strongly influenced by other contemporary and past writers on evolution. *In Memoriam*'s famous invocation of 'Nature, red in tooth and claw' (56: 15) looks forward to Herbert Spencer's later doctrine of the 'survival of the fittest', and anticipates him in imagining a world in which man, like the dinosaurs discovered and named in the early Victorian period, is constantly threatened with extinction or reversion into the beast. Indeed, one of the key anxieties in *In Memoriam* is that man is purely a material, animal being, and hence has no spiritual part and – crucially – no afterlife. In a poem that is deeply concerned with the question of whether Tennyson will ever encounter Hallam again, and what form Hallam could exist in after the decay of his physical body, the issue of afterlife is at the heart of religious and scientific considerations. It is not until section 120 that Tennyson ends his agonizing and defiantly asserts that men are '[N]ot only cunning casts in clay', and that even should science prove this, he is determined not to 'shape/His action like the greater ape' (120: 5, 10–11) but to live life according to older and more positive Christian beliefs.

While the poet constantly restates his faith in God, he expresses this in terms that leave that faith in doubt, for instance in section 55:

> I stretch lame hands of faith, and grope,
>   And gather dust and chaff, and call
>   To what I feel is Lord of all,
> And faintly trust the larger hope. (55: 17–20)

The imagery of touching hands that runs throughout the poem, expressive of Tennyson's loss of Hallam's human touch, here resonates in a wider context as the poet receives no response from God. The tentativeness in 'I *feel*' and '*faintly trust*' indicates a lack of certainty about God's presence, as does the alienating use of 'what' rather than 'who': the human figure of Christ is often oddly absent in *In Memoriam*'s evocation of the supreme being. If Tennyson's 'feeling' that God exists seems a dubious basis for solid faith, however, the poem ultimately concludes that it is only through personal felt experience that faith can be proven. In the climactic section 95, marking a major turning point in the poem, Tennyson experiences a moment of visionary connection to Hallam through re-reading his letters, and this moment leads to a simultaneously physical and spiritual perception of the movements which underlie all things: 'The deep pulsations of the world' (95: 40). Similarly, in another crucial section, section 124, the insinuations of doubt are countered by the poet's heart responding 'I have felt' (124: 15–16), a response that leads to an experience of God's touch: 'And out of darkness came the hands/That reach through nature, moulding men.' (124: 23–4).

In Memoriam can be frustrating in its constant self-contradiction and reluctance to make definite assertions but, as Tennyson states in section 48, at least some of this tension is deliberate:

> If these brief lays, of Sorrow born,
>   Were taken to be such as closed
>   Grave doubts and answers here proposed,
> Then these were such as men might scorn (48: 1–4)

One of the most modern aspects of the poem is, as stated here, its refusal to accept the idea of neat closure, whether to the messiness of grief or to the pressing religious, scientific and poetic questions of the day. Another is Tennyson's self-consciousness about the poem as text, seen here in the typical dismissiveness of 'brief lays', and in his worry about reader response. As in sections 5, 123 and 55, he uses deceptively simple language here to express ambiguous and complex ideas; when reading *In Memoriam*, it is always worth remembering T. S. Eliot's famous observation: 'Tennyson's surface . . . is intimate with his depths' (337). Looking past the surface of *In Memoriam* always reveals new possibilities for interpretation, and new relations between the poem and various historical and critical discourses.

Kirstie Blair

Further Reading
See work by Amigoni and Wallace and Young in **Darwinism**, by Armstrong and Bristow in **Poetry**, and by Armstrong in **Science and Technology**.

Charles Dickens, *Bleak House* (1853)

Edition cited: *Bleak House*, in *The Oxford Illustrated Dickens*, Oxford: Oxford University Press, 1996.

The Novel and the Nation
Bleak House was Dickens's ninth novel, appearing in instalments between 1851 and 1853. The novel is remarkable for its innovative dual narrative technique, switching between the first-person retrospective narrative of the character Esther Summerson and a more sinister present-tense voice of an unknown omniscient narrator. These two voices represent one of *Bleak House*'s central concerns, the relation between the public and the private world.

 Bleak House is often regarded as a transitional novel, marking Dickens's descent into what have been termed the 'dark' novels of the 1850s. The 1850s were a difficult time in Dickens's life, as he became increasingly disillusioned with the state of his marriage and more and more despondent about the state of

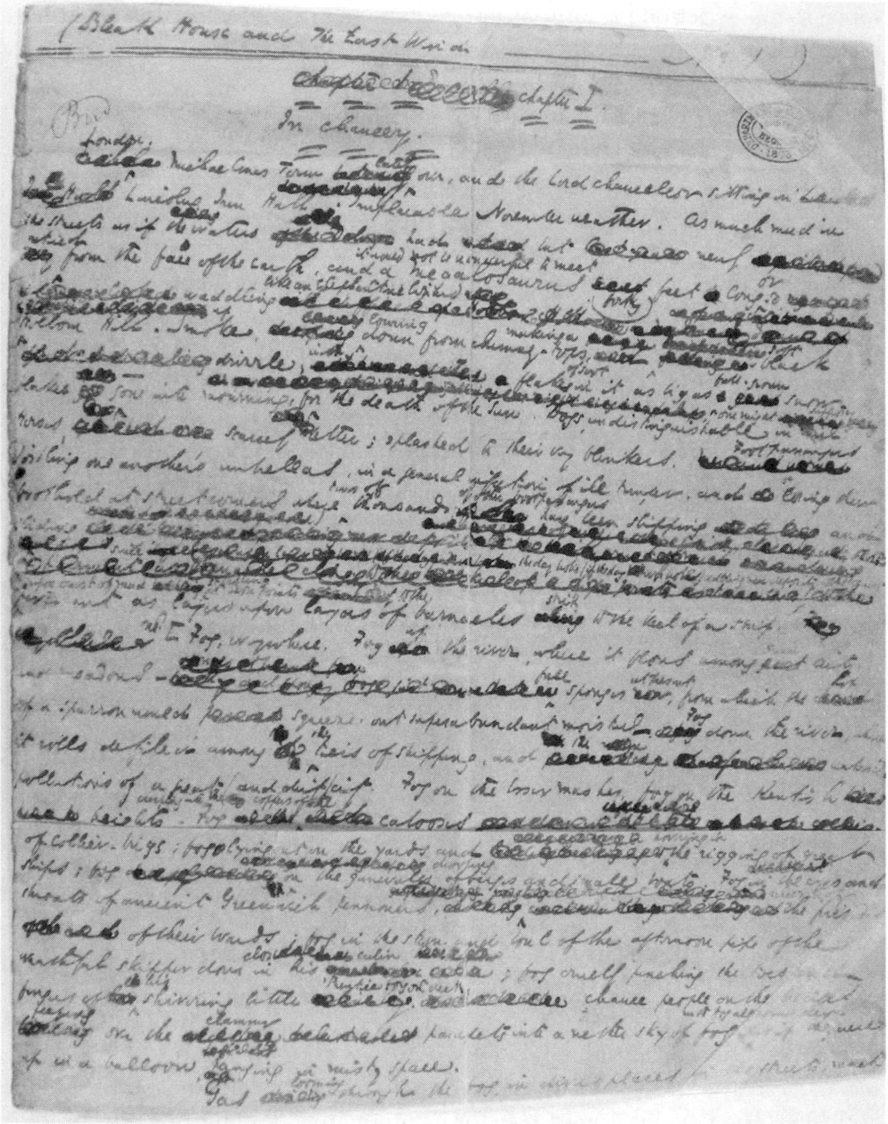
Bleak House and The East Wind

Chapter I

In Chancery.

London.

Figure 3: The first page of Charles Dickens's *Bleak House,* in manuscript. From a photograph in the collection of the Editors.

the nation. As Paul Schlicke notes, 1851 was the year of the Great Exhibition at the Crystal Palace in Hyde Park, London (49). Designed as a festival dedicated to international peace and understanding, as well as a testament to British ingenuity and organization, Dickens was appalled at this attempt to convey a message of national prosperity while so many still lived in extreme poverty.

The *Bleak House* of the novel's title became, as J. Hillis Miller has suggested, an ironic synecdoche for the real-life Crystal Palace, as well as representing a number of extremely bleak houses within the novel itself (12). *Bleak House* famously opens with a fog-smothered, mud-drenched evocation of a London that is dripping with urban pestilence. This picture of the nation's capital city is directly at odds with the glittering splendour of the Crystal Palace and, on a realist level, reflects contemporary concerns about urban decay. In his dramatic opening, Dickens figures London as a primal swamp in which 'it would not be wonderful to meet a Megalosaurus, forty feet long or so, waddling like an elephantine lizard up Holborn Hill' (1). He also presents both the city and the nation as a whole as a decomposing corpse. The issue of urban decay was an important one for social reformers including Henry Mayhew and Edwin Chadwick and while the mud 'accumulating at compound interest' (1) may seem like hyperbole to the modern reader, it represented the reality of the disease-ridden capital.

Dickens's decision to split the narrative in two represents his frustration with the middle classes and their retreat from the muddy, grubby public world into a smug, private domesticity. Like his friend and mentor, Thomas Carlyle, Dickens recognized that somebody needed to take responsibility for the state of the nation. While Carlyle looked back nostalgically to the days of tyrants and heroes who seized power through the very force of their personalities, Dickens looked to the bourgeoisie to take control of Britain and her many problems. In *Bleak House* and *Little Dorrit* (1855–57), Dickens vents his anger at the people Carlyle termed 'the governing class who do not govern' (*Past and Present*, 152).

The Law

Dickens seizes the opportunity to attack a number of official institutions in *Bleak House*, but the novel is often regarded primarily as an indictment of the complicated British legal system. As Edgar Johnson has noted in his classic essay '*Bleak House*: The Anatomy of Society', '[T]he key institution of *Bleak House* is the Court of Chancery, its key image the fog choking the opening scenes in its dense, brown obscurity and pervading the atmosphere of the entire story with an oppressive heaviness' (73). Johnson goes on to comment that the law and the fog have merged together to become 'symbols of all the ponderous and murky forces that suffocate the creative energies of mankind' (73). The fog and the law certainly seem to be in danger of completely engulfing the world of the novel as the story unfolds. There is almost nobody in the narrative who has not been touched by the ongoing Jarndyce and Jarndyce case and, like the fog, the law is a pestilence that contaminates everyone it touches. We see the law's ghastly contagion when Krook, the mock lord chancellor, spontaneously combusts, leaving behind only grease and foul air and signaling the corruption at the very heart of the legal system. Furthermore, figures like the crazed Miss Flite, who has clearly sacrificed her sanity to the case, represent the ways in which the legal system can take over entire lives, sometimes for generation after generation. Those who attempt to avoid the case altogether, like Mr Jarndyce, are shown to be as eccentric as Miss Flite and ultimately fail in their bid to avoid being tainted by the case, as is exemplified through Jarndyce's grief at Richard Carstone's death. Dickens presents the legal system and its emissaries as parasitical and even vampirical. The novel's denouement, in which the Jarndyce and Jarndyce case finally ends, only to have completely absorbed itself in costs, points to Dickens's vision of the law as functioning only to line the pockets of solicitors and barristers. This concern is reinforced through characters like the legal advisor Mr Vholes who is represented as a vampire, feeding from Richard's slowly dying body.

The Character of Esther

For Dickens, the affluent but complacent middle classes needed to take responsibility for the nation they were bleeding dry, and his depiction of middle-class domesticity in the novel highlights the dangers of ignoring the wider world. The novel's heroine, Esther Summerson, may be viewed as the epitome of Victorian femininity in her devotion to good works and duty. However, many critics, including George Orwell, have regarded her as somewhat cloying and ingratiating. In a bid to 'win some love' for herself (25), Esther devotes her life to good works, firstly at the school where she works as a governess and later when she becomes Mr Jarndyce's housekeeper at Bleak House. One of the problems, however, with Esther's goodness is that it is almost completely restricted to the private sphere and, for the most part, she only endeavours to help those in her immediate vicinity. We very rarely see Esther in the public world at all and, on the occasions when she ventures out onto the streets with philanthropic intent, she is always met by disaster. Her visit to the brickmakers' cottages ends with the death of the sickly baby she has come to see, while her later pursuit of her mother through the labyrinthine streets of London ends in Lady Dedlock's death.

Chris Brooks has argued that with her enormous bunch of jangling keys, Esther may be regarded as a jailer, whose business is to intern people in Bleak House (see *Signs for the Times: Symbolic Realism in the Mid-Victorian World*, London: George Allen and Unwin, 1978). According to Brooks, so chaotic is the public world of the novel, that a single charitably disposed figure like Esther is unable to bring about change. Esther's acts of kindness are therefore limited to those that she can perform on an individual basis. She cannot change the world around her, so she draws her projects into Bleak House, as is exemplified by her attempts to care for Jo, the crossing sweeper. The inadequacy and downright danger of efforts such as Esther's are registered when she contracts smallpox from her contact with Jo, suggesting that the diseased public world will only contaminate the domestic sphere if it is drawn in. This is a concern that Dickens was to return to with greater force in *Little Dorrit* where he offered an extended satire of the government's laissez-faire attitude to issues like poverty, disease and urban decay.

Public and Private Roles

Bleak House contains numerous other philanthropists, but they are each, in their own way, shown to be ineffective. Following her attempt to save her mother, Esther retreats into the new Bleak House, where she focuses her attentions upon her family. In spite of the numerous deaths – John Ruskin counted nine and commented that they were 'a properly representative average of the statistics of civilian mortality in the centre of London' – Esther declares to Mr Jarndyce that everything is 'just the same' (879) and the reader is left with the impression that Esther will not venture forth into the public world again. Thus, her philanthropy is stifled by the hostilities of the real world. Far more pernicious than the well-intentioned but ineffective Esther are figures like Mrs Jellyby and Mrs Pardiggle, who exemplify much more dangerous forms of charity.

Mrs Jellyby is identified as a 'telescopic philanthropist', a phrase coined by Dickens at the very beginning of his career to define anyone with what he regarded as misplaced priorities. As early as *Sketches by Boz* (1833–6) and *The Pickwick Papers* (1836–7), Dickens attacked those who set their sights overseas when there was work to be done at home. Mrs Jellyby's obsession with the Boorioboola Gha project, which takes up all of her attention and energies, leads to her complete blindness to the state of her own family. Her jumbled house and unkempt family represent the severely neglected children of England like Jo, the crossing sweeper, whose plight is ignored because it lacks the exotic interest of colonial subjects. While Mrs Pardiggle does, admittedly, concern herself with the urban poor, her attitude towards them is so patronizing and lacking in understanding that it would almost be better if she left them alone. She too is distracted by projects beyond British shores, forcing her resentful children to surrender their pocket money to causes including the Infant Bonds of Joy and the Tockahoopo Indians, and failing to register their utter misery at the prospect. While Mrs Jellyby is airily oblivious to the disintegration of her domestic world, Mrs Pardiggle is presented as nothing more than an egotistical bully, and both are shown to be complicit in the wretched state of the nation.

Bleak House is a novel in which the characters largely fail to connect with one another, a condition which is emphasized through Mrs Pardiggle's lecturing of slum dwellers when she takes Esther to the brickmakers' cottages in Chapter 8. Her 'great show of moral determination . . . talking with much volubility about the untidy habits of the people' (106) serves only to alienate those she claims to want to assist and reinforces the chasm between what Benjamin Disraeli termed the 'two nations', the rich and the poor. As Chris Brooks has noted, almost all of the novel's characters are solipsistic in the extreme and it is notable that figures like Jo are only able to connect with those around them through infection. Even when Esther briefly succeeds in confining Jo to Bleak House, Skimpole rapidly removes him and he is left to wander the streets, being endlessly 'moved on'.

The only character who successfully straddles the public and the private worlds of *Bleak House* is Inspector Bucket, who is able to adapt himself as each situation requires. Bucket is arguably the first professional detective to appear in English literature, and one of his roles is to mediate the demands of the public and the private worlds. Bucket skillfully negotiates the strains that his public role as a detective place upon him as a privately benevolent man; a process which is exemplified when he takes Trooper George into custody. Instead of making a scene, Bucket quietly leads George away from the Bagnets' home, having partaken of the family's hospitality and joined in their revelry (see Chapter 49).

Bucket's mantra, 'Duty is duty, and friendship is friendship. I never want the two to clash, if I can help it' (677) ultimately becomes a coping mechanism for all of the characters. By the end of the novel Esther and her circle have completely retreated from the public sphere, leaving the likes of Bucket to do what they can in the wider world. Although ostensibly presenting a happy ending, when read alongside Dickens's other works of the 1850s, it leaves the reader with a bleak picture of a world in which almost nobody will take responsibility for anyone else.

Grace Moore

Further Reading
See work by Nead in **The City**, by Himmelfarb in **Class**, by Frank in **Crime, Underworlds and Detective Fiction**, and by David, Flint and Johnson in **The Novel**.

 ### George Eliot, *Middlemarch* (1872)

Edition cited: *Middlemarch*, Oxford: Oxford University Press, 1998.

Contexts
First serialized in eight half-volume parts from December 1871 to December 1872, George Eliot's most ambitious and panoramic work of fiction, *Middlemarch: A Study of Provincial Life*, is set in a fictitious country town in the

Midlands during the years immediately preceding the first Reform Bill of 1832. Its clearly defined timeline stretches from September 1829 to the end of May 1832. A historical novel that focuses on pressing issues of the recent past, *Middlemarch* thus describes a trajectory of social, scientific and political discourses that were of central concern throughout the nineteenth century. It combines social critique with a profound investigation of the key themes of vocation, disillusionment and hypocrisy. At the same time, it is also one of the most important marriage novels in British literature. It famously induced Virginia Woolf to praise it as Eliot's most mature work, as 'the magnificent book which with all its imperfections is one of the few English novels written for grown-up people' (168).

The central theme of disillusionment links together the closely interwoven main plots, while the juxtaposition of two failing marriages articulates a preoccupation with the entrapment of the individual by the demands of society. Foiled aspirations for higher goals, both personal and specifically related to social responsibilities on a larger scale, structure the interconnected narratives. It is a structure that brings out the very connectedness, or interdependence, of individuals in what is fascinatingly represented as a panorama of misdirected ambitions and consequent disenchantment. Thus Dorothea's bright visions of assisting in her husband's scholarship fade away quickly against the dull realities of 'the stifling oppression of that gentle-woman's world, where everything was done for her and none asked for her aid – where the sense of connexion with a manifold pregnant existence had to be kept up painfully as an inward vision' (257). As she gazes at the miniatures hanging in her boudoir, she reflects at once on domestic confinement in general and on unfulfilled hopes of her role in her husband's life and work in particular. The 'disenchanted' room encapsulates her emotional state:

> In the first minutes when Dorothea looked out she felt nothing but the dreary oppression; then came a keen remembrance, and turning away from the window she walked round the room. The ideas and hopes which were living in her mind when she first saw this room nearly three months before were present now only as memories: . . . Each remembered thing in the room was disenchanted, was deadened as an unlit transparency, till her wandering gaze came to the group of miniatures, and there at last she saw something which had gathered new breath and meaning: it was the miniature of Mr Casaubon's aunt Julia, who had made the unfortunate marriage – of Will Ladislaw's grandmother. Dorothea could fancy that it was alive now. (258)

The passage welds together the foiling of expectations and the desire and need to counter disenchantment with new hope. The shift is externalized by images of light and darkness. Oppression manifests itself in a room 'deadened' and 'unlit', and yet its transparency highlights the transformation of her memories of disappointed expectations by suggesting a source of future consolation. Thus Dorothea's affinity with Will Ladislaw's grandmother already projects her future relationship with him. It is a disturbing moment, embedded as it is in the description of a failing marriage, and yet the very innocuousness that underpins the collapsing of Dorothea's first set of visions divorces her longing for a connectedness through the portrait of a woman who married for love from the adulterous desire that Casaubon's codicil later undeservedly seems to accuse her. The theme of disenchantment, in fact, becomes intriguingly counterpoised by the novel's consistent emphasis on the significance of the visionary, of fancy, within the mundane. The need for compromise is acknowledged with resignation rather than endorsed. Marriage becomes a leading metaphor for this negotiation of expectation, compromise and retention of individual visions of connectedness.

Marriage

'Marriage is so unlike everything else', comments the recently widowed Dorothea when advising Rosamond, the likewise disappointed, socially ambitious wife of the young doctor, Tertius Lydgate, towards the end of the novel: 'There is something even awful in the nearness it brings' (748). As the leading protagonists need to realize, marriage brings home the pressures of society, while it disrupts personal ambition, ironically in particular when its goal is the common good. Dedication to the advancement of science as well as to traditional scholarship engenders a revealing parallelism that further underscores the ways in which the Casaubon–Dorothea and the Lydgate–Rosamond marriages incorporate a central conflict. This overarching dilemma is less about the dynamic between individual and society than about the complexities of expectations and chances at large. Both Lydgate's project of setting up a fever hospital that is to make the provincial town of Middlemarch the centre for medical research, and Casaubon's desire to write up his life-long study are shown to fail. Although Lydgate himself traces the disruption of his work exclusively to his marriage, it is vitiated by 'spots of commonness' (141) that are ingrained in him.

The central bifurcation in the novel's structure is indeed crucial to the scope of the social panorama, bringing together the landed gentry, provincial tradesmen and the rising professional classes. The original conception of the two main plots casts an important light on what clearly constitutes the pivotal concerns of the novel as a whole. As can be traced from her notebooks, in late 1869 George Eliot started a novel with the working title 'Middlemarch'. It was to be set in a provincial town and to concentrate on a physician. In 1870 Eliot began writing 'Miss Brooke,' which came to be the plot focusing on Dorothea

Brooke, her marriage to the elderly would-be scholar Casaubon and her growing interest in and love for his young cousin Ladislaw. The successful fusion of what had thus originally been conceived as two separate works hinges on the paralleled aspirations of Dorothea and Lydgate to do good, and yet with equal significance also on the identification of Lydgate's scientific projects and Casaubon's plans for a massive work that is to encompass dissections of ancient belief systems, to provide *The Key to All Mythologies*.

Education

The *Bildungsroman*, or novel of education, that traces Dorothea's growth is thereby projected onto various closely interwoven narrative strands. Hence the search for something noble or worthwhile and the ways it is thwarted may characterize the dreams of Dorothea and Lydgate most insistently, but the theme of vocation pervades the projects of almost all protagonists. They range from the ridiculed political ambitions of Dorothea's uncle, a notoriously irresponsible landowner who wishes to stand for the Liberal side in the coming election, to Rosamond Vincy's visions of marrying a newcomer to Middlemarch. Yet Rosamond's 'social romance' (109), it is repeatedly emphasized, has nothing to do with matrimonial speculation. It spawns genuine visions as powerful and single-minded as that of Lydgate himself: 'There was nothing financial, still less sordid, in her previsions: she cared about what were considered refinements, and not about the money that was to pay for them' (110). To underscore the prevalence of individuals' parallel, and yet disconnected, ultimately often opposing or divergent expectations, her imaginative constructions 'of her wedded life, having determined on her house in Middlemarch' (110) within minutes after meeting Lydgate for the first time are then immediately juxtaposed with her brother's hopes of an inheritance: 'But – those expectations! He really had them, and he saw no agreeable alternative if he gave them up' (111). Their hopes become as concentrated on such emphatically worldly visions as are the equally self-absorbing concepts of disinterestedness entertained by Lydgate and Dorothea.

The irony of this treatment of social ambition as personal vocation extends to the overall structure of the novel's treatment of disillusionment as its key theme. While it welds together the main plotlines, the search for self-realization and the attendant threat of disappointment are simultaneously shown at once to connect and to separate individuals: the shared predicament sets them apart. The redeeming love Rosamond's scapegrace brother Fred feels for Mary Garth, young Ladislaw's search for fulfilment in politics and love and Bulstrode's carefully concealed past as a *Bildungsroman* gone wrong are woven into the central plots on various levels.

One of Victorian fiction's most powerfully evoked religious hypocrites, Bulstrode, in fact, acts as a catalyst for a theme that permeates the novel.

Ominously introduced as 'the philanthropic banker' (82), he is shown to denounce Vincy's choice of the Church as a profession for his son. He similarly speaks out against Farebrother, a clergyman who has missed his vocation as a naturalist, and who supplements his income by gambling. This twofold condemnation of gambling and a lack of dedication to what Bulstrode perceives as the right religion (his appropriation of providence to suit his own needs and desires) becomes particularly ironic when his dark past as a fraudulent speculator is revealed by a man named Raffles, an apt embodiment of chance. Fred Vincy ultimately decides not to enter the Church, finds a more suitable, less ambitious occupation by working with Mary Garth's father and is consequently rewarded with Mary's love. But he first needs to overcome the disappointment that has arisen from his expectations of inheriting old Featherstone's estate. Yet the end of the novel sees Fred become the owner of its stock and furniture; Featherstone clearly has not managed to keep the estate away from him. Casaubon's codicil similarly fails to prevent Dorothea from marrying Ladislaw. In referring to the last wills of both Featherstone and Casaubon, 'The Dead Hand' (Book Five) effectively holds together two parallel plotlines that furthermore bring out the novel's analysis of hypocrisy.

Disillusionment and Sympathy
As J. Jeffrey Franklin has compellingly argued, that Lydgate self-consciously defines himself against fashionable physicians who are like hypocritical philanthropists (138) is deeply ironic since 'neither Lydgate nor the reader will know for 500 pages yet that this is a chillingly accurate description of Bulstrode' (46). Bulstrode, it is crucial to note, is not one of the 'coarse hypocrites' who consciously affect beliefs (581). He is genuinely convinced by the virtue of his very acquisitiveness. Yet if Bulstrode is by far the most fully fledged realization of single-minded faith in his life's (and especially his financée's) centrality in the scheme of providence, it is really only a more explicit version of the same self-absorption that is shown to be natural in the choice of a vocation. It is a universal trait that connects individuals while it keeps them apart, absorbed, like Casaubon, in their own appropriation of the providential:

> [i]f he was liable to think that others were providentially made for him, and especially to consider them in the light of their fitness for the author of a *Key to all Mythologies*, this trait is not quite alien to us, and like the other mendicant hopes of mortals, claims some of our pity. (78)

What makes the novel so compelling as an analysis of disillusionment linked to the related theme of disconnectedness is, in fact, both the emphatic sympathy with which otherwise uncongenial characters, rendered so by their very function as the main protagonists' foils, are treated and conversely, by the spots of self-delusion that permeate society. In an ironic twist, they connect individuals. Thus, it is not only that Casaubon's self-absorption renders that of Lydgate and Dorothea explicit, it also echoes Bulstrode's personal claiming of providence. For Casaubon, moreover, his isolation becomes his project's failure. Ignoring an extensive part of current research, working outside a community of scholars, while at first limiting and then abusing Dorothea's enthusiastically envisioned assistance, he becomes a failure as a scholar and as a husband. Self-absorption, in short, is shown to lead at once to seclusion and to exploitation. The novel's structure further bears out this inability to connect. As it is pointedly put at the convergence of Dorothea's and Lydgate's narratives, 'any one watching keenly the stealthy convergence of human lots, sees a slow preparation of effects from one life on another, which tells like a calculated irony on the indifference or the frozen stare with which we look at our unintroduced neighbour' (88). This passage introduces one of the most memorable and powerful images of the novel: 'Destiny stands by sarcastic with our *dramatis personae* folded in her hand' (88). Instead of a providence that can be adapted to individual interpretation – as most pointedly in Bulstrode's spiritual bookkeeping – this personification of destiny is at once secretive and sarcastic. All may be mapped out, sketched for a performance in which the world acts as a stage, but the outcome remains unknown: the account of the characters and their fate is a closed book, in destiny's hand. Yet the image works on multiple levels, as in an equation of chance and providence, desire for a specific vocation is undercut by the individual's helplessness as well as by human fallibility, by the 'spots of commonness'.

What makes *Middlemarch* such a powerful marriage novel is likewise precisely the sympathy with which these spots are presented. Casaubon certainly is 'a dreadful warning to all those who try for a life of learning' (Birch 208), but he is more than simply an embodiment of 'the lifeless order of pedantry' (Van Zuylen 100). In a persuasive reading of the novel's treatment of monomania, Marina Van Zuylen has suggested that *Middlemarch* not only 'diagnoses single-mindedness as an escape from life's quotidian realities', but that it associates Dorothea's initial, emphatically abstract, concept of marriage (to Casaubon and his work) with 'faith' so as to highlight the pervasiveness of self-delusion (100, 112). Just as there are affinities between the futility of Casaubon's and Lydgate's projects, there is an eerie resemblance between Rosamond's 'social romance' and Dorothea's longing for a vocation. Like the marriages it depicts, the novel ends in a list of compromises. It projects Lydgate's career as a fashionable physician who has abandoned medical reform, and while it sees Dorothea united to the political idealist Ladislaw, the range of her own enthusiasm is strangely muted:

> Certainly those determining acts of her life were not ideally beautiful. They were the mixed result of young and noble impulse struggling amidst the conditions of an imperfect social state, in which great feelings will often take the aspect of error, and great faith the aspect of illusion. (784)
>
> *Tamara Wagner*

Further Reading
See work by Beer in **Darwinism**, by Franklin and Leavis in **The Novel** and by Shuttleworth in **Science and Technology**.

Oscar Wilde, *The Importance Of Being Earnest* (1895)

Edition cited: *The Importance of Being Earnest*, London: Collins, 1996; 2003.

Theatrical Strategies

When audiences for *The Importance of Being Earnest* heard Jack's final riposte to Lady Bracknell, 'On the contrary . . . I've now realized for the first time in my life the vital Importance of Being Earnest', they probably recognized both the truth and falsity, the seriousness and the triviality of Jack's remark (307). On the one hand, the play affirms earnestness, a core value of respectable Victorians, but it also suggests that Jack's conversion to earnestness is accidental and in name only. I would suggest that this tactic of affirmation/negation shapes the play as a whole and that Wilde, with some helpful editing by George Alexander, the director of the St James Theatre (where the play first appeared on 14 February 1895), crafted it to be, as Hesketh Pearson wrote in *The Life of Oscar Wilde*, 'correctly risky' so that they might become 'the talk of the social world that was correctly risky' (Donohue 50).

There are a number of reasons which no doubt influenced Wilde to adopt this artistic strategy. *The Importance of Being Earnest* was his fourth effort to write for the commercial theatre, something he needed to do to achieve the fame he desired and the wealth he needed to support his family and his luxurious lifestyle. He found that writing poetic, experimental or serious drama was not the way to wealth. The way, he found, was to write intelligent plays that appealed to the correctly risky, well-to-do audiences who attended the West End theatres, plays which mixed wit and comedy with some attention to the social, political and domestic problems of the day. *Lady Windermere's Fan, A Woman of No Importance,* and *An Ideal Husband* preceded *The Importance of Being Earnest* to these theatres and all were popular and financial successes. When he earned £7,000 from *Lady Windermere's Fan* in the first year, Wilde realized the vital importance of being an earner (Raby viii).

But at the same time that he sought popularity and commercial success, Wilde remained deeply critical of the respectable institutions and values of Victorian society and committed, at least intellectually, to radical social change and to the creation of subversive and unconventional forms of art. Wilde is popularly, and properly, known as a critic who espoused 'art for art's sake' and championed Aestheticism and the Arts and Crafts movements in the last decades of the century. But his revolt against the highly moralized and didactic arts of the previous generation had its roots in cultural criticism which aimed at improving society. He was developing and adapting the ideas of Matthew Arnold, Walter Pater and John Ruskin, critics he knew either personally or from his studies at Oxford University.

Like Arnold, Wilde was a poet and a classicist who believed that the Hellenic ideal (Arnold's 'sweetness and light'), the creation and appreciation of beauty, harmony and intellectual playfulness, was badly needed to counterbalance the very practical, materialistic and heavily moralized character of respectable Victorian society. What Arnold called 'sweetness and light' Wilde called 'pleasure' and in the conclusion of his important, but often neglected work of cultural criticism, 'The Soul of Man Under Socialism', Wilde claimed a biological justification for the pleasure principle in culture: 'Pleasure', he wrote, 'is Nature's test, her sign of approval. When man is happy he is in harmony with himself and his environment' (*Works* 1,104). Wilde recognized Darwin as one of the two thinkers (the other is Ernest Renan) who changed the course of history and his social and political views are rooted in evolutionary theory. In 'The Critic as Artist' he explained the connection between aesthetics and social improvement: 'Aesthetics, like sexual selection, make life lovely and wonderful, fill it with new forms, and give it progress, and variety and change' (*Works* 1,058). Aesthetics, with its emphasis on pleasure, was an engine of progress. Darwinian theory gave his cultural criticism a thoroughly modern and more powerfully authoritative basis than Arnold's morally based cultural criticism. Once again it is the goal of social harmony, what he called the 'new Hellenism,' which justified the pursuit of pleasure. A society which achieves this 'perfect harmony,' he wrote, 'will be what the Greeks sought for, but could not, except in thought, realize completely' (*Works* 1,104).

Wilde's emphasis on pleasure and sceptical view of conventional morality certainly sharpened – rhetorically and politically – the cultural dialectic which Arnold described. For Wilde, pleasure certainly included sweetness and light, but it had hedonistic implications which were distinctly edgy and risky. He wrote at a time when the social, political and ethical compromises, the assumptions of the dominant, mid-Victorian orthodoxy, were being challenged. In 'The Soul of Man Under Socialism' Wilde rejected the institutions of marriage, the family, the class system and private property (and the moralizing about them) because they impeded social transformation. In *The*

Importance of Being Earnest Wilde's characters cast cold but witty eyes on these institutions and their moral justifications.

This was not easily accomplished. In 'The Soul of Man Under Socialism' Wilde discussed the power of repressive official censors and public opinion to stifle creativity and criticism, but he also noted the creative strategy that would free his social criticism, the use of comedy to gild the bitter pill: 'delightful work may be produced under burlesque and farcical conditions, and in work of this kind the artist in England is allowed very great freedom' (*Works* 1,091). Critics and scholars have identified possible dramatic influences for *The Importance of Being Earnest* including the well-made play, W. S. Gilbert's *Engaged* (1877), and Arthur Pinero's *The Magistrate* (1885) and *Dandy Dick* (1887). He also seems to have stolen some ideas from the topsy-turvy world of Gilbert and Arthur Sullivan's comic operetta, *The Mikado (1885)*.

Wilde's strategy was to create a plot which confirmed the conventional forms and values of respectable society and, at the same time, revealed their emptiness and absurdity in the characters' conversations. In describing the earliest version of the play to Alexander, Wilde wrote that 'The real charm of the play, if it is to have charm, must be in the dialogue . . . The plot is slight, but, I think, adequate' (Donohue 36). In fact, the plot in *The Importance of Being Earnest* is quite conventional and Wilde used it to affirm the conventional values of his audience. It is all about sexual selection. Two young men (Jack and Algernon (Algy)) and two young women (Gwendolyn and Cecily) fall in love (some before first sight!) and desire to marry.

To do so they must overcome the obstacles of family background (a question of class) and bad reputations (made absurd by the young women's insistence that they must be named Ernest). In Act II we see the couples quarrel but eventually reconcile their various jealousies, misunderstandings and differences. By Act III the couples are determined to marry despite Lady Bracknell's serious opposition to Jack's family background: it seems his handbag, with or without handles, is not suitable for a suitor. But Jack's financial and legal power to block Algernon's marriage, and his amazing discovery that he is Algernon's brother (named Ernest) and Lady Bracknell's nephew, resolves the problem of class and brings about the celebration of future marriages. The plot, that is, confirms conventional institutions, social arrangements and beliefs: that romantic love will lead to, and is compatible with, marriage; that wealth and breeding will be united; that duty and pleasure are not at odds, that a respectable married life will solve all frustrations and alienation, symbolized by secret lives and imagined diaries. And, of course, that it is vitally important to be earnest. In all, these are a nice summary of late Victorian bourgeois aspirations.

Comedy and Convention

But the plot does not tell the whole story; it provides an overarching structure and theme. What is missing, and what makes the play distinctive and unsettling, is its wit and comedy which work locally, that is from moment to moment in the play, to provide an ironic counterpoint to the conservative values suggested by the plot. It is the dialogue which convinced Eva Thienpont that *The Importance of Being Earnest* 'is the most radically subversive of Wilde's plays' (115). Writing to Robert Ross about the 'philosophy' of *The Importance of Being Earnest* Wilde suggested 'we should treat all trivial things very seriously, and all the serious things of life with sincere and studied triviality' (Ellmann 422). That is, it is this topsy-turvy attitude towards the respectable and the conventional (and the trivial) which reshapes this popular dramatic form closer to Wilde's dialectical vision.

We can see an example of this unsettling quality in the opening conversation of Act I between Algy and Lane, his manservant, when they discuss marriage, class relations, petty theft, pleasure and moral responsibility. Algy sees marriage as 'demoralizing' because these households have inferior champagne. Lane's response is to describe this demoralizing state as 'very pleasant', but adds that he is uninterested in his own family life: 'I never think of it myself.' This Algy finds 'very natural' but he laments, after Lane exits, the lack of moral responsibility in the working class (253–4). While conventional social relations between master and servant are enacted, the characters' ideas about marriage, family, pleasure, class characteristics and duty are unconventional, if not confusing.

The conversation between Jack and Algy which follows also plays with conventional ideas and forms. Jack presents himself as an idealistic, morally upright gentleman, who believes in romance, true love and taking the responsibilities of guardianship seriously. Cynical, impecunious and worldly Algernon offers anti-conventional commentary. Of Jack's marriage proposal he says, 'I thought you had come up [to town] for pleasure? . . . I call that business' (254). As the conversation continues Jack plays the polite moralist with conventional ideas while Algernon, greedily eating cucumber sandwiches, provides the humour by offering his critical insights ('If I ever get married I'll certainly try to forget the fact, 'Divorces are made in Heaven', 'in married life three is company and two is none' (255).

Wilde also complicates the conventional dramatic form, with its simple distinctions between good and bad and, in this case, between Jack as the conventional idealist and Algy the cynic. When Algy unmasks Jack's double life (virtue and duty in the country, pleasure in the city), it is Jack who makes a rather devastating critique of conventional morality:

JACK: 'When one is placed in the position of guardian, one has to adopt a very high moral tone on all subjects. It's one's duty to do so. And . . . a high moral tone can hardly be said to conduce very much to either one's health or one's happiness.

That, Jack says, is 'the whole truth pure and simple', to which Algernon adds a further complication: 'The truth is rarely pure and never simple' (258).

We see similar complications of the simple contrast between Gwendolyn as a 'brilliant, clever, thoroughly experienced young lady', and Cecily as a 'sweet, simple innocent girl' (292). Some of Gwendolyn's early comments ('Algy, you always adopt a strictly immoral attitude towards life. You are not quite old enough to do that') are knowing and sophisticated (270). Yet they mix incongruously with her conventional romantic sentiments: 'But although [Lady Bracknell] may prevent us from becoming man and wife, and I may marry someone else, and marry often, nothing she can possibly do can alter my eternal devotion to you' (270).

By contrast Cecily offers an innocent and high-minded explanation for her desire to meet Ernest: 'We might have a good influence over him, Miss Prism' (272). But when she meets him, it is his wickedness which interests her. When Algernon admits to being 'very bad in my own small way', Cecily remarks, 'I don't think you should be so proud of that, though I am sure it must have been very pleasant' (275). Duty simply masks a desire for the mating dance. Furthermore she thinks Jack's 'higher sense of duty and responsibility' make him 'a little bored' and 'not quite well' (272).

The play continues in this vein: desire and/or pleasure motivate characters, rather than a sense of duty. Conversations pepper the audience with critical comments on society from characters who nevertheless act in conventional ways. Even at the play's conclusion Jack asks Gwendolyn if she can forgive him for 'speaking nothing but the truth'. She replies, 'I can, for I feel that you are sure to change' (307). That is a rather risky and unconventional response from a Victorian lady, but it is quite in line with Wilde's belief in the value of lying, by which he meant creativity.

Does this play suggest the values of the 'new Hellenism'? Certainly pleasure, both aesthetic and erotic, trumps duty in the lives of these characters. The play itself mocks the moralizing mania of Victorian people and, with its campy conclusion, their popular art. Instead the plot offers the kind of formal balance and symmetry, the harmony, which Wilde (and Arnold) might consider aesthetic and Hellenic.

The minor conflict between Algy and Jack over Cecily in Act I is balanced by the minor conflict between Gwendolyn and Cecily over Ernest in Act II. The more significant conflict between Jack and Lady Bracknell is introduced near the end of Act I and then becomes central to the resolution in Act III. Two men court two women. Both pairs imagine or live alternative lives. There are two older women (Lady Bracknell and Miss Prism) who have shaped the lives of these characters, two homes, two diaries, two butlers and, of course, the twins to be christened by Chasuble. The power of commerce is pitted against the power of a relatively impoverished aristocracy (the opposing political powers of the century) and they are united by the forthcoming nuptials of the two couples: harmony is restored to this never-never land. There are so many parallels and contrasts (so much symmetry) that Wilde seems to be playing with this aesthetic idea. But more than anything there is Wilde's wit. Sweetness, light and the free play of the mind: these are the qualities that made *The Importance of Being Earnest* a pleasure, and keep it that way.

Michael Helfand

Further Reading
See work by Koven in **The City**, by Hill in **Degeneration and the fin de siècle**, various in **Drama and Theatre**, by Dellamorra in **Gender and Sexuality** and Gagnier in **Politics and Economics**.

Case Studies in Reading Critical Texts

Miriam Elizabeth Burstein, Martin Danahay, Carol Margaret Davison and Solveig C. Robinson

---

Chapter Overview

This chapter considers a selection of key critical texts (that is, book-length works of literary and cultural analysis by leading academic scholars) that are widely regarded as having had a significant influence on the way we now think about the Victorians and their literature. The selection includes Sandra Gilbert and Susan Gubar's *The Madwoman in the Attic*, Patrick Brantlinger's *Rule of Darkness*, Mary Poovey's *Making a Social Body*, Linda K. Hughes and Michael Lund's *The Victorian Serial*, Isobel Armstrong's *Victorian Poetry and Poetics* and Kate Flint's *The Woman Reader*. In writing about these works, the contributors to this chapter have attempted to show how, in different ways, it is possible to evaluate their content. This type of critical review of academic work is at one remove from the analysis of Victorian literature that was exemplified in the previous chapter. Here, other critics offer an analysis *of an analysis* of a literary text or texts. Being able to comment profitably on existing academic criticism is a vital part of the study of Victorian literature. It shows an awareness of the ongoing debates on a particular piece of literature and an ability to find a place for personal analysis within prevailing critical opinion. It is unusual (outside the review pages of academic journals) to undertake an extensive reading of a single critical work, as the contributors do here. Nevertheless their examples of what it entails to comment effectively on the work of other scholars – close reading, contextualization within critical paradigms, evaluations of structure and content, consideration of inclusions and exclusions, succinct summary – provide a series of useful touchstones for critical examinations of any, and all, Victorian scholarship.

Sandra M. Gilbert and Susan Gubar, *The Madwoman in the Attic: The Woman Writer and the Nineteenth-Century Literary Imagination*

Edition cited: *The Madwoman in the Attic: The Woman Writer and the Nineteenth-Century Literary Imagination*, New Haven: Yale University Press, 1979.

Context

Sandra M. Gilbert's and Susan Gubar's monumental study *The Madwoman in the Attic* (1979) emerged out of the feminist scholarship that sought to restore women writers' place in English literary history. To explain both the omission of women from literary history and the thematic patterns they perceived in women's literature, Gilbert and Gubar drew on critic Harold Bloom's theory, described in *The Anxiety of Influence* (1973), that literary history consists of a kind of Oedipal conflict between strong equals, with emerging authors attempting to challenge and shake off the influence of their literary predecessors. However, as Gilbert and Gubar explain, Bloom's theory is predicated on the assumption that 'author' means father, progenitor, procreator, owner, or possessor of his works. 'Where does such an implicitly or explicitly patriarchal theory of literature leave literary women?' they ask. 'If the pen is a metaphorical penis, with what organ can females generate texts?' (7) Furthermore, they note that the models of female behaviour depicted in male-generated texts are often terribly confining: women are figured as either angels or monsters, or they are silenced, trapped, 'killed into art'.

Twisting Bloom's theory, Gilbert and Gubar posit that instead of an 'anxiety of influence', a women writer experiences an 'anxiety of authorship', a 'radical fear that she cannot create, that because she can never become a "precursor" the act of writing will isolate or destroy her' (48–9). Women who sufficiently overcome their anxiety of authorship often produce texts that are 'odd' by traditional (patriarchal) critical standards, as the women writers enact 'a uniquely female process of revision and redefinition' that subverts the literary traditions in which they are working (73). To overcome her anxiety of authorship, Gilbert and Gubar suggest that a woman writer must look for female predecessors who will enable her to 'legitimize her own rebellious endeavours' (50), and they offer as a positive image for women writers that of the Sibyl, the 'primordial prophetess who mythically conceived all women artists' (97).

This theoretical framework is laid out in the first part of *The Madwoman in the Attic*. The remaining parts examine how various thematic patterns are expressed in the works of major nineteenth-century women authors, both British and American and drawing examples from earlier and later centuries as well. Gilbert and Gubar note that women's literature of this era is filled with 'images of enclosure and escape, fantasies in which maddened doubles functioned as asocial surrogates for docile selves, metaphors of physical discomfort manifested in frozen landscapes and fiery interiors . . . along with obsessive depictions of diseases like anorexia, agoraphobia, and claustrophobia' (xi). In each chapter, they explore the significance of these themes for the given writers and point out how various literary traditions have been challenged or subverted by women artists.

Gilbert and Gubar begin with Jane Austen, whose earliest writings play with the seduction plots that form the basis for both Byron's and Richardson's tales and for the Gothic novel. Austen acknowledges that Romantic and Gothic literature include some truths about the struggle between the sexes, but she embeds the traditional 'seduced-and-abandoned' plot within another more complex one: the seduction plot is generally an 'interpolated tale' *told to* the heroine, rather than what *happens to* her (3). In *Northanger Abbey*, Austen rewrites and challenges the conventions of the Gothic tale, showing how women like the hapless Catherine Morland 'have been imprisoned more effectively by miseducation than by walls and more by financial dependency . . . than by any verbal oath or warning' (135). In her later fiction, Austen creates heroines who reach a mature self-awareness, thus rising above the angry older women and tragicomic younger ones who play various supporting roles in the stories. This self-consciousness liberates them and enables them to become 'exquisitely sensitive to the needs and responses of others', thereby preparing them for the transition from daughter to wife (163). In *Persuasion*, Austen's last novel, greater self-awareness on the part of both male and female characters even makes possible an 'egalitarian society in which men value and participate in domestic life, while women contribute to public events', and heroine Anne Elliot enters into a marriage 'that represents the union of traditionally male and female spheres' (180–1).

Gilbert and Gubar next explore the influence of *Paradise Lost* on women writers, offering *Frankenstein, Wuthering Heights, Shirley, Middlemarch* and *Goblin Market* as powerful 'misreadings' of Milton's epic in which the rebels Satan and Eve are reclaimed. 'If both Satan and Eve are in some sense alienated, rebellious, and therefore Byronic figures', Gilbert and Gubar suggest, then 'the woman writer, in fantasy if not in reality, must often have "stalked apart in joyless revelry," like Byron's heroes, like Satan, like Prometheus' (203). In George Eliot's *Middlemarch*, for example, Dorothea takes on an Eve-like role when she offers to become her husband's amanuensis (as Milton's daughters were for their father). While she suggests to Casaubon that she learn Latin and Greek in order to transcribe his work, it is clear that she desires the knowledge for her own sake as well. In Mary Shelley's *Frankenstein*, the male characters Walton, Victor Frankenstein and the Creature all have more in common with Milton's Eve than with God or Adam, as they seek knowledge denied to them. Gilbert and Gubar claim that Emily Brontë is 'the fiercest, most quenchless of Milton's daughters' (308). Brontë's *Wuthering Heights* reverses Milton's heaven–hell dichotomy, privileging hell.

Central Thesis

The section on Charlotte Brontë gives Gilbert and Gubar's study its title and central metaphor. Brontë's fiction reveals how doubles and enclosure function as 'complementary signs of female victimization' (443). Jane Eyre is an active agent, engaged in a *Pilgrim's Progress*-like quest for herself, and Bertha Mason serves as a powerful double of Jane, since each of her appearances in the novel is associated with an experience of anger (or repression of anger) on Jane's part. Similarly in *Shirley*, active Shirley Keeldar is paired with passive Caroline Helstone, again illuminating restrictions on women. In sharp contrast with Jane, Shirley or even Bertha, Lucy Snowe, the heroine of *Villette*, is fundamentally passive and 'from first to last a woman *without* – outside society, without parents or friends without physical or mental attractions, without money or confidence or health'. Her story, Gilbert and Gubar claim, is 'perhaps the most moving and terrifying account of female deprivation ever written' (400). The authors also argue that the indecisive endings of Brontë's novels suggest that Brontë was unable to envision 'viable solutions to the problem of patriarchal oppression' – perhaps because none of her contemporaries 'could adequately describe a society so drastically altered that the matured Jane and Rochester could really live in it' (369–70).

The section on George Eliot begins with an examination of her much-neglected poetry and its theme of the difficulty of artistic expression. In 'The Lifted Veil' (1859), Latimer is granted poetic abilities but denied the power to create, so that he lives out 'the classic role of women who are denied the status of artist because they are supposed to become works of art themselves . . . or because they are destined to remain merely artistic, channeling their capabilities into socially acceptable accomplishments' (450). 'Armgart' (1871) tells of a female singer who loses her voice and is thus reduced to being an ordinary woman; she prefigures the characters of Mirah and Princess Halm-Eberstein in *Daniel Deronda*, other women artists who have to compromise their art (454–5). Gilbert and Gubar suggest that all these compromised artists may reflect Eliot's ambivalence about her own accomplishments (466).

Moving to Eliot's fiction, Gilbert and Gubar note that the titles of Eliot's novels generally provide a masculine or sociological 'camouflage' for dramatic plots that are in fact centered on 'portraits of female destiny' (491). (*Romola* is the exception.) For example, the title of *Scenes of Clerical Life* suggests vicars and deacons, but the stories actually focus on the plights of Milly Barton and Caterina Sarti Gilfil, who both die in childbirth, and of Janet Dempster, trapped in an abusive, alcoholic marriage. Gilbert and Gubar suggest that the self-renunciation practiced by many of Eliot's heroines – from Maggie Tulliver to Romola to Dorothea Brooke to Gwendolen Harleth – may be partly self-hatred, but it also reflects 'how the injustice of masculine society bequeaths to women special strengths and virtues, specifically a capacity for feeling born of disenfranchisement from a corrupt social order' (498). In effect, every negative female stereotype protested against by Charlotte Brontë is transformed to virtue by Eliot. Gilbert and Gubar claim that what redeems these novels is the sympathy among the women characters: by recognizing their potential for becoming each other, Eliot's women 'define the heroism of sisterhood within patriarchy' (517).

In the final section, Gilbert and Gubar focus on poetry, first addressing the misogynistic nature of much criticism of women poets:

> While the woman novelist may evade or exorcise her authorship anxieties by writing *about* madwomen and other demonic doubles, it appears that the woman poet must literally *become* a madwoman, enact the diabolical role, and lie melodramatically dead at the crossroads of tradition and genre, society and art. (545)

Part of the difficulty lies in generic distinctions. Historically, fiction has been 'commercial rather than aesthetic, practical rather than priestly', requiring 'reportorial observation instead of aristocratic education' and, as a result, it has been more open to women (546). By contrast, lyric poetry requires more education, familiarity with aesthetic models and traditions, plus 'a strong and assertive "I"' (547–8). While Christina Rossetti and Elizabeth Barrett Browning had the necessary education and access to tradition, they struggled with the inherent conflict between the assertive poetic 'I' and Victorian notions of passive womanhood. Citing its plaintiveness, Gilbert and Gubar claim that Rossetti's work suggests 'only renunciation, even anguish, can be a suitable source of song' for women poets (572). Barrett Browning found a more positive but still traditionally feminine mode of expression, substituting 'a more Victorian aesthetic of service for the younger woman's somewhat idiosyncratic aesthetic of pain' (575), notably in *Aurora Leigh*, where Aurora's rescue and support of Marian Erle and her child is what finally leads to self-fulfillment and reunion with Romney.

Gilbert and Gubar make a special case of poet Emily Dickinson. Dickinson did not follow Rossetti's and Barrett Browning's attempts to accommodate societal expectations about women while pursuing their poetic art; instead she largely opted out of society, metaphorically killing herself into art:

> Dickinson must have half-consciously perceived that she could avoid the necessity of renouncing her art by renouncing, instead, that concept of womanliness which required self-abnegating renunciation . . . she must have decided that to begin with she could try to solve the problem of being a woman by refusing to admit that she was a woman. (590–1)

In essence, Gilbert and Gubar suggest that Dickinson's childlike persona and characteristic white dress were strategies by which Dickinson 'incarnated the paradox of the Victorian woman poet – the Self disguised as the Other, the creative subject impersonating the fictionalized object' (621). Dickinson's creation of a new Sibyl-like self and her creation of a new art thus went hand in hand.

Summarizing Influence
Gilbert and Gubar's study is very much of its time. Some of their conclusions about nineteenth-century women authors (particularly Dickinson) now seem rather strained, and contemporary readers may find their arguments about the oppressive weight of patriarchal culture on women writers overdetermined or unconvincing. However, *The Madwoman in the Attic* is one of the studies that expanded and improved the status of women authors in the canons – providing the female precursors necessary to future woman artists – and that firmly established the legitimacy of feminist criticism. As such, its influence can be traced through many branches of contemporary critical thought and in many works on the history and psychology of nineteenth-century literature. Gilbert and Gubar thus appear to have freed successive scholars from the 'anxiety of authorship' they so carefully illuminate.

Solveig C. Robinson

Further Reading
See other work in **Gender and Sexuality**.

Patrick Brantlinger, *Rule of Darkness: British Literature and Imperialism, 1830–1914*

Edition cited: *Rule of Darkness: British Literature and Imperialism, 1830–1914*, Ithaca: Cornell University Press, 1988.

Defining Principles

Patrick Brantlinger's now classic study, *Rule of Darkness: British Literature and Imperialism, 1830–1914* (1988), was written as a response to the critique that his earlier monograph, *The Spirit of Reform: British Literature and Politics, 1832–1867* (1977), focused on domestic politics to the exclusion of imperial politics. Crafted as a sister study to *The Spirit of Reform*, *Rule of Darkness* is a work of cultural history grounded in the Foucauldian idea that discourse is a form of power. It examines what Brantlinger characterizes as the cultural impact of the widespread and evolving ideology of imperialism, 'the chief enabling factor that made the political support for and expansion of the Empire possible' (x). *Rule of Darkness* consciously follows in the tradition of two contemporary, groundbreaking works of scholarship that countered longstanding claims that Victorian Britain was anti-imperialist and theorized about the role of imperialist ideology on European and American culture – Edward Said's *Orientalism* (1978) and Martin Green's *Dreams of Adventure, Deeds of Empire* (1979). Drawing on Green's claim that adventure tales furnished the energizing myths of English imperialism, Brantlinger argues that while imperialist adventure fiction may seem to be located at the opposite pole from the more serious tradition of domestic realism, they are actually 'a single system of discourse, the literary equivalents of imperial domination abroad and liberal reform at home' (12). Brantlinger repeatedly exposes the nature of the dialectic underpinning this discourse: while imperialism furnished a reservoir of utopian images and alternatives that energized the domestic reform agenda, reformist ideas informed and bolstered the imperial project. Further, Brantlinger argues that 'it was largely out of the liberal, reform-minded optimism of the early Victorians that the apparently more conservative, social Darwinian, jingoist imperialism of the late Victorians evolved' (27).

Rule of Darkness is structurally symmetrical and astute. Its nine chapters are divided into three historically arranged sections respectively entitled 'Dawn' (Chapters 1 to 2), 'Noon' (Chapters 3 to 7), and 'Dusk' (Chapters 8 to 9). The opening two chapters devoted to early Victorian attitudes to imperialism parallel the closing two examining the *fin de siècle*. Brantlinger justifies his focus on the 1850s in the middle chapters on the basis that this decade marked a turning point in imperialist ideology before a new imperialism emerged during the scramble for Africa and other uncolonized countries (1880–1914).

Opening Visions

Chapter 1, 'From *Dawn Island* to *Heart of Darkness*', provides an overview of his subject and contrasts early and *fin-de-siècle* Victorian attitudes to imperialism. Brantlinger notes that despite the fact that the term 'imperialism' only came to be used in the 1890s and early Victorians did not label themselves imperialists, their agenda to extend free trade, commerce and Christianity globally essentially fulfilled that mission. He observes, further, that imperialism grew increasingly self-conscious, racist and vociferous with the waning of Victorian faith in free trade and liberal reform as the century progressed.

The second chapter, 'Bringing Up the Empire: Captain Marryat's Midshipmen', examines the novels of Captain Frederick Marryat, a writer whose works Joseph Conrad characterized as uneven – undeniably great until they venture on shore. Marryat established the pattern for Victorian imperialist adventure fiction ranging from the seafaring writers of the 1830s and the historical romances of Charles Kingsley, to the later varied works of Stevenson, Haggard, Kipling and Conrad. Brantlinger notes how, in a decade of social and domestic reform (1830s/1840s), Marryat's conservative fiction revitalized heroism and aristocracy, nostalgically recalling Britain's military triumphs during the Napoleonic Wars. Ironically, as Brantlinger highlights, such works as *The King's Own* (1830), *Newton Forster* (1832) and *Mr Midshipman Easy* (1836), feature youthful protagonists who actively escape social hierarchies only to find themselves caught up in naval and military hierarchies. Unlike their offspring, Marryat's novels regard miscegenation and 'going native' as positive events that combine the best characteristics of Britain and its colonies.

Brantlinger's third chapter, 'Thackeray's India', takes William Makepeace Thackeray's life and works as its focus while providing an overview of early and mid-nineteenth-century attitudes towards, and literary treatments of, India. The long-standing association of India with despotism, luxury and decadence in British literary texts, from Christopher Marlowe's *Tamburlaine the Great* (1587) to Robert Southey's *Curse of Kehama* (1810), is shown to have endured well into the Victorian era. William Wilberforce's view of India as a degenerate country driven by cruelty and lust echoes James Mill's assessment of that nation as one ruled by despotism and priestcraft. Thomas Babington Macaulay's claim that India requires domination likewise finds reverberations in John Stuart Mill's advice that Britain rule India with benevolent despotism.

Enter Thackeray who, in stark contrast to Marryat's representations of the empire as a romantic playground, disdained military and imperial adventure and cast India as an inferior nation and dumping ground for his less talented compatriots. As Thackeray lost the bulk of his estate in the collapse of the great Indian agency houses, India serves as the backdrop for his plots involving illegitimate commerce. In this regard, Brantlinger chronicles the changing face of the East India Company after scandals of greed and corruption seriously marred its image in the late eighteenth century. It was thereafter transformed from a militarily protected trading concern into a virtual branch of government that further cultivated the popular philosophy that Britain possessed a special duty to civilize India. The highlight of this chapter is Brantlinger's reading of Philip Meadows Taylor's *Confessions of a Thug* (1839), a then little known yet, in Brantlinger's view, great Victorian crime novel. This generically noteworthy work combines the traditional Newgate novel with confessional fiction and a Benthamite reformist agenda, and is recounted to a British police official by a captured member of the Thuggee, a secret Kali-worshipping cult of professional thieves and murderers.

A Broader Empire

In Chapter 4, 'Black Swans; or, Botany Bay Eclogues', Brantlinger turns his attention primarily to Australia, a popular colonial backdrop, he claims, for some of the most complex treatments of 'the conversion motif' – a two-pronged theme that portrays the British colony as a site both for the subjugation and conversion of natives, and the colonial master's possible redemption. Despite the establishment of the penal colony at Botany Bay in 1788 and the ongoing debates relating to criminality and the efficacious nature of transportation, much Victorian literature set in Australia – such as Henry Kingsley's *The Recollections of Geoffrey Hamlyn* (1819) and Edward Bulwer Lytton's *The Caxtons* (1849) – recounted colonial success stories. Brantlinger notes the exception of Charles Dickens who offered up contradictory representations of Australia as both a place of transportation and retribution and a land of promise and social rehabilitation. The climax of the chapter comes in Brantlinger's analysis of Marcus Clarke's then little known work, *For the Term of His Natural Life* (1874). Clarke, a schoolboy friend of Gerard Manley Hopkins, believed – as did many – that the primitive peoples of Australia were doomed to extinction. He emigrated to New South Wales in the 1860s where he wrote an unrelentingly realistic tale of nine escapees who resort to murder and cannibalism. This 'remarkable novel' thus radically undermines the possibilities of conversion and redemption.

Chapter 5, 'The New Crusades', offers a brief assessment of the role of the East and the Near East in the Victorian imperial worldview. From the time of Napoleon's invasion of Egypt in 1798, to the Crimean War (1853–56), the First World War and beyond, this region was, Brantlinger rightly states, 'a hotbed of intricate diplomatic maneuvering, espionage, and frequent war'. Commencing in the 1840s, it was transformed by the modern tourist industry with many Britons flocking to the Holy Land and the pyramids. Apart from a somewhat reductive synopsis of Benjamin Disraeli's views on the East, Brantlinger focuses on Richard F. Burton, a noted explorer, gifted Orientalist and an uncredited founder of the new science of anthropology, a field disputably defined as 'the social science discipline of imperial domination' (166).

Chapter 6, 'The Genealogy of the Myth of the "Dark Continent"', considers how that myth fed into a larger discourse about empire and constituted a projection of 'the darkest impulses' of Europeans onto Africa. The chapter examines the singular, hugely popular genre known as the explorer narrative. David Livingstone's *Missionary Travels* (1857) and Henry Morton Stanley's *In Darkest Africa* (1890), which made their authors wealthy, famous and national heroes, are basically, Brantlinger argues, non-fiction quest romances that fed Britain's reformist self image. Brantlinger also reveals how various Victorian intellectuals, in fields ranging from the scientific to the sociological, fed the imperial project. The discovery of quinine as a prophylactic against malaria facilitated the British exploration of Africa in the late 1850s. Similarly, socio-logical theory was marshalled to justify the imperial enterprise. Some main-tained that Africans were a natural labouring class; others, like Benjamin Kidd in his book *Social Evolution* (1894), drew on Darwin's speculations and proph-esied that, in the struggle for survival, Britons would eventually exterminate the weaker races. Brantlinger astutely notes the particularly 'adolescent quality' of much imperialist fiction: 'Africa was a setting where British boys could become men, and British men, like Haggard's heroes, could behave like boys with impunity' (190).

Resistance to Empire

Chapter 7, 'The Well at Cawnpore: Literary Representations of the Indian Mutiny of 1857', revisits India by way of an event that generated much public hysteria. As Brantlinger's noteworthy breadth of primary and secondary source reading illustrates, the mutiny remained a hugely popular topic from the publication of Sir George Trevelyan's epic entitled *Cawnpore* (1865) and George Lawrence's *Maurice Dering* (1864), to G. A. Henty's two novels for adolescent readers and *fin-de-siècle* productions by Henry Merriman, Hume Nisbet and Flora Annie Steel. Brantlinger charts a major shift in Victorian attitudes from a black and white moralizing interpretation of events whereby the mutineers were damned as villains and the British represented as victims, martyrs and heroes, to a more even-handed moral assessment figuring the mutiny as a response to imperial domination. Brantlinger again highlights the literary work of Philip Meadows Taylor, whose *Seeta* (1872), the last volume in a trilogy, offers 'the most fully imagined account in any Victorian novel both of the scope and of the motives for the Mutiny' (212).

Brantlinger's greatest insights emerge in Chapter 8, 'Imperial Gothic: Atavism and the Occult in the British Adventure Novel, 1880–1914'. In his overview of texts from H. Rider Haggard's *King Solomon's Mines* (1885) to John Buchan's *Greenmantle* (1916), he coins the term 'Imperial Gothic' to describe the novelistic sub-genre that registered anxieties about Britain's waning imperial hegemony. It combined 'the seemingly scientific, progressive, often

Darwinian ideology of imperialism with an antithetical interest in the occult'
(227) at a time when imperialism came to assume a pseudo-religious role. Such
anxieties manifested themselves in works like Bram Stoker's *Dracula* (1897)
and H. G. Wells's *The War of the Worlds* (1897) in the form of three principal
Imperial Gothic themes: (1) 'going native'/individual regression; (2) invasion-
scare narratives featuring attacks on civilization by barbaric/demonic forces;
and (3) the diminution of opportunities for adventure and heroism.

The closing epilogue, 'Kurtz's "Darkness" and Conrad's *Heart of Darkness*',
considers how imperialism influenced 'the often reactionary politics of literary
modernism' (257). In response to Chinua Achebe's 1975 lecture deeming
Conrad's *Heart of Darkness* racist and urging its exclusion from the curriculum,
Brantlinger theorizes about Conrad's fundamental ambivalence towards
imperialism: this novella possesses an anti-imperialist message that is
undercut by racism. This self-critical work gestures towards a moral idealism
it does not seem to contain. Brantlinger daringly suggests that Conrad, the
writer, also identifies with and ironically admires Kurtz, the empire builder,
for his ability to stare 'into an abyss of nihilism so total that the issues of
imperialism and racism pale into insignificance' (270).

Rule of Darkness compellingly exposes how the fictions of empire were key
to the construction of British national identity. Despite its minimal examination of such regions as Canada, New Zealand and the West Indies, this critical
study prompted the republication of various powerful, once popular Victorian
classics. Brantlinger's ongoing fascination with Victorian imperialism has
been in evidence most recently in his 2003 publication, *Dark Vanishings:
Discourse on the Extinction of Primitive Races, 1800–1950*. This work, examining
'extinction discourse' – 'a specific branch of the dual ideologies of imperialism
and racism' (1) – cogently extends his insights from *Rule of Darkness*.

Carol Margaret Davison

Further Reading
See Green, Said and other work in **Colonialism, Imperialism and Race**.

**Mary Poovey, *Making a Social Body: British Cultural
Formation, 1830–1864***

Edition cited: *Making a Social Body: British Cultural Formation,
1830–1864*, Chicago: Chicago University Press, 1995.

Understanding Society
Mary Poovey's *Making a Social Body: British Cultural Formation, 1830–1864* is a
collection of essays, many of which are republished journal articles, that show

the full range of her inquiry into Victorian social history. The essays extend the scope of her previous book, *Uneven Developments: The Ideological Work of Gender in Mid-Victorian England,* into areas such as public health, poor law reform and individualism in the novels of Charles Dickens and Elizabeth Gaskell.

Her essays on 'Domesticity and Class Formation: Chadwick's 1842 *Sanitary Report*', 'Homosociality and the Psychological' and 'Speculation and Virtue in *Our Mutual Friend*' are closest in topic to *Uneven Developments* in that they focus on gender issues. Two of the essays deal with masculinity and the ways in which Victorian discourse informed even apparently dry and objective documents like Edwin Chadwick's *Report on the Sanitary Condition of the Labouring Population of Great Britain.* Chadwick's *Report* was an apparently objective effort to understand the living conditions of the poor through statistics. However, Chadwick focused on the homes of workers, or the 'domestic sphere' in Victorian terms, and established the married working-class man as the implicit norm for his *Report.* Defining the normal man as heterosexual and married, Chadwick then went on to represent working-class male organizations and associations as deviant: in other words the *Report* applied a heteronormative model to working-class households. There is clearly a political agenda at work in the apparently objective tables and statistics that make up the report.

In addition, the model of marriage applied to the working classes was middle class. Poovey does not focus on gender alone, but also triangulates her analysis with class and, in some essays, Victorian ideas of 'race'. Thus in 'Curing the Social Body in 1832: James Phillips Kay and the Irish in Manchester' Poovey again focuses on a government report, James Phillip Kay's *The Moral and Physical Condition . . . of the Working Classes . . . in Manchester* (1832). The report uses a medical vocabulary of disease and contagion to describe the 'condition' of the working classes; as Poovey says, this language 'helps assimilate the politicized violence of laborers and trade unionists to the violence of cholera' (59), configuring social problems as the result of disease. Furthermore, Kay focuses on the Irish as a 'race' of 'barbarians' and as the source of contagion in Manchester. Kay's focus on the Irish transfers the apparently innocuous medical discourse into the realm of England's fraught relationship with Ireland, both wishing to repudiate the Irish and maintain control of the country at the same time. Calling the Irish a 'race' apparently makes them radically different from the British, but Kay's descriptions actually reinforce how similar are the poor in Manchester, whether British or Irish (70–1).

Uniting these essays is a concern with creation of a British 'cultural identity' in the period from 1830 to 1864. Poovey is not only concerned with overtly nationalist discourse like that in Kay's *Report,* but also the 'formation' or 'making' of a collective identity in texts as diverse as government reports and novels. The strength of Poovey's approach lies in her refusal to deal in stark dichotomies but to insist instead on the 'unevenness' of the discourse on British identity. She views it as a complex terrain of competing political and economic interests that led to contradictory positions in reports and novels, just like Kay's contradictory attitudes toward the Irish. As Poovey says, the discourse is 'always internally fissured and contradictory' (19) and such fissures are her primary subject matter.

The Social Body

At the heart of the formation of a British cultural identity according to Poovey is the concept of 'population'. 'Population' does not just mean 'people' but what Poovey refers to as a 'social body'. The term implies that the government needs to concern itself not only with economic issues, but also morality, health, sanitation and nutrition, or in other words the welfare of its citizens in all aspects of their lives. The old metaphor for the nation as a whole was the 'body politic,' a term that denoted an essentially political and economic attitude toward the government of the country, but Poovey argues that this concept in the Victorian period shifted into a new register. Crucial in this shift was the redefinition of political and economic issues as 'social' problems. The end result was the creation of a 'social body', an imaginary space of the nation as a collective in need of care and sustenance, rather than the nation as a purely economic or political entity.

Poovey describes this as a simultaneous process of 'aggregation' and 'differentiation'. People had to be aggregated into groups like 'the poor' (which was distinguished from the earlier term of 'pauperism') in legislation like the New Poor Law of 1834. Poovey's topic here is much like Gertrude Himmelfarb's *The Idea of Poverty* that charted the 'discovery' of poverty as an area of social reform. Poverty became a cause for concern because it was seen as an issue that affected national welfare. This 'emergent social domain' (11) thus came under government control and the subject of a whole array of 'experts' who collected facts, gathered statistics and made reports like those submitted by Chadwick and Kay.

Although she does not name it as such, Poovey's essays trace the emergence of a vast Victorian bureaucracy and the attitudes that normalized its intervention into all aspects of the life of its citizens. Here her work is close to that of Michel Foucault on 'governmentality'. For both Poovey and Michel Foucault 'governmentality' is not a question of the creation of government organizations so much as state of mind that enabled a bureaucratic consciousness that can be found in novels as well as in reports like Chadwick's. Poovey deals with this topic most directly in her chapter on 'The Production of Abstract Space'.

In this chapter Poovey sketches the 'new organization of space' enabled by a conceptual apparatus that had its origins in the scientific method. She argues that methods of analysis formulated in scientific disciplines, especially geometry, were applied to social problems (28).Geometric models assumed that 'space was continuous and uniform in all directions' and thus subject to mathematical laws; this assumption was translated in political economy into 'functional equivalence' and that 'individuals are functional equivalents within the state' (29). The nation as an imaginary space that was uniform and continuous was thus brought under the surveillance and control of government programs.

Poovey analyzes Adam Smith's *The Wealth of Nations* for the way in which social relations were made abstract and applicable to rich and poor. Furthermore an analysis like Smith's made the nation homogenous so that laws were applied to the nation as a whole. His analysis is thus part of the 'British cultural formation' that is the overarching subject of her book. As part of its mandate to ensure both national prosperity and health the poor came under increased surveillance and the subject of concern over their morality. In the interests of 'efficient morality' (35) the habits as well as the hygiene of the poor were deemed a governmental responsibility.

Poovey's argument intersects most closely with Foucault's concept of 'governmentality' at this point; part of the mission of 'efficient morality' was to create 'self-governing individuals'. A quotation from Robert Chambers captures this movement most succinctly when he argues that 'on every man, no matter what his position, is imposed Individual Responsibility . . . from the power of universal self-management and self-reliance . . . must ever spring the chief glory of the state' (22). The 'self-management' of the individual is seen as a social responsibility that also ensures the prosperity of the state. The individual must, in other words, internalize principles of 'governmentality' that make the interests of the state and of the individual coterminous.

Poovey illustrates this in detail in her chapter on 'Speculation and Virtue in *Our Mutual Friend*'. Dickens's novel explores such 'typically masculine traits as economic autonomy and muscular strength' but does so through the figure of the 'masculine woman' Lizzie Hexam (168). Poovey argues for a 'crisis of masculinity' caused by the sudden explosion of credit and speculation in the 1860s. The new economic climate both enabled speculation without traditional economic and moral restraints, and pitted men against each other in intense competition (176). Dickens's novel, Poovey argues, represents an attempt to pit a nostalgic representation of femininity and domesticity against this threat posed by economic forces. She sees the plot of Dickens's novel drawing both upon representations of gender and of race in the wake of events like the Indian Mutiny of 1857 and the Jamaican Uprising of 1865.

Poovey reads the novel as an 'individualizing technology'; that is, the novel as presenting models of subjectivity. This is not to say that the novel is necessarily oppressive, but rather that it can be seen as helping to create habits of mind that accord with broader economic and political changes in Victorian society. Dickens's novel is written in the context of the 'government promotions of self-help programs like savings banks, friendly societies and insurance schemes' (22). Again, her approach here is akin to Foucault; the term 'disciplinary individualism' (10) captures the Foucauldian argument that power in industrial and bureaucratic societies is not imposed from above but rather is internalized by its 'subjects' who act voluntarily in ways that help the state.

Poovey's analysis is made more complex by the double movement of 'aggregation' and 'differentiation' (8–9). While the concept of 'population' brought people into larger units such as the nation, 'differentiation' led to the creation of new disciplines like economics, political science and anthropology that created new 'domains' of knowledge (5). Thus Dickens, while his novel may address economic issues, does so in terms of the domestic and individual relationships. Broad economic issues would be seen as a separate domain from that of that of the novel; government reports could address economic and public health issues while the novel would be seen as focused on the 'domestic'. However, in 'Homosociality and the Psychological' Poovey reads Disraeli's *Coningsby* and Gaskell's *Mary Barton* as attempts to address broader social issues which can only do so through 'disciplinary individualism' because of the 'differentiation' of 'social' from 'purely' economic issues.

Uneven History

Uniting all these essays is Poovey's emphasis on 'unevenness,' the concept that also underlay *Uneven Developments*. In 'uneven' development, older forms such as the patriarchal model of relationships between men and women found in Dickens's fiction coexist with newer forms of subjectivity such as that engendered for men by speculation and credit. This idea is also termed 'relative autonomy' by Poovey (13) when she asserts that in historical processes while 'extrainstitutional determinants will always be mediated through language, practices and priorities of an institution, that institution will never free itself completely from which it emerged and in which it continues to operate' (13). An 'institution' here could be a governmental office or a novel, both of which have their own conventions of discourse.

A prime example of this situation can be found in the career of James Phillip Kay (he later changed his last name to Kay-Shuttleworth) who moved from the area of public health to the position of first secretary to the Committee of Council on Education in 1839 (12). Kay used an older evangelical vocabulary to explain both his recommendations for public health and education. Although these were later to become purely secular issues, in early Victorian Britain they showed traces of the religious context from which they emerged. Kay's career also showed the permeable boundaries in this period between the 'private' and the 'public' which had yet to be completely differentiated from each other (13).

As this close analysis makes clear, and as Poovey herself admits, this is social history 'from the top down', in contrast to such studies as E. P. Thompson's *The Making of the English Working Classes* which examined what the working classes themselves had to say about such issues as the sanitary movement. Poovey says that her interest in broad epistemological changes has led her to 'focus on the dominant rather than the oppositional side' of the historical issues (18). However, as she says, her emphasis upon the power exerted by institutions is always contradictory, and insights into the limits of power can be found by examining the internal fissures in governmental reports and Victorian novels.

Martin Danahay

Further Reading
See other work in **Gender and Sexuality** and also Poovey's and others' work in **Politics and Economics**.

 ## Linda K. Hughes and Michael Lund *The Victorian Serial*

Edition cited: *The Victorial Serial*, Charlottesville: University Press of Virginia, 1991.

Publishing Fiction
Linda Hughes and Michael Lund's 1991 study *The Victorian Serial* reasserts the importance to Victorian literature and culture of serialized publication. While contemporary readers generally think 'fiction' when they think of serials, the Victorians published and read every genre in serial form: fiction, non-fiction prose (everything from biography to cookbooks) and even poetry. Published weekly, monthly, quarterly or sporadically over a long stretch of years, Victorian literature came to its readers in pieces, with enforced interruptions. Recent critics have tended to elevate the 'finished' single-volume editions of Victorian texts; as Hughes and Lund observe, 'anything that appeared in installments was fragmentary, inferior', seeming to be 'loose and undisciplined' (13).

However, serialization was not only the usual means of publication in the Victorian age, but it embodied a particularly Victorian view of the world. This view encompassed a range of significant cultural changes in the areas of economics, time and science. In the economic sphere, the Victorians believed in growth and the value of investments over time, in 'the perseverance and delay of gratification necessary for middle-class economic success' (4). Hughes and Lund suggest this at least partially explains their patience with serial reading: the time invested in reading each part would pay off as the complete

Figure 4: *The Illustrated London News* (1859). Reproduced courtesy of the British Library.

narrative gradually took shape. The Victorians were also the first generations to experience time simultaneously speeding up (as railroads and industrialization shrank distances and accelerated processes) and slowing down (as discoveries in geology and archaeology extended the earth's and humankind's timelines). Hughes and Lund point out that an 'analogous contraction and expansion in reading time can be observed in serial literature', as readers encountered short installments of multi-volume (and even multi-year) texts (5). Finally, developments in such fields as geology, embryology, politics and history convinced Victorians that both natural and human events generally proceeded through short, stepwise changes rather than through the catastrophic upheavals assumed by previous generations. This, too, influenced their sense of how to read and appreciate texts. The result was a distinct form of reading: 'Victorian literature, because of its parts structure, was engaged much more within the busy context of everyday life. Readers repeatedly were forced to set aside a continuing story and resume everyday life' (8–9).

The Values of Serialization

While the Victorians read their serialized literature with a different kind or quality of attention, they also brought to it (and saw expressed in it) a different set of values. In each of their chapters, Hughes and Lund concentrate on a different key Victorian value – home, history, empire and doubt – and examine how it was exemplified in several serialized texts of the age.

Victorian home virtues constituted endurance, perseverance and patience. The long periods associated with serial publication meant that the readers who persisted through the long runs of given texts 'lived on intimate terms with characters of the imagination . . . sharing their acquaintance with others outside the pages, and so extending a kind of intimacy also associated with home' (16). This long intimacy significantly shaped readers' responses to the works in ways that cannot be appreciated by readers who only know the one-volume, 'fixed' work. For example, Coventry Patmore's poem *The Angel in the House*, serialized over nine years (1854–63), is a more interesting and interactive poem than the static 1886 edition, not least because the heroine Honoria is an active collaborator and critic in the creation of the narrative. Florence, the heroine of Dickens's *Dombey and Son*, can be 'unsatisfactory' for volume readers, but she was loved by serial readers as 'an active and evolving spirit of patient understanding' (33–4). The gradual developments in Florence's character and understanding took place over a realistically long space of time for the novel's serial readers, as did the restored, rewarding domestic life. Similarly, Thackeray's *The Newcomes* 'posits from its earliest numbers a world of great time and space across which relationships must somehow reach if a final and probably temporary happiness for the characters is to be found'; although readers of the earliest instalments complained about the lack of plot, those who continued with the narrative ultimately found the intensity of detail and relatively slow development paid off (44–7). In each case, Victorian readers entered into intimate relations with the characters, whose fictional lives ran parallel with their own.

Hughes and Lund point out that Victorian explorations of history took on 'additional resonance when they were embodied in serial publication' because 'a serial work is itself embedded in the linear unfolding of time, yet – especially in the case of novels and poetry – also aspires to a wholeness of shape and meaning' (60). The Victorians had a sense of being between times: a vast history stretched behind them, a vast future stretched ahead. Reading serial literature echoed that experience: 'being between numbers or at the end of the entire text was inhabiting one of those moments at which one glimpses or creates larger patterns, fixing oneself more securely within a scheme of history' (61). Historical fiction particularly helped to make those connections real for contemporary readers. In Dickens's *Tale of Two Cities*, the commenting character Jarvis Lorry stands in for readers as someone who is caught up in and also apart from the historical events the novel describes. George Eliot's novel *Romola* also stresses identification with the characters' sense of being within a historical moment: readers of the serial version 'often felt themselves to be in a position similar to Romola's, understanding with unusual clarity what had happened in the fiction to that point, yet less able than expected to predict how the story was "to be continued"' (74). And Robert Browning seems explicitly to have used the publication method to shape readers' responses to his epic poem *The Ring and the Book*: 'I want people not to turn to the end, but to read through in proper order', he wrote to William Allingham, 'Magazine, you'll say: but no, I don't like the notion of being sandwiched between Politics and Deer-Stalking, say' (89–90). The compromise was to issue the poem in four parts of three monologues each, so that readers approached it like reading court proceedings unfolding in a newspaper. Upon completion, readers could grasp the poem's meaning as a whole, 'leaping across the physical boundaries of each volume's cover to perceive the triadic structure still emphasized today' (108).

Progress and the Pause

Empire was another important Victorian value, and serialization worked as a metaphor to support Victorians' sense of themselves at the centre of a vast colonial network: like an empire, a serial 'starts with a single, limited part, then grows through the issue of additional installments, and finally comes to a conclusion with the appearance of the whole work' (110). Trollope's *The Prime Minister* is one work that actually represents the civil service of empire, as Plantagenet Palliser gradually assumes the reins of power and discovers how to lead a coalition government properly. The slow, journalistic unfolding of the plot garnered criticism but also steadily increased the novel's readership. Like *The Prime Minister*, George Eliot's *Daniel Deronda* also shows how leadership takes a long time to develop, although *Daniel Deronda* only depicts the start of Daniel's career. Like Browning's *The Ring and the Book*, the part publication of Eliot's novel also ensured that readers could not (as an 1876 *Weekly Dispatch* review suggested they would) 'rush to the end to see what becomes of Gwendolen Harleth'; instead, serialization ensured that readers would pay attention to the 'gradual development of character' (155). Hughes and Lund note that the long-drawn-out, cyclical nature of Tennyson's *Idylls of the King* validated for Victorian readers 'the ability of an Arthur to return' and the 'potential within Arthur's realm for renewal, growth, and expansion from a clear centre' (128) – and, by extension, that potential within the British Empire. Many Victorian readers quite literally grew up with both Arthur and empire: the inordinate length of time for completion of the sequence meant that 'A youth of twenty who read the "Morte d'Arthur" eagerly in 1842 would have been sixty-three when the *Idylls* assumed the form we know now. The poem was not just an artwork but an inextricable part of readers' own lives' (154).

But the Victorians were not just about progress, they were also about caution, and Hughes and Lund suggest that 'the characteristic alternation between progression and pause in serials' publication intensified hesitation and progression in the stories themselves' (175). Serialized works such as Trollope's *The Way We Live Now* presented difficulties for readers that paralleled the real ambiguities of the nineteenth century: there were no easy black–white contrasts of paired characters, characters themselves were often internally mixed, and the many plots were interwoven and almost never linear. William Morris's poems *The Earthly Paradise* and *The Pilgrims of Hope* also reflect Victorian society's reservations about accepted beliefs and cautious approach to the world. The plot and structure of *The Earthly Paradise* reinforce the idea of resistance: although the Wanderers 'must move forward from Norway into unknown lands to preserve their lives . . . if they persist in moving forward they simply move closer to death' (192–3). The work's part publication helped extend the internal patterns of 'doubt and hope, reversion and progression' (208–9). That this chimed with the Victorian zeitgeist is supported by the fact that after 1,500 pages of poetry over three years, Morris's serial readers were eager for more. Hughes and Lund suggest that Morris's *The Pilgrims of Hope*, published only in the pages of the socialist paper *Commonweal*, may have been both an aesthetic and a political statement: 'Leaving the poem in unassembled parts amidst the Socialist news and messages surrounding them implicitly paralleled the work's insistence on subordinating individualism to a larger, socially conscious group' (211). And George Meredith's novel *Diana of the Crossroads* demonstrates how even the exigencies of serial publication – padding or, in this case, cutting to fit available space – could reinforce the Victorians' sense of caution, in this case about what was the proper format for fiction, especially fiction based on fact. (Contemporary readers would have remembered the scandal surrounding Caroline Norton and thus could have anticipated episodes in the serial.)

Finally, as the case of *Diana of the Crossroads* suggests, not just themes but the very process of serialization itself expressed values within Victorian society, values that were challenged as the age drew to a close. Writers began to conceive of narratives that jarred with the dynamics of serial literature, and these new narratives demanded a new form, 'the single volume, an autonomous whole, in which all parts found their places in a unity of theme and effect' (230). But the new form was overlaid on the old distribution system, so that authors began to plan one-volume works that would be substantially reworked for 'final' publication. The resulting tensions can be seen in Hardy's *Jude the Obscure* and *The Dynasts* and Conrad's *Lord Jim. Jude the Obscure* began in serial form first as *The Simpletons* and then as *Hearts Insurgent*, and Hardy's efforts to make each instalment a whole rather than an episode advancing the continuing story helps to explain why much of Hardy's serial audience abandoned him. Conrad's *Lord Jim* shares some of the problems of Hardy's novel: originally envisioned as a 'sketch' in three numbers, *Lord Jim* instead ran to 14 instalments, all of which reprise the main event in Jim's life (the jump) rather than progressing the narrative. Hardy's *The Dynasts* fared somewhat better, perhaps because its mixed genre (a drama blending dialogue, prose, verse and scenes) and intermittent serialization raised different reader expectations, and because its content and outlook vacillated between Victorian and modernist sensibilities – as did society at the time the work appeared.

Serialization continues in soap operas, movie sequels, popular fiction and in some periodicals. The shared sense of suspense, anticipation and completion experienced by consumers of contemporary serials can help us to appreciate the appeal for the Victorians of their primary mode of publication. Hughes and Lund suggest that reading Victorian serials as serials help us better approximate the Victorians' experience of those texts and of the world.

Solveig C. Robinson

Further Reading
See other work in **Periodicals, Serials and Publishing Culture**.

Isobel Armstrong, *Victorian Poetry and Poetics: Poetry, Poetics and Politics*

Edition cited: *Victorian Poetry and Poetics: Poetry, Poetics and Politics*, London: Routledge, 1993.

Investing in Poetry

The novel looms large over Victorian studies. Victorian poetry might not be the shivering orphan waif that Victorian drama is, but it nevertheless remains a relatively ignored child – or, as Isobel Armstrong bluntly observes at the beginning of *Victorian Poetry and Poetics*, 'the major critical and theoretical movements of the twentieth century have been virtually silent about Victorian poetry' (1). Armstrong intends *Victorian Poetry and Poetics* to be not just a critical study of its titular subject, but more importantly an intervention in the overall composition of Victorian studies itself. Most obviously, Armstrong wants to clear a space for considering Victorian poetry as an object of interest in its own right, not simply as a disappointing sequel to Romanticism or a superseded precursor to Modernism. But Armstrong also proposes a historicist mode of reading that remembers the 'ambiguities' of poetic language and form.

It is worth considering the theory before moving on to the practice. Armstrong's project combines new historicism with deconstruction. Victorianists were relative latecomers to new historicism, which had already moved from its early modern roots in Stephen Greenblatt's *Renaissance Self-Fashioning* (1980) into the work of Romanticists such as Marjorie Levinson and Alan Liu. Strictly speaking, *Victorian Poetry and Poetics* is not the first important new historicist account of its subject; Anthony Harrison's *Victorian Poets and Romantic Poems: Intertextuality and Ideology* (1990) covers some of the same territory in its discussion of Spasmodic poetics. Indeed, Alan Sinfield's *Alfred Tennyson* (1986), with which Armstrong engages at some length, also combines historicism (more precisely, cultural materialism) with deconstruction. Armstrong, however, wrestles far more overtly with the contradictions between new historicist and deconstructive techniques.

Readers who believe that all deconstructive readings naturally collapse into a murky puddle of irreconcilable meanings may wonder how deconstruction and historicism could possibly co-exist. For Armstrong, deconstruction highlights the clash of conflicting discourses within the same text; the reader of Victorian poetry faces not *meaninglessness* but a plurality of meanings, the legacy of poetic language. These discursive struggles within poetry both shape and respond to struggles in other arenas – religion, radical politics, philosophy and so forth. Armstrong's argument here partly reflects her long-standing position on Victorian critical practices, laid out in her critical anthology *Victorian Scrutinies: Reviews of Poetry 1830–1870* (1972): for the Victorians, there is rarely such a thing as aesthetics without political, moral or other cultural content. Moreover, because poetry is a form of politics – by which Armstrong means not party politics, but all the processes of engagement with the world – poetics itself becomes a political act.

Deconstruction's hand reveals itself further in one of Armstrong's most significant claims: that which she calls 'the double poem' flourished during the Victorian period before giving way at the end of the nineteenth century. The seeds of Armstrong's 'double poem' are already visible in her earlier book, *Language as Living Form in Nineteenth-Century Poetry* (1982), a formalist study characterized by an intensively rigorous programme of close reading. There, doubleness did not *define* nineteenth-century poetry so much as it frequently manifested itself at moments of great poetic crisis. In *Victorian Poetry and Poetics*, however, the double poem – manifested most notably in various forms of dramatic poetry – is the Victorian period's most significant poetic innovation. According to Armstrong, the double poem is 'a deeply sceptical form': 'It draws attention to the epistemology which governs the construction of the self and its relationships and to the cultural conditions in which those relationships are made. It is an expressive model and an epistemological model simultaneously' (13). That is, in the double poem, the reader encounters both a lyric expression of the self and the poem's reflections on how that self comes to be known – at the same time. This simultaneity is important, because Armstrong insists that the poem's expressive and epistemological movements act and react upon each other, remaining in flux rather than solidifying into *the* meaning. With the rise of modernist poetics, Armstrong claims, the double poem disappears, to be replaced by 'the poetry and poetics of symbol and ambiguity' (480).

Despite this overarching historical narrative, the book itself does not offer a straightforward account of Victorian poetry. Instead, Armstrong divides it into three chronologically arranged parts – the 1830s, the mid-nineteenth century and the 1860s and after – which are themselves subdivided into essays on poetic forms and major figures. The reader thus experiences a tension between the book's movement through time and its lack of interest in telling a critical 'story'. As one might expect, Alfred (Lord) Tennyson and Robert Browning play prominent and determinant roles, but Armstrong also devotes individual chapters to Matthew Arnold, Arthur Hugh Clough, Gerard Manley Hopkins, William Morris, Algernon Charles Swinburne and James Thomson. George Meredith appears together with the Pre-Raphaelite poets, while women poets are shoehorned into their own chapter. Reviewers criticized this somewhat awkward arrangement when *Victorian Poetry and Poetics* first appeared; in retrospect, given Armstrong's extensive recent work championing eighteenth- and nineteenth-century women's poetry, it seems even more puzzling. Not surprisingly, given Armstrong's interest in the double poem, the book focuses most intensely on the fortunes of that most Victorian of genres, the dramatic monologue, with its ironic investigations of what initially appear to be lyric speakers. But Armstrong also extends her reach to dramatic poetry more generally, as in her reading of Tennyson's *Maud*.

Tennyson and Browning

Armstrong devotes Part I to Tennyson and Browning, who serve as representative types of conservative and radical aesthetics – both of them 'avant-garde'. She begins by delineating two intellectual environments: the dissenting, politically radical culture, represented by the highly influential W. J. Fox and his *Monthly Repository*; and the Anglican, politically conservative (but 'subversive' (27)) culture, represented by the Cambridge Apostles. Fox, a significant force in Browning's intellectual development, was himself interested in the Utilitarian philosopher Jeremy Bentham, and Armstrong finds Bentham's theory of language behind much of the Fox circle's poetics. In Bentham, Armstrong argues, 'language is at once the greatest conjuror of illusion and the greatest social invention. Language for Bentham is made rather than given, since it creates "fictions", that is, words such as "soul", for which there is no corresponding entity in reality' (35). By contrast, Armstrong claims, the Apostles tried to avoid the linguistic instabilities of Bentham's model by substituting 'the continuity of history' as a guarantor of 'meaning' (35). At the same time, however, Armstrong finds several points of contact between the two apparently opposing sides, ranging from their attempts to conceptualize the intellectual's role in early Victorian culture to their belief in the significance of gender (37). Note that Armstrong's interest in doubleness and its self-deconstruction extends to her characterization of Victorian intellectual history: we have two authors who represent two sides of a particular debate, and yet each side raises points of controversy which link them to the other.

Although Armstrong identifies Tennyson and Browning with conservative and radical aesthetics, she nevertheless distinguishes the former from what she terms the 'reactionary' Tory poets and the latter from the theories of drama on offer from Fox and John Stuart Mill. Armstrong finds the Tennyson of the 1830s and 1840s revealing that the 'poetry of sensation' – among other things, 'the Romantic account of the unity of mind and world, subject and object' (79) – is a fiction. There is no natural, immediate connection between, say, nature and the perceiving subject; any such apparent unities actually derive from the work of the creative mind. More trenchantly, Armstrong's account of Browning's early dramatic monologues takes on the standard literary historiography of that genre, including Robert Langbaum's *The Poetry of Experience: The Dramatic Monologue in Modern Literary Tradition* (1956), Herbert Tucker's *Browning's Beginnings: The Art of Disclosure* (1980) and Loy D. Martin's *Browning's Dramatic Monologues and the Post-Romantic Subject* (1985). Reading Browning against W. J. Fox, Armstrong argues that just as Tennyson deconstructs the post-Romantic, Tory fashion for the poetry of sensation, so Browning deconstructs Fox's enthusiasm for dramatic poetry by following Bentham's line of thought on fictions. Armstrong repeatedly invokes the word 'sceptical' to describe the poetics of Browning's dramatic monologues, which she interprets as 'a dare with the status of the fiction, an analytical process which ceaselessly investigates the nature of utterance and its representations and their cultural meaning' (154). What, in other words, does it mean to speak – to make and experience fictions about the world?

After 1848

In Part II, Armstrong examines the poetry that emerged during and after the revolutionary movements of 1848. Not surprisingly, she argues that the poetry of this period, exemplified here by Arnold, Clough, Morris and the women poets, engages critically with Tennyson and Browning while it also embodies the upheavals of the age. Even language becomes uncertain:

> The question of representation is more tentatively explored as a gap between sign and meaning; language becomes that which possesses an independent life eluding consciousness. It is seen as that which makes communal understanding impossible by its inherent ambiguities and fatal capacity to invite misprision. (168)

In Clough, the 'radical', the double poem explores the nature of language itself – specifically, the interplay of dialects and their capacity to stratify or unify society. (Armstrong goes on to compare Clough's project with that of the contemporary Chartist poets.) Arnold, who exemplifies the 'liberal', tries to counter Clough with his own theory of the 'grand style', which, Armstrong argues, 'in its simplicity was intended to be *universal* and thus generally accessible, enabling the moral effect of poetry to be widely experienced' (217). Nevertheless, Arnold's poems reveal not just this quest for an absolutely purified style, but also the 'terror' (219) that lies behind Arnold's attempt to keep everything else out. Finally, in Morris, as well as in Browning, Armstrong sees a version of John Ruskin's theory of the medieval grotesque at work. The grotesque, as Armstrong sees it, is 'abberant' (236) or 'a form of play' (237): through its drastic manipulation of difference, it forces the reader or viewer into a heightened consciousness of form. In particular, the 'enslaved Grotesque' (239), created out of workers' oppression, offers an especially dramatic and unsettling attempt to work through the horror of everyday existence. Armstrong sees Morris adapting Ruskin's theory to his own poetry and reworking it to lay bare other modes of cruel domination, such as those that lie within gender relations.

After returning to Tennyson (whom she sees engaging in increasingly critical dialogue with the late Arthur Henry Hallam) and Browning (whom she sees refining the politics of the grotesque through the dramatic monologue), Armstrong finally takes on the women poets. Although Armstrong critiques blunt-edged feminist interpretations of such poets, she nevertheless argues that women poets occupy their own 'tradition', one which developed out of the late Romantic poetry of Felicia Hemans and Letitia Elizabeth Landon (323). Armstrong argues that women's poetry relies on but also interrogates the conventions of nineteenth-century expressivism, remaining 'always deeply concerned with struggle and limit, transgression and boundary, silence and language' (344). Expressivism becomes key precisely because it is gendered feminine: women turn to expressive theory because it is somehow 'appropriate' for them to do so, but also critique its inconsistencies and even its potential oppressiveness. For Armstrong, the poet who best embodies this intricate dance with expressivism is not Elizabeth Barrett Browning, the Victorian period's most famous female poet, but the early Christina Rossetti. Rossetti, she argues, transforms 'limit' into its own strange form of freedom.

Sensation and the Grotesque

Finally, in Part III, Armstrong traces the afterlife of both the poetry of sensation and the grotesque in the work of Swinburne, Hopkins, Meredith and Thomson. In all four cases, Armstrong finds poetic language undergoing another crisis. Armstrong argues that Swinburne and Hopkins effectively invert the political implications of the poetry of sensation and the grotesque, but do so by exploring 'the breakdown of language, which they express in terms of the collapse of form and content, the breaking apart of sign and referent' (403). Swinburne and Hopkins's radical experiments in poetic language thus link what appear to be two very different poets – politically, religiously and otherwise. Similarly, Meredith's theory of comedy, critical because 'it is about people who do not *know* about the contradictions in which they live' (444), enables him to dismantle upper-class 'fictions' of love, gender and sexuality. Finally, Thomson's *The City of Dreadful Night* (1874) turns religious language against itself, the better to imagine a new atheism – only to imagine that atheism, too, might perpetuate its own disabling structures of oppression.

Concluding with the relatively minor Thomson may seem strange at first, but for Armstrong he conveys the sense of an ending: for one, the collapse of Victorian certainties about faith. Armstrong almost entirely skips the 1890s; her postscript briefly sketches out how the double poem unraveled in the early twentieth century, in poems which frequently *refuse* to engage in self-critique. An important exception is Thomas Hardy's massive epic drama, *The Dynasts* (1904–8), which Armstrong interprets as a Victorian siren song of sorts, 'the last great revolutionary poem of the "Grotesque" tradition, and possibly the last great double poem to be written' (484). As Armstrong hints at the end, after Hardy, the First World War puts its own stamp on the fate of post-Victorian poetics.

Miriam Elizabeth Burstein

Further Reading
See Armstrong, Harrison and other work in **Poetry** and Armstrong's other work in **Science and Technology**.

Kate Flint, *The Woman Reader, 1837–1914*

Edition cited: *The Woman Reader, 1837–1914*, Oxford: Clarendon Press, 1993.

Reading Women
Kate Flint's *The Woman Reader, 1837–1914* investigates the enduring debate about what (or whether) women should read. The private nature of most reading provoked questions about women's mental processes, particularly about the moral, sexual, religious and ideological dangers inherent in such an absorbing pursuit. Flint examines theories of women's reading, the social context of the Victorian and Edwardian debate, specific reading practices as revealed by contemporary women and the significance of sensation and New Woman fiction. Contemporary commentators 'chose to believe or desire that women read in certain ways', but Flint's investigation of a wide range of documents – medical and psychological works, advice manuals, educational

works, periodical reviews and articles and autobiographies, journals and letters – suggests that for nineteenth-century women, the practice of reading 'provided a site for discussion, even resistance,' rather than conformity (vi–viii).

In Part I, Flint identifies several concerns about women's reading: first, that reading would corrupt women (especially younger ones) by fueling a desire for romance and excitement; second, that reading would waste time better spent on domestic responsibilities; and third, that reading would lead women to question their roles within the family and society. What began in the eighteenth century as a largely sociological concern became a biological one in the early nineteenth century. Increasingly, the debates about women and reading turned upon the belief that a woman's biological predisposition to sympathy rendered her particularly susceptible to textual influences. This susceptibility opened women to positive influences, and advice manuals, educational materials and self-improvement programmes and societies were created to direct women's social and moral development, but it also rendered women prey to negative religious, social and moral influences, particularly through the agency of fiction.

Reading Practice and Influence
Nineteenth-century critics believed that 'reading had more effect on an individual's private and moral life than on his or her public concerns', and thus belonged more to the domestic than to the public sphere (47). In general, readers of both sexes were urged to read 'the best books' and to ingest a 'wholesome diet' of sustaining literature (history, biography, classics, moral works), rather than to over-indulge in the 'sugar-plums' of lighter fiction or poetry. As one of the functions of the domestic sphere was to provide a retreat for men from public life, escapism was an important part of reading's appeal – but critics worried about the dangers to women of such 'self-indulgent' reading. Flint cites medical and psychological texts to illustrate nineteenth-century beliefs about the different physical constitutions of men and women's brains, explaining that women were deemed to be in a permanent state of semi-adolescence, more sensitive and 'especially liable to the perturbing effects of literature calculated to shock and surprise' (55).

In Part II, Flint paints 'a picture of widespread assumptions about what, when and how a woman should read' (73), turning first to Victorian advice manuals and other instructional works. Many didactic writers were concerned that women read uncritically and that too much fiction would raise false expectations or breed dissatisfaction, particularly in inexperienced girls. (Poetry was regarded as less dangerous because it was less likely to be directly applied to a woman's own situation.) Educators suggested that girls' reading should be guided by their mothers, and some advice texts served as 'proxy mothers' by offering reading suggestions. While most critics assumed girls needed protection from certain kinds of literature, others thought that girls' 'natural' purity would protect them from making bad choices or from understanding potentially harmful passages.

Overall, contemporary theorists expressed a preference for 'efferent' reading over 'aesthetic' reading. Many urged women to practice self-control with regard to their reading: they should set aside their books until other work was done, resist reading the next instalment of a serial as soon as it arrived and even give up novels during Lent. More positively, they championed reading as an investment in domestic life, with women educating themselves to teach their children or reading aloud to strengthen family bonds, or as an insurance against boredom and inactivity. While much of the debate about women's reading focused on the middle classes, after the 1870 Education Act advice was also directed towards the working classes. Servants were admonished to respect books in the households in which they were employed, and employers were advised about which kinds of books to supply. In general, working-class women were advised to read the Bible, wholesome magazines and non-fiction, especially history and biography.

Where women read was often as contested as *what* women read. For the middle classes, a library at home was often a masculine preserve, but some authors recommended that it be redecorated to function as a family space. Outside the home, reading clubs were recommended as a way to help direct individual reading plans, and reading aloud was recommended as an accompaniment to communal sewing, or as part of parish work. As the century progressed, women's reading rooms and libraries were increasingly available, and public libraries offered separate tables or reading rooms for women. Debates about the functions and offerings of libraries increased, including debates about women's use of the British Museum Reading Room, where the presence of women was thought to be disruptive to 'serious' male scholars. Women were also strongly cautioned against indiscriminate browsing.

The expansion of women's education prompted debates about what girls should know, how literature should be studied and about the relationship between formal and leisure reading. Flint notes that the debates were usually based on the assumption of a girl's eventual marriage and maternity, but other factors could also apply. For example, the systematic study of English literature was valued not only 'because of the humanist influences which it might impart', but also because it could foster 'a sense of both national identity and continuity' (133). Flint notes that where girls were concerned, 'scholarly practices in reading literature were seen . . . as de-feminizing the subject of study', yet at the same time, 'using literature to cultivate both the imagination, and the powers of subjective response to emotional and aesthetic factors, meant encouraging precisely those non-critical reading practices which induced concern in both protective and feminist commentators alike' (136).

Flint also examines how the contemporary press joined the debate. In reviews and articles, the 'woman reader' functioned variously as a point of reference for judging the literary merits of texts, as an object of scorn, or as a subject of investigation. Because 'the dominant critical standard was tacitly assumed to be male, and hence the reader . . . was habitually thought to be male as well' (147), when women readers did enter into the picture, they were generally regarded as shallow; thus, certain works and authors that sought to be regarded as more serious and demanding were marketed as being *not* for women. However, some reviewers – often women themselves – did assume that women read for more serious purposes, and that they especially sought female role models and exempla.

The religious and feminist presses represented the poles of the debate about women readers. The evangelical press was often firmly opposed to women readers, especially of the working classes, and it was particularly opposed to women's novel reading, stressing fiction's power 'to engender false standards and expectations and to promote frivolity' (149). By contrast, the feminist press consistently urged a greater breadth of reading for women. By the 1890s, papers like *Shafts* urged the critical analysis of texts, exhorting women to consider 'their own point of view with relation to the principles at stake' and to compare the information given in a text – fictional or otherwise – 'with their own knowledge of facts' (153).

What to Read?
In Part III, Flint addresses the complicated issue of what women were actually reading. At the turn of the century, several surveys attempted to determine this, and the results raised concerns about the debasement of women's literary taste from the mid-nineteenth century. (Critics mostly blamed an increase in women's discretionary income and the growth of public libraries.) Noting that the survey results might nevertheless have reflected '"suitable" rather than accurate responses' to questions, Flint turns to evidence of women's reading in autobiographies, letters and journals. These primary documents reveal both the 'extreme heterogeneity of readers and their texts throughout the period' and 'the specificities of circumstance . . . which militate against establishing neat patterns of generalization' (187). Overall, however, women's reflections on their reading show that they felt keenly the difference between the aridity of educational reading and the pleasures of aesthetic reading. Many women expressed gratitude to their mothers for introducing books or authors, or simply for encouraging their reading habits, and they also commented on the importance of their fathers' influence and libraries. Women recorded both the influence of particular books and the thrill of seeking out and reading prohibited texts. Flint notes that the commonality of much of their reading provided an important link in women's experiences: "The sheer frequency with which

certain texts recur in women's memories as having been significant to them is testimony to this', she observes, 'to have responded to [these works] is to have shared a relationship with others: to have broken down some of the barriers which divide public and private worlds' (249). She concludes that reading allowed the Victorian or Edwardian woman 'to assert her sense of selfhood, and to know that she was not alone in doing so' (330).

Fiction, a flashpoint for the debate about women and reading, is the focus of Part IV of Flint's study. In general, fiction was important because it both depicted reading as an activity, thereby creating a cultural milieu, and because it drew attention to the ways in which texts and reading were deployed by characters, thus serving as a lesson to the reader. Both of these functions assumed a (woman) reader who was in the know.

However, two sub-genres – sensation fiction and New Woman fiction – loomed large in the contemporary debates. Sensation fiction, which reviewers presented as 'being devoured by women', 'deliberately catered to compulsive forms of consumption' (274). Critics assumed that such works 'jaded the palate', but Flint asserts that this notion is undercut by the breadth of literary and cultural reference within some of the novels. The authors assumed their reader to be 'an alert interpreter, not one who will be content with passive consumption, but whose literary knowledge is called upon, and challenged, in the process of unraveling the complexities of the text' (287). Much anxiety was expressed about sensation fiction's sexual content, especially when it was written by women, but Flint suggests the real danger of the genre was 'the degree to which it made its woman readers consider their positions within their own homes and within society' (276). The later New Woman fiction was largely attacked on sociological grounds – 'such writing would cause women to question marital and family values, and hence would damage society's necessary structures' – but it was also seen as symptomatic of 'wider social decay' (294), at least partly because its typical *Bildungsroman* structure encouraged readers to identify with its main characters. However, the criticism of the effects of New Woman fiction on women readers was somewhat blunted by a shift in assumptions about how women read. By the 1890s, there was no longer so much emphasis on the interdependency of mind and body, or on controlling women's physical responses to her reading; instead, there was a greater emphasis on the critical skills women learned through reading, so that they 'were encouraged to apply the criteria they would employ when reading a novel to the society around them' (315).

Flint's study is an important addition to the literature on reading practices in the Victorian and Edwardian eras, as well as to feminist scholarship. The breadth of her investigation helps scholars to navigate the shifting ground of the opposition to women's reading and to see and appreciate the wealth of materials and ideas explored by the women readers themselves. Along the way she raises interesting questions about power, particularly the 'authority to speak, to write, to define, to manage, and to change not just the institutions of literature, but those of society itself' (43).

Solveig C. Robinson

Further Reading
See other work in **Gender and Sexuality** and Flint's other work in **The Novel** and **Visual Culture**.

6 Key Critical Concepts and Topics

Alexandra Warwick (ed.)

Childhood

Although the lives of very many children were spent in harsh conditions, the Victorian period saw the development of the 'cult of the child' and of ideas of the special nature of childhood that have their roots in Romanticism. In reality, infant mortality was high and legislation that limited the employment of children was slow in coming. The Act of 1847 only limited child labour to 10 hours a day, and it was not until 1870 that the Elementary Education Act made schooling compulsory for those under 13. At the end of the century concerns about the vulnerability of children – and particularly child prostitution – led to two adjustments of the age of consent, from 12 years of age to 13 in 1875, and then in 1885 from 13 to 16. Although legally a child could start work earlier, the establishment of the age of consent is effectively the establishment of the duration of childhood, as by this point in the century it is associated with the maintenance of innocence, specifically of sexual innocence.

There are two distinct areas in which a notion of childhood functions: the first is in relation to the production of literature for children themselves, and the second is the use of the figure of the child in fiction and art that is not intended for the child reader. As children were seen as unformed beings, the literature produced for them often had a didactic purpose. Similarly, in literature for adults, the child was able to represent both innocence and the danger of corruption in ways that were both about the plight of children themselves and metaphors for the human condition. The legacy of Romanticism suggested that the innocence of children was an ideal state that should be preserved, while a more evangelical way of thinking believed that the child should be educated strictly and swiftly to prevent a possible fall into sin. Dickens's child figures are good examples of the different uses of childhood: in *Oliver Twist* (1837), for example, Oliver is an example of the harsh effects of the Poor Law, and Fagin's gang of boys suggests other dangers facing the unprotected child, but Oliver, as an orphan who has lost his family, also represents the dissociation and rootlessness of contemporary society.

After Darwin, ideas of evolution also become tangled with ideas of childhood, so that whole groups of people are considered to be at a stage of civilization equivalent to childhood or adolescence, in relation to the developed 'adult' society of the white Europeans. This view licences paternalistic positions on the part of government and philanthropists towards the working classes in Britain, and towards other countries and peoples in the Empire. At the end of the century too, a clear gendered division arises in the treatment of the child and in the production of separate literatures for boys and girls.

Alexandra Warwick

Class

Class is a notoriously difficult concept and our modern sense of it emerges to some extent from the Victorian ideas of Karl Marx and Friedrich Engels, where class is defined as a group relation to the means of production; that is, whether a group is made up of workers or owners, and its share of the wealth created through work. But however complex, it is clear that people are in very different relations to the structures of wealth and power and that their place in that structure has a profound effect of their experience of existence. The Victorian period saw the development of a language of class and an increasingly finely graded sense of its existence and significance. Nineteenth-century commentators usually spoke of 'the working classes' or the 'middle classes': the pluralizing of the term suggesting a perception of the variations within it. The literature and art of the period increasingly came to represent figures of differ-ent social groups and to engage with the issues arising from class division.

The three broad classes that emerged during the nineteenth century were the upper class (the aristocracy and gentry), middle class (professionals, manufacturers) and the working class. In the mid-nineteenth century the middle class was relatively small; made up of men from the professions such as bankers and merchants, it was sharply divided from the working class. By the end of the century, however, the division was blurred by the emergence of a new class somewhere between the two: the lower middle class. Produced by the commercial expansion of the economy, it consisted of huge numbers of workers in the service sector: insurance, banking, accounting and trading. This class is perhaps most representative of what have come to be called Victorian values, closely identified with the Liberal ideals of individual achievement. They valued merit, respectability, competition, money and efficiency.

The upper class did associate itself with commercial expansion, but princi-pally in the areas of banking and finance rather than in 'trade' itself and, while a certain snobbery persisted against those who had made their money rather than inherited it, the aristocracy did sustain itself by being open to the more newly wealthy families, who themselves aspired to join rather than oppose the ranks. The upper classes were closely associated with an idea of leisure, and this was not endearing to the greater mass of people whose basic values resided in hard work and self-help.

The extremely poor constitute quite a different group from the working classes, functioning alternately as objects of fear representing disease and criminality and objects of pity and charity. By the end of the century the increasing significance of an idea of race was also applied to the destitute, who came almost to be regarded as a different type of humanity. The fear of poverty was also present in the working class itself, where the dividing line between relative comfort and respectability and destitution was uncomfortably close.

Alexandra Warwick

Degeneration

In the post-Darwinian period degeneration is a loose yet pervasive set of ideas that diagnose and describe an apparently regressive development at the level of the individual, society and the nation. Degeneration theory had a basis in biology, where instead of the increasing complexity of structure expected in the evolution of an organism, scientists observed simplification. In conditions that were no longer challenging or where environmental dominance had been gained, organisms were sometimes seen gradually to lose complex and higher order features.

As with Darwinism itself, the biological model of degeneration was rapidly extrapolated beyond the strictly scientific and applied in a wide range of contexts. Its diffusion and apparent explanatory power indicate its status as something like myth, capable of accounting for a great diversity of phenomena. Its strength was precisely in its lack of clear definition, as it could be deployed to explain many of the paradoxes that the Victorians felt keenly in the tensions between ostensible progress in material terms and perceived worsening of other conditions.

In the individual, degeneration was seen as both physical and mental, and bodily form was a key indicator of mental state. Thus the stunted bodies of the poor were easily seen as correlations of their stunted moral and intellectual growth. The anxiety about the degenerate was that his or her qualities could be transmitted, either by the mechanism of heredity or by a subtle form of contagion, thus eventually spreading more widely in society. Again, there is a confusion of the physical and mental, in which traits such as alcoholism or criminality are seen to be transmissible through the body.

In society the threat of the degenerates was that they would outnumber the 'fit', and thus the whole of the social body would slide backwards, losing its forwardly progressive momentum and high state of development, becoming less complex and ordered. In the late nineteenth century the fear of degeneration acquired a particular national aspect, in which the developing theories of race were placed against the imperial project. The imperial race was threatened with degeneration, thus placing the Empire's future in peril and promising a decline from high civilization to barbarism.

Alexandra Warwick

Darwinism

Although there were ideas about evolution before Darwin, his publication of *On the Origin of Species* in 1859 was crucial because it identified the mechanism by which evolution happens – natural selection. He argued that different species emerged as a result of variations in an organism that made it better adapted to its environment, thus more successful in reproducing itself and transmitting its variation to the next generation. Those organisms without the successful variation would either adapt in different ways (eventually becoming other new species) or become extinct. The idea of evolution through natural selection was potentially a very serious challenge to the prevailing description of creation given in the Bible. The biblical account of creation is of species created in seven days and already distinct from one another. In particular, humans are created separately and specially. Darwin hardly mentions humanity at all in *On the Origin of Species*, but his idea is quickly applied to it by others. Although the theory was controversial, it was not as devastating to the Church as is sometimes believed, with many churchmen and religious believers assimilating science with faith and reading the biblical account as metaphorical rather than literal.

Darwin's idea of natural selection is also rapidly taken up in many areas other than science or religion. The now familiar definition 'survival of the fittest' was not Darwin's own, (he initially used the more neutral term 'struggle for existence') but that of Herbert Spencer, and it was Spencer's version that had great impact on social and political thought. In this interpretation 'best adapted' comes to be seen just as 'best' with moral and practical value attached to it, suggesting that the 'fittest' are deserving and the 'unfit' are not. This 'Social Darwinism' argued that modern society worked against the principles of natural selection by supporting the unfit, and that this interference in a natural process would be detrimental because it would allow the unfit to multiply instead of becoming extinct. The unfit would then be a burden on the rest of society and would decrease its efficiency, provoking further and steeper social decline.

The political and social uses of Darwinism were persuasive because they appeared to have a scientific basis and a corollary in the natural world. If nature proceeded on the basis of slow change tested over time, then a similar process could be justified in human society, arguing against revolution or other sudden changes. In the sphere of Social Darwinism it was a theory that could be employed against state or private philanthropic enterprise and in support of the social status quo.

Alexandra Warwick

Gender

Victoria was the Queen, Empress, head of the Church, head of state and chief of the Army. At her accession to the throne her female subjects could not, among other things, vote, own property, enter into legal contracts, gain custody of their children, study for a degree or qualify for any profession. Their place and function in society was governed by ideas of what constituted womanhood or femininity. Although gender is the term usually used to denote the social role of men and women the assumptions that structure it are deeply rooted in other assumptions about the physical body and its influence on the self.

Nineteenth-century ideas of gender inherit much older beliefs such as the passive, nurturing and emotional character of women and the active, aggressive and rational nature of men. Although a belief in the fundamental difference of the sexes remained, the period saw the development and change of ideas about what that difference was and what it signified. Crucial to this was the change in Victorian society itself; as the public sphere of politics, business and the professions expanded hugely its separation from the private domestic world became sharper and women, who already had little public place, grew further confined to that private sphere. As the consumer society developed and class-consciousness became more acute, the leisured, decorative wife served as a marker of her husband's success and status. The home also became idealized as the place of morality. In his well-known articulation of the idea of the separate spheres, *Sesame and Lilies*, John Ruskin wrote:

> The man, in his rough work in open world, must encounter all peril and trial: -to him, therefore, the failure, the offence, the inevitable error: often he must be wounded, or, subdued, often misled, and *always* hardened. But he guards the woman from all this; within his house, as ruled by her, unless she herself has sought it, need enter no danger, no temptation, no cause of error or offence.

Men, by their nature and their occupation, are always compromised by exposure to the world, whereas women, because of their distance from the rough public arena remain sources of moral and spiritual comfort. In Ruskin's description though is a telling phrase: 'unless she herself has sought it' and this is one of the paradoxes of gender, that the greater purity of women is always threatened by her association with the body (as opposed to the 'mind' of men) and her weakness. Thus she is in greater danger of moral 'fall'. In the circular logic often deployed in thinking of gender, it then becomes crucial to protect women from temptation by further restriction of their activities and knowledge. The right to knowledge becomes key: the kind and amount of knowledge women should be allowed to have forms part of debates on, for example, education, marriage, medicine, sexuality and prostitution.

These questions indicate another fact that should never be overlooked in discussions of gender: that the 'angel in the house' was a middle-class ideal. Millions of working-class women were actually present in the public world of work, and many thousands had more than just a theoretical knowledge of the existence of prostitution. In terms of the bourgeois ideal, working women appeared not to be women at all, and the special considerations of protection that were thought vital for their middle-class sisters were not extended to them.

There were social changes for all women during the course of the nine-teenth century. In the climate of mid-century liberalism the 'Woman Question' was also debated and there were changes to legislation governing divorce, property rights, marital violence and custody of children. Women were also gradually gaining access to education and, by the end of the century, to work in offices and other 'respectable' employment. What characterizes all these changes is an underlying recognition of a woman's right to independence and self-determination, even if still fairly limited. The appearance of what became known as the New Woman was still controversial and, at worst, she was regarded as a sign of the imminent collapse of society.

One of the reasons for the latter view is that, parallel to the changing ideas and realities of women, there were shifts in notions of masculinity. Since the bourgeois ideal of femininity is the one that came to be codified as *the* ideal of femininity, the pressure of middle class values also affected the idea of masculinity. The values of sobriety, decency and hard work that constituted the broad moral shift in society also produced the ideal of the man as the hard-working provider and head of the family. The 'gentleman' came to describe an ideal no longer confined to the upper classes. In fact, a model of upper-class masculinity became a source of suspicion, since the upper classes were associated with leisure and idleness. No longer participating in the energizing struggle for existence they were seen as decadent, morally weak and potentially corrupting, particularly after the series of (homo)sexual scandals that culminated in the trials of Wilde. At the other end of the spectrum, there was another kind of anxiety, articulated most clearly in W. T. Stead's 1885 series of articles for the *Pall Mall Gazette*: 'The Maiden Tribute of Modern Babylon'. Here masculinity featured as a caricature of its qualities of strength and dynamism: as bestial, aggressive, violent and sexually exploitative.

At the end of the century masculinity and femininity were troubled categories as they seem to many commentators to be detaching themselves from biology, with women becoming masculinized through their entrance into the public sphere and men becoming feminized by the undermining of their roles and the contagion of decadence. The crisis was bodily too: for women in the disturbance caused to their reproductive systems by direction of physical energy to the brain and for men in their weakness brought about by leisure and inactivity. The exaggerated *fin-de-siècle* fear of degeneration saw the possibility of the collapse of gender difference and a resulting inability or unwillingness to reproduce that could lead, at worst, to the end of the imperial race. Renewed ideals of gender emerged, strongly focused on children and particularly on boys, in which masculinity is defined by decency, duty and the military and sporting values of courage, physical bravery and team loyalty – an ideal that was to prove devastating in the First World War.

Alexandra Warwick

Imperialism

Imperialism in the Victorian context was constituted by the appropriation or annexation of distant, foreign territories, ruled over by a metropolitan centre and by the imposition of a military order, the control of indigenous resources and the cultivation of an external culture. Colonialism, often a product of imperialism, involved the cultivation of settler communities on distant territory. By 1900, Britain controlled the world's largest empire and its possession was crucial to the nation's sense of its identity. The late nineteenth century is

Figure 5: Map of Empire: The Imperial Federation World Map.
The Graphic Magazine, July 1886. Reproduced courtesy of the British Library.

often described as a period of 'high imperialism', when it was the dominant force in European politics and the European nations vied for control of the African continent, known as the 'Scramble for Africa'.

The acquisition of the empire was not a deliberately programmatic enterprise: some parts of it were gained by invasion and military conquest, some were the result of Christian missions, some were trading areas brought under political control, others were settler colonies. The impulse of imperialism was similarly mixed: the encouragement of emigration, for example, was seen as a solution to the 'problem' of the working classes in Britain, while the expanding economy needed both new sources of raw material and new markets to continue its growth.

As well as the empire having material existence it carried an immense weight of imaginative and ideological significance: imperialism was cultivated at home and abroad by cultural production aimed at promoting the notion of adventure with the prospect of wealth, the desire to foster Christianity abroad (the 'civilizing mission'), and the propagation of nationalistic fervour, described as jingoism. The Empire functioned as an object of knowledge, providing a wide ground for scientific inquiries of very different kinds. Exploration was not always carried out for obvious personal or national gain, although there was a good deal of money to be made and status to be acquired from the sales of books giving accounts of travels. For female travellers, empire could provide an escape from social constraints at home: Mary Kingsley, Amelia Edwards and Gertrude Bell all published their anthropological and archaeological explorations.

Although political discourse was obviously important, for the majority of the British population the empire was encountered primarily as an object of the imagination. Attitudes to the empire were not undifferentiated; the areas of white settlement for example, were imagined (and governed) in different ways from Africa, which in turn was represented very differently from the Indian subcontinent. Written and visual texts were important media for these representations of distant people and places, and for the cultivation of popular images of them. While early and mid-Victorian literature was less explicit about imperial concerns, it has been argued that they are nevertheless a crucial unspoken presence (for example in *Jane Eyre*). Late Victorian imperialism, however, coincided with the growth of an increasing literate population in Britain, and the development of popular magazines. The increasing prominence of imperialism in the political arena is paralleled in cultural production, and in the last decades of the century the empire features more and more directly. This is obvious in texts like H. Rider Haggard's *King Solomon's Mines* or in the many short stories in the newly founded *Boy's Own Paper*, where fictional accounts sat alongside factual ones, further blurring the boundary between the real and the imaginary in the cultivation of an adventuring spirit. Imperialism also generated certain anxieties in fiction as fears of invasion or collapse surface, and there is a distinct thread that has been identified in *fin-de-siècle* texts in which the motion of colonization is reversed and the arena of imperial conflict is Britain. This can be seen in a text like Conan Doyle's *The Sign of Four* where the consequences of actions taken in the Indian Rebellion are played out in London, and often in Gothic fictions, such as *Dracula* or Richard Marsh's *The Beetle*, where the alien other is found at the heart of the Imperial capital.

Catherine Wynne

Industrialism

The transformation of Britain into an industrialized society was very obviously manifested in its changed appearance. The new towns and cities dominated the landscapes in which they sat, and by the middle of the century the majority of the population lived in urban areas such as these. The transport links of canals, roads and, most conspicuously, railways cut across the countryside. Industrialization changed the atmosphere as pollution blackened buildings and contributed to dense fogs. It also radically changed the conditions of the ordinary people whose lives were now led very differently. Such profound change would obviously have an impact on literary and cultural production and in the Victorian period this is apparent in a number of different ways.

Non-fictional prose is an important nineteenth-century form, and the first engagement with new conditions is found in the works of writers like Thomas Carlyle, whose *Signs of the Times*, published in 1829, is a passionate polemic on the new industrial society. The debates continue, even in unlikely areas such as art history, where John Ruskin's work frequently considers the effects of working conditions on art, architecture and cultural life. Matthew Arnold's *Culture and Anarchy* is another crucial intervention in the discourse.

Novelists soon become concerned with similar issues and an identifiable genre – known variously as the industrial novel, the social problem novel or the condition of England novel – developed. Such work was usually a depiction of the conditions in new towns and cities, often designed to raise consciousness of the plight of the people in them, with recurrent themes and scenes such as employer/worker conflict, strikes, riots and starvation and disease among workers.

These are only the most explicit of engagements however, as even in the non-industrial novel ideas of work assumed a new importance. Honest hard work, diligence and purposeful activity were highly valued and those outside the group that embodied such values were increasingly regarded with suspicion and even fear. The very poor and the aristocracy were two poles of idleness, detached from the central activities of bourgeois capitalism, who frequently represented physical and moral threats to the rest of hard-working society.

As well as the physical changes brought about, there was also a perception that the character of the people had altered. Thomas Carlyle commented that it was not an 'Heroical, Devotional, Philosophical, or Moral Age, but, above all others, the Mechanical Age'. Marx, too, famously suggested that conditions shape consciousness and his account of the alienation of labour describes how the way in which work is done robs men and women of pride and fulfilment, substituting only the gratification of money. Alongside older organic or familial metaphors for describing society, a new metaphor of society-as-machine becomes influential.

Although many people largely accepted industrialism, albeit with the hope that the worst effects could be ameliorated, there were those who wished to reject it altogether. William Morris, for example, envisioned a pre-industrial socialist utopia in his fantasy fiction and Richard Jefferies's *After London* exemplifies a sub-genre of the post-industrial. By the end of the century, too, a general shift towards an idea of heritage, seen in the foundation of organizations like the National Trust and societies for the preservation of folk music and dance, encompassed the countryside as the place of tradition and the past.

Alexandra Warwick

Marxism

'All I know is that I am not a Marxist', insisted Karl Marx according to his friend and collaborator Friedrich Engels. Marxism as an ideology, in the limited sense of a self-contained intellectual system or fixed set of political beliefs, was effectively an invention of the Second International (1889–1914), a European federation of socialist parties that dominated the late nineteenth-century labour movement, not of Marx himself. In fact, for all the totalizing ambitions of his theoretical labour, and in contrast to the caricature manufactured in both the East and West throughout the twentieth century, Marx always emphasized the changing, historically specific character of his thought. It is also important to note that that, although Marx now appears to us as the most important of left-wing thinkers, there were many others (such as Charles Fourier, Robert Owen and Louis Blanqui) who were equally well known in the nineteenth century, and whose influence was then arguably as influential.

The question of Marx's 'Victorianism' is also interesting. He was, of course, not British, coming to London as an exile in 1849, aged 31. The foundations of his thought were in European philosophy and did not initially arise from observations of the conditions of Victorian industrial Britain, although the empirical research of his collaborator Friedrich Engels and British economic theory were both important to it. Marx's work has very little, if any, noticeable impact on Victorian literature or art in its own time. It has, however, been one of the crucial influences on the study of the Victorian period. Two books in particular: *Culture and Society* by Raymond Williams (1958) and *The Making of the English Working Class* by E. P. Thompson (1963), both of which proceed from Marxian premises and deal substantially with the nineteenth century, were instrumental in the re-vivification of Victorian studies.

Marx first came to prominence as a leading figure and principal renegade among the Young Hegelians in Germany in the early 1840s, when he developed a humanistic conception of communism influenced by both French Utopian Socialists, like Fourier (1772–1837) and German materialist philosophers, especially Ludwig Feuerbach (1804–72). Yet, philosophically, he always remained profoundly indebted to the thought of Georg Hegel (1770–1831), from which he developed his own distinctive notion of what the latter called the dialectic. This emphasized a conception of social and historical reality as a phenomenon that proceeds through the production and overcoming of contradiction. Marx's materialism, summarized in the formula 'Life is not determined by consciousness, but consciousness by life', was the premise from which he critiqued Hegel's supposed 'idealism', and it formed the basis of his own mature philosophy. It was, however, in the field of political economy that Marx concentrated his epochal intellect, accumulating the materials for a devastating critique of capitalism, both on a theoretical level, in his constructive criticisms of

Adam Smith (1723–90) and others, and on a practical level, in his detailed accounts of the ordinary depredations of industrial production. More practically still, as the *Communist Manifesto* (1848) programmatically announced, Marx was actively committed to the revolutionary working-class struggle. The eleventh of his 'Theses on Feuerbach' for this reason remains his most apposite formulation: 'The philosophers have only interpreted the world, in various ways; the point is to change it'.

Matthew Beaumont

Race

The concept of race is relatively new. Although there is long history of writing in English about non-European peoples, the word 'race' is rarely used before the nineteenth century in describing or thinking about the differences of the world's population. The Romantic movement of the early nineteenth century gave impetus to a more recognizably contemporary view of race, in which it was thought that there were natural and unchanging differences between social groups and that those differences formed the history and destiny of the people. Romantic ideas of race tended to concentrate on European peoples and the development of their particular spirit, but the widespread practice of slavery appeared to lend plausibility to the sense that there were fundamental differences in the constitution of people that explained their very different fortunes in the world. Darker skin came to be a 'natural' outward sign of inner moral and mental inferiority. The Romantics were also responsible for the articulation of the idea of the 'noble savage' – a person or people untainted by civilization and living in an ideal relationship with the natural world.

Early Victorian writers on race continued in the circular logic of ascribing the success of particular groups or nations to a natural superiority, and the increasing success and prosperity, particularly of Britain, to its place at the top of a hierarchy. Writers like Robert Knox in *The Races of Men* (1850) suggested that all historical change could be attributed to race, and that the superiority of British industry and commerce was simply one indicator of its supremacy in all things. The idea of race helped to provide an explanation for the difficult question of progress, as it implied that progress was inevitable – part of the natural history and destiny of the race. It was, in the early part of the century, a source of confidence that a natural order supported the human construct of society.

Interpretations of Darwinism gave impetus and 'scientific' ballast to the elaboration of theories of race, as did the growing practice of archaeology which, as well as attempting to recover historical remains, focused sharply on the illumination of prehistorical development and the origins of humanity. After Darwin, race increasingly came to be seen in evolutionary terms, with different peoples positioned at stages along an imagined curve of increasing complexity and sophistication. Civilization is a key term that encapsulates these ideas.

As Britain expanded its empire, the sciences of anthropology and ethnology emerged and were often pressed into the service of justifying the imperial project. Theories of race and civilization become more complex and finely detailed in the differentiation of peoples and underpin political decisions and attitudes, for example in the kinds of government with which a country could (or could not) be entrusted. The concept of race was not originally solely associated with skin colour and this re-emerges to some extent in the latter years. Victorian society had its own class stratification, and this was projected in imperial terms too, whereby the monarchs, chiefs and ruling families of other countries were seen as having a closer relation to the British ruling classes than the British working class. Class division was another set of 'natural' differences, and the inferiority of the lower classes was common to every race. In late nineteenth-century writing the mapping of race onto class is frequent, and the East End slum-dweller is often understood in racist terms as irrational, superstitious, lazy, criminal, sexual, violent, childlike and inhabiting strange, unknown regions.

Alexandra Warwick

Realism

In the simplest definition, Realism attempts to come as close as possible to depicting life, but these simple terms are not necessarily helpful. This definition implies that literature and art are simply passive mirrors of life, rather than having any part in its construction, and other kinds of questions arise about the nature of the 'reality' being depicted. Typically, Realist fiction contains a wealth of material detail of clothes, furniture, buildings and landscapes, all of which tempt the reader to see it as an almost photographic rendition of what 'life was really like' in the period. To some extent this must actually be the case, but the belief in the truth of material detail can also then be extended to belief in the 'truth' of the characters or the accuracy of the whole novel as showing what it was 'really' like to be, for example, a Victorian factory worker. The latter assumptions are ones that should be carefully questioned.

It is perhaps more useful to think of Realism as a mode of representation that has its own recognizable conventions, rather than being something that accurately or completely captures 'real' existence. Georg Lukács offers a useful distinction between Realism and Naturalism in the nineteenth-century novel. While naturalism tends towards a pure descriptiveness, Realism is distinguished by what he calls a 'perspective of totality', in which the depiction of characters and events is directed towards portraying the social and historical whole. Hence, for instance, the particular law case of Jarndyce versus Jarndyce in Dickens's *Bleak House* may be read as standing in for a representation of the Victorian legal system as a whole.

In literary terms, Realism is often identified as beginning in France with a movement towards depicting contemporary life and experience without the stylization of Romanticism. While in France realism came to concentrate more on 'low' life and more desperate human experience, in Britain it developed into the representation of ordinary people and their lives. It was to some extent a product of the rationalist mood of Victorianism with its privileging of fact and empirical observation, and was influenced by the political and social changes taking place in the industrializing of the nation. Realism tends to view the human being as formed and motivated by context, rather than by larger spiritual or metaphysical forces and attempts to capture that process and context in its representation. It has also been attributed to the self-consciousness of the Victorians and their interest in themselves and their times, although this could also be seen as an example of the complex relationship between life and art, as the dominance of Realism in the novel could be contributing to that self-consciousness rather than merely just satisfying it.

In Realist work the emphasis is placed on the individual in his or her environment, and the experience and interactions of that individual form a context, as in Lukács' suggestion, for the larger interrogation of human values and motivations. For this reason, Realism is a mode that is well suited to the consideration of moral questions, and even for more didactic instruction through example. Again this contributes to its popularity with the Victorian reading public. It should also be remembered, however, that purely Realist fiction is very difficult to locate, and even those writers often cited as examples, like Dickens, are not without elements of romance, sensation, Gothic or other apparently non-Realist forms.

Alexandra Warwick

Sexuality

Like a number of other terms discussed here, our contemporary understanding of sexuality owes a great deal to ideas current in the nineteenth century. It is also intricately enmeshed with ideas of gender. Some words, especially those used to describe sexual pathology such as nymphomania or masochism, are used for the first time in the period. This indicates the emergence of 'sexual science', in which the description and classification of sexual behaviour is intensified. The influential theories of Michel Foucault suggest that the end of the nineteenth century is the point at which sexuality comes to be considered as defining element of identity. He argues that prior to this there were sexual acts, but that they were not necessarily seen as defining an individual's personality, thus, he says 'the homosexual' is an identity created at the turn of the century. The codification of sexuality at this time is not limited to what was seen as 'abnormal', but encompasses all practices.

It can be argued that the development of sexual science is related to an increasingly economic view of sexuality. This is evident earlier in the century where government surveys of the living conditions of the working classes often drew moral conclusions, for example that over-crowded housing leads to greater and earlier sexual activity, which in turn produces large families and further worsens poverty. A strong view arose that men should be abstinent until financially able to support a family. The economic concern was present in ideas about 'abnormal' sexuality too, which is seen as unproductive – not leading to the birth of children and therefore threatening the population needed to produce and consume in industrial society. This fear was most often directed at the middle class, and lies behind some of the antipathy to the New Woman.

Female sexuality was centred on motherhood, with female desire, in so far as it was acknowledged, being directed to this end. Disruptions of the direction of female sexuality to motherhood are seen to produce physical and emotional disturbance, such as hysteria, that are the result of the distortion of the desire for children. In an often complex counter to the notion of the passivity of female sexuality, questions also clustered around the social, moral and political question of prostitution (indeed, the characterization of marriage as 'legal prostitution' threatened to collapse distinctions between these Victorian sexual classifications). Most notably, this debate centred on the Contagious Diseases Acts of the 1860s (eventually repealed in 1886). Designed to combat the prevalence of venereal disease among the military, they became notorious as a symbol of distasteful double standards and were the focus of passionate campaigning by feminist philanthropists, such as Josephine Butler. The cultural presence of prostitutes ('fallen women') and quasi-prostitutes was extensive and reached across painting, non-fiction writing, sensation fiction and theatre practice (an area that vigorously reconfigured its association with prostitution).

A critical moment in considering Victorian sexuality is the passage of the Criminal Law Amendment Act in 1885. It came about partly in response to the moral panic produced by W. T. Stead's 'The Maiden Tribute of Modern Babylon', and as well as attempting to give greater police power against prostitution, it raised the age of consent for girls to 16. A late addition to the Bill, the so-called Labouchère Amendment, created the legal offence of gross indecency between men, the first time that any specific offence of male homosexuality (rather than the more general offence of sodomy) had been criminalized. The elements of the Act indicate clearly the major concerns of the late century in their increasingly precise regulation of both male and female sexuality. As in Foucault's thesis, however, the articulation of such regulation also provided the possibility of what he calls 'reverse discourse' where the availability of terms of definition (even when apparently negative in their effect) allowed individuals to speak about and define themselves. Alongside moral panic and legislation there is also the emergence of writing that more positively theorizes homosexuality (though much more focused on men than on women), such as the work of John Addington Symonds and Edward Carpenter. Although the writing of some sexologists is implicitly or explicitly judgemental of what was called sexual inversion, others, like Havelock Ellis, can be more liberal.

The most dramatic result of the Criminal Law Amendment Act was the trial of Oscar Wilde in 1895 when he was found guilty on seven counts of gross indecency and sentenced to two years' hard labour. The press and public reaction to the trial manifests many of the questions that have arisen in the re-conceptualization of Victorian sexual practice and identity through political, economic and social frameworks as well as more familiar moral or religious understandings. The variety of their treatments, then, is testament to the fluidity and approximation held within the notion of 'sexuality' in general, and in Victorian discourse in particular.

Rhian Williams and Alexandra Warwick

7 Changes in the Literary Canon

Jane E. Thomas

The Idea of the Canon

The literary canon is a contentious concept. The canon of Victorian literature is no exception, and the critical debate that has sought to define and redefine it is probably at its liveliest among scholars working in this field. The canon is largely the product of complex relationships between authorized literary, historical and cultural institutions, such as literature departments in universities and colleges, and publishers. The media – especially television and the film industry – also plays an interesting role in the consolidation and dissemination of the canon and the popularization of specific items within it. Film and television adaptations of 'classic' Victorian texts account for a marked upsurge of interest in writers such as Charles Dickens, Anthony Trollope, George Eliot, Elizabeth Gaskell and Thomas Hardy among students, independent scholars, book-group members and sometimes lecturers compiling syllabuses for courses and modules.

The canon is also implicated in a symbiotic and sometimes dialectical relationship with evolving critical and theoretical practice, in that how we read and why we read has a direct bearing on what we read. Current scholarly discourse is particularly directed towards defining, delimiting or reassessing the canon and predicting its shape in the light of new approaches to the literature of the period. Terms such as 'literature', 'period', 'Victorian' and 'nineteenth century' have been subject to intense scrutiny and speculation. Indeed the very term 'canon' is under interrogation – and some would say under threat – as the lines and boundaries that demarcate it are progressively erased and redrawn.

For obvious reasons – mostly administrative – syllabuses tend not to be immediately reactive to canonical revision, although university literature and cultural studies departments inevitably review their provision in the light of current critical interventions. The cutting edge of canon formation can be most easily tested in bibliographical reviews of a narrative or qualitative nature such as *The Year's Work in English Studies*, *The Yearbook of English Studies* and leading scholarly journals and periodicals that pride themselves on being at the sharp edge of the debate and where seminal moments in the review and reformation of the canon can be clearly discerned.

The term 'canon', originally used to designate those works by a particular author that were generally recognized as genuine (OED), describes a list of highly regarded works comprising 'our Western society's literary inheritance'. Tricia Lootens reminds us that the notion of the canon, and its role in the creation of cultural icons, has its roots in the 'traditions and rhetoric of religious legend in creating its own saints' which originates in folklore and oral tradition. The canon carries with it 'powerful traditions of sanctification and suppression' which are discernible in what she calls the 'conservative collective authority' of canonizing texts such as teaching anthologies.[1]

Conservative canonists defend the idea of intrinsic literary, and even moral, worth and cite the durability of certain authors and texts as proof of their value. Such works may be seen to constitute a legitimate national experience and to reflect the 'character' of a nation. Distinctions are drawn between 'high' culture, defined according to notions of aesthetic quality, and 'low' or 'popular' culture whose profile is largely the result of its economic success. Lootens and James Najarian question the assumption that literary value is inherent in a text, preferring to see it as 'an attributed quality' resulting from the consensus of authorized institutions at a particular moment and, therefore, a highly contingent and contentious concept.[2]

The idea of the canon has been increasingly scrutinized by revisionists who challenge the hegemony of powerful academic institutions or, at the very least, seek to instil a sense of responsibility and self-awareness in those who help to shape it. Their project is to reveal the ideological determinants of canon formation, its genre and gender biases, and to champion the claims of marginalized authors, or literatures that deal with experiences traditionally deemed peripheral. The effect of such revisionism is to undermine the idea of a canon in favour of new ways of classifying and combining texts and authors.

Defining the Victorian Canon

Hugh Walker was one of the first literary historians to attempt to define the Victorian literary field in *The Age of Tennyson*, first published in 1897 and reissued, significantly, in 1914. The Victorians, Walker declares, were defined by the failure of the French Revolution and concerned, above all, with the construction of a modern democracy. The spread of education from 1870 onwards, especially the education of women, and the extension of the franchise to working men is testimony to this. Although the social and economic position of the poor 'pressed upon the imagination' of writers such as Carlyle, Mill, Hood, Barrett Browning and Kingsley, the 'age of Tennyson', he concludes, was primarily an age of reconstruction in which the Chartists and the Anti-Corn Law League 'merely rippled the surface of social order'.[3] Walker distinguishes between Dickens, Eliot, Thackeray and Meredith, and 'the fat classes who minister to the wants of the popular audience' drawing a clear moral and evaluative line between 'high' and 'low' culture. However, class and political agitation are firmly placed beyond the pale of the canonical concerns. Alongside Carlyle, Tennyson and Browning, he lists Letitia Landon, W. M. Praed, Laman Blanchard and Thomas Hood as 'minor' writers.[4] Novelists of the early and middle Victorian period include Bulwer Lytton, Disraeli, G. P. R James, Captain Marryat, Samuel Warren, Dickens, Thackeray and the Brontës (Charlotte and Emily) and Mrs (sic) Gaskell. Under the heading 'Historians and Biographers' he lists Carlyle, Macaulay, Arnold, Connop Thirlwall, George Grote and J. A. Froude. Keble, Newman, Pusey, Jowett, Mark Pattison, Mill, Lewes and Spencer appear under 'Theology and Philosophy', and Lyell, Darwin and Wallace under 'Science'. 'Criticism and Scholarship' includes the 'Intellectual Poets': Matthew Arnold, Anna Jameson, Ruskin, Clough, Tennyson, Robert Browning, Barrett Browning and Edward Fitzgerald. Walker also mentions, in a separate category, the Pre-Raphaelite poets – Dante Gabriel Rossetti, Coventry Patmore and William Morris – and the 'Spasmodics' – Aytoun, Dobell and Smith. 'Minor' writers include S. F. Adams, William Allingham, William Cory, Dora Greenwell, Edward Lear, Adelaide Ann Procter, Caroline Norton and Menella Bute Smedley. George Eliot, Mrs Henry Wood, Dinah Craik, Kingsley and Charles Reade appear under 'Later Fiction'.

In a later edition Tennyson and Browning take centre position in Walker's congregation of saints supported by the 'lesser' women poets. Sara Coleridge, Caroline Norton, Felicia Hemans, Sarah Flower Adams and Fanny Kemble supplement Barrett Browning and Christina Rossetti, and under the heading 'later Poetesses' he lists Dinah Craik, Eliza Cook, Dora Greenwell, Emily

Pfeiffer, Jean Ingelow, Augusta Webster and Constance Naden. The Pre-Raphaelites feature strongly as Thomas Gordon Hake, Thomas Woolner, William Bell Scott and J. Noel Paton join Rossetti, in addition to Richard Watson Dixon, Roden Noel and Arthur O'Shaughnessy. James Thomson appears under the heading 'The Poetry of Pessimism'. Walker expands his list of novelists to include George Du Maurier, Margaret Oliphant and Charlotte Yonge. Henry Kingsley and Albert Smith also feature and the category 'New Romantics' includes Stevenson, Walter Besant, Samuel Butler and George Gissing.

Although Walker's aims are avowedly conservative, this surprisingly capacious and eclectic list testifies to the high regard in which women writers were held in the early twentieth century. He includes more than 40 women in his survey of the field. While there is no overt consideration here of issues of race, nationality or class, imperial concerns are gestured in under the heading of 'Patriotic Verse', which features Arnold and Clough, and Walker creates a new category of 'Celtic Poets' to include Aubrey de Vere, William Allingham, George MacDonald and Robert Buchanan but fails to register the political implications of such a grouping. Recent contemporary interest in travel writing is anticipated by over half a century with the inclusion of Stanley's African writings; Speke and Lane on Egypt and the Nile; Lafacdio Hearn on Japan; Borrow on Spain, Wales and the Gypsies; Burton's *Arabian Nights* and Samuel Baker on Abyssinia. Walker also includes the sporting writers, the critics, the historians and biographers.

At the start of the new century the debate was focused not so much on what the Victorian literary canon should consist of but whether any of it was worth reading at all. In 1918, Lytton Strachey criticized the age for its hypocrisy, cant and pious hagiography, attacking its preoccupations with Church, public school and empire, and initiating the postmodern turn to the 'Victorians' as the 'Other' against which the present defines itself.[5]

Six years after the publication of *Eminent Victorians*, Stewart M. Ellis dismissed the debunking of the Victorians as 'an amusing pastime rather than a meaningful criticism; the distortion of a past culture representing little more than the evasion of a present problem'.[6] The writers of the period, he claimed, were largely engaged in modifying or discarding attitudes that they had themselves inherited: Tennyson, in particular, he suggests, 'speaks to an enquiring mind'.[7]

Ellis is particularly critical of those 'journalistic young men', and the 'tube-like' and 'shingled' women who lampoon their grandmothers and great-grandmothers: independent women whose desire to lead their own life was equally as strong as that of their young detractors. Ellis's witty and amusing attack on the 'Young Barbarians' may seem a little strident, but it was a timely reminder that the Victorians were often their own severest critics.

Oliver Elton's 1920 survey of the period of 1830 to 1880 is predictably defensive. He subdivides writers into 'Prose Writers', 'Poets' and 'Novelists', slightly revising his list in 1924. The 'Prose Writers' include Carlyle, Mill, Comte, Spencer, Darwin, Huxley and Leslie Stephen as 'Thinkers' or 'Sages'; Bagehot, Lecky, Macaulay, Froude, Arnold and Seeley as 'Historians'; the 'Tractarians' Pusey and Newman; Ruskin, Arnold and Pater as 'Critics' and the 'Essayists' Jefferies, Butler and Borrow. 'Poets' include Tennyson, Swinburne, 'the Brownings' and 'the Rossettis', and the 'Novelists' are represented by William Morris, Bulwer Lytton, Dickens, Wilkie Collins, Charles Reade, Thackeray, Eliot and Trollope. Elton also makes space for the Brontës (Charlotte and Emily), Gaskell, Charlotte Yonge, Mrs Oliphant, Mrs Braddon, Mrs Henry Wood and Dinah Mulock, as well as Kingsley and Meredith. Hardy is not included, perhaps because he is seen as primarily a novelist of the late Victorian period and a twentieth-century poet. Elton concludes: 'I hope at least to have shown that more Victorian prose and verse deserves to live than is sometimes imagined'.[8] Again women feature strongly and a clear distinction is made between prose and fiction writers, and between historians, critics, essayists and 'Sages'. In terms of aesthetic value, poetry takes pride of place for both critics.

The issue of the literary and spiritual value of Victorian literature was still alive in the 1930s. For John W. Cunliffe the Victorian age was primarily distinguished by the conflict between 'the authoritative spokesmen of revealed religion and the protagonists of scientific research which has revolutionised modern thought'.[9] Batho and Dobrée extend the period to include the years up to 1914, pertinently declaring at the outset: 'it has become a platitude to say that an age is reflected in its literature . . . an age is often much better represented by what is no longer read'.[10] While apologizing for perceived errors and admissions, citing 'the difficulties of normal, and still more of scholarly English life in the years 1939–45', they champion the novels of Emily Eden and 'John Oliver Hobbes' (Pearl Craigie). Marie Corelli, 'Ouida', Mary Braddon, Dinah Mulock and Mrs Henry Wood are cited as bestsellers 'now unjustly derided' and high praise given to May Sinclair (1863–1946) for demonstrating 'good and sincere craftsmanship' and a 'richer and more solid intellectual background than is possessed by many of the contemporary novelists'.[11] Interestingly, they compare Kipling with Flora Annie Steele, suggesting that the latter 'shows the difference between ability and genius but the ability was great', and praise Elizabeth Gaskell whose novels were 'considered dangerous and subversive by her contemporaries'.[12] Harriet Martineau, Ann Thackeray and Frances Trollope join the canon of Victorian novelists, and women poets are equally well represented. Already by the late 1930s the chronological boundaries of the Victorian period were being extended.

Consolidation and Expansion

By the 1950s Victorian literature was steadily growing in popularity and Holloway reported that 'the fashion for thinking that in Victorian Culture there was nothing of any value . . . is happily passing'.[13] Despite their 'blindness', 'taboos', 'wildness' and 'crudity' the Victorians are to be praised for their attempts to deepen their culture. Holloway singles out Carlyle, Disraeli, George Eliot, Newman, Arnold and Hardy for their ability to 'express notions about the world, man's situation in it, and how he should live'.[14]

Revising *The Victorian Temper: A Study in Literary Culture* (1951) for republication in 1969 Jerome Hamilton Buckley notes that in the past decade 'the Victorian period has become one of the major areas of research and criticism with half a dozen journals exclusively devoted to its poetry or fiction, periodicals, bibliography etc'.[15] The term 'Victorian' is no longer 'a shield for the conservative and a target for the modernist' who, like that 'eminent debunker' Lytton Strachey, detects in all Victorian life 'a manifestation of the anal complex' operating upon a group psyche.[16] A degree of nostalgia appears to have set in: 'the epithet "Victorian" has acquired increasingly positive connotations until it may now frequently designate an exuberance and amplitude scarcely to be recovered yet devoutly to be wished for'.[17] Buckley notes a distinct shift away from poetry to the novel, and applauds Lewis Carroll 'for attacking the jungles of nonsense' which made up the daily life of the adult.[18]

The 1960s saw definite moves to define and consolidate the Victorian canon around Dickens, Eliot, the Brontës, Thackeray, Trollope, Hardy, Hopkins, Swinburne, Tennyson, Browning, Clough, Hopkins, Meredith and Wilde. In reviewing the year's research for 1968, Michael Timko notes the preponderance of biographical and bibliographical scholarship over critical studies of the period testifying to the canonical activity of the period. Winifred Gerin's *Anne Brontë* (1959), Inga-Stina Ewbank's seminal study *Their Proper Sphere* (1966) and R. B. Martin's *The Accents of Persuasion* (1966) stimulated a critical revaluation of the Brontës, and a rejection of the 'Purple Heather School of Criticism' in favour of an assessment of them as women working in a predominantly masculine industry and the 'sexless sphere of disinterested intelligence . . . and autonomous personality'.[19] This was a timely intervention as the wealth of women poets and novelists accumulated in the early years of the century began noticeably to diminish although Barrett Browning still commanded attention and Ann and Patrick Branwell Brontë joined their more famous sisters. New studies of Gaskell demonstrating the conflict between her professional and domestic role, critical analyses of the role of women and a reassessment of the work of Margaret Oliphant constituted the first steps by feminist scholarship towards full and proper representation of women writers.

In the 1960s, the interest in alienation and despair, characterizing literary surveys and critical works of the previous decade, gave way to serious concern with class and socialism. A major exhibition of the Kelmscott Press at Brown University late in 1959 directed attention to William Morris, augmented by the centenary of the founding of 'Morris and Co.' and the first issue of *The Journal of William Morris Studies* in 1962. Taking up the challenge of E. P. Thompson's *William Morris: Romantic to Revolutionary* (1955) and R. P. Arnot's *William Morris: The Man and the Myth* demonstrates how the concerns of the volatile 1920s resurfaced in the 1960s as Morris's social and political vision was reassessed alongside his aesthetics. The Pre-Raphaelite poets continue to be popular in their own right.

The Victorian social and political novel comes into its own in this decade. The first major treatment of the genre, Kathleen Tillotson's *Novels of the 1840s* (1954), is succeeded by new studies of Disraeli and major reassessments of Gaskell.[20] Lukács' *The Historical Novel* (1937), is published in translation in 1962 along with a new edition of Arthur Morrison's *A Child of the Jago*. The Catholic revival, also prominent in 1940s and 1950s scholarship, is superseded by discussions of religious doubt and Arnold and Leslie Stephen displace Newman and Pusey as leading canonical figures. The popularity of Beardsley, Ibsen, Wilde, Shaw, theatre and melodrama, prompts controversy over the precise meaning of the term 'decadent', the consolidation of 'the Nineties' as a distinct period, and one of the earliest studies of the *Yellow Book*.[21] Kipling's centenary (1965) stimulated interest in imperialism, and the portrayal of Africa in English fiction. The twenty-first century's critical investigation of sex and sexuality is anticipated by Steven Marcus's *The Other Victorians* (1966) and the publication of the transcript of the trial of Walter's *My Secret Life* at Leeds Assizes.[22] Sensation fiction remains of central scholarly concern – especially the novels of Mary Braddon and Wilkie Collins – and Arthur Conan Doyle haunts the canonical margins.

The Politics of the Canon

The 1970s was a turning point in Victorian studies. By 1974 enthusiasm and scholarship had grown to the point where it was no longer practical for the *Year's Work in English Studies* to include the period from 1837 onwards within the general category of the nineteenth century and scholars, and critics continue to consolidate the established canon under the name of the monarch. There are dissenting voices, however, especially in the areas of class, gender and the newly emerging area of colonial or imperial studies. The term 'litera-ture' is also under scrutiny, and an awareness of the importance of the social and historical context to an understanding of the period anticipates our own century's move towards interdisciplinarity and cultural studies.

Literature and politics are seen as inextricably intertwined, and the term 'sociology of literature' gains currency following the 1978 University of Essex Conference on '1848'. Studies of the British Trade Unions, the Chartist movement, Tory radicalism, the cotton industry, Victorian Lancashire, broadside ballads, the rural and urban working class and class conflict generally dominate the early 1970s, adding context and a political edge to critical appreciations of the industrial novels of Gaskell and Disraeli. The perceptible shift from conservative to radical and left wing revaluations of the canon culminates in the publication of Terry Eagleton's *Myths of Power (1975)*, a Marxist study of the indisputably and enduringly canonical Brontës.

Feminist critics, stimulated by Kate Millett's *Sexual Politics* (1970), highlight the gender discrimination of the previous two decades. Vineta Colby's *The Singular Anomaly* (1970) instigates the recovery of forgotten or marginalized women novelists, the reassessment of those present in the canon and the challenging of the sexist bias of readings of their work. The field is dominated by contextual studies of adultery, marriage, prostitution, dress reform, the 'Woman Question' and the first studies of the 'New Woman' fiction of the period by Gail Cunningham and Lloyd Fernando. Revisionist studies of rebellious fictional heroines feature alongside evaluations of women characters in the work of male novelists such as Hardy and Gissing, whose *The Odd Women* was reprinted in 1971.

Biographical criticism of women writers ensures their visibility and paves the way for the serious consideration of their work which will persist and develop through the closing decades of the twentieth century and into the twenty-first, although critics begin to take sides over the respective merits of Rossetti and Barrett Browning. Colonial studies become increasingly analytical in the early years of the decade and explores British imperial aggression and arrogant cruelty towards other races. Kipling and Haggard are at the centre of this debate, at once the targets of anti-imperialist critique and the beneficiaries of guarded defence or rehabilitation. The romantic view of the so called 'Celtic' poets hardens to an analysis of the portrayal of the Irish in literature and cartoons. Further attempts are made to identify the 1890s as a distinct period of study and define terms such as 'aestheticism', 'decadence' and 'symbolism', and Stoker's *Dracula* and Conan Doyle's Sherlock Holmes stories become prominent. Growing interest in the 1890s, coupled with an unwavering enthusiasm for the sexual dimension of the lives and work of the Victorians, contributes to Oscar Wilde's reputation, and Rupert Croft-Cooke's *The Unrecorded Life of Oscar Wilde* (1971) ushers in 'queer' studies. The *Year's Work in English Studies* reviewer notes the book's 'persuasive colloquial prose' freely sprinkled with such words as 'drag', 'butch', 'queer', 'queen' and 'camp'.[23] Hopkins's sexuality is debated and Bram Djikstra's groundbreaking study of the androgyne in nineteenth-century literature identifies 'a counter offensive among artists against the economic motivation behind . . . the sexual stereotyping of bourgeois industrial society'.[24] The canonical 'core' remains largely unchanged although the publication of a special edition of *Agenda* magazine in 1972 dedicated to his poetry, and the first new edition of his collected poems since 1930, gives Hardy special prominence as a major poet as well as a novelist.[25]

In the 1980s, Newman, Pusey and the Church historians lose their canonical status although Pater, Ruskin and Carlyle survive. The Browning/Rossetti debate gains momentum and there is an increasing demand for serious attention to be paid to the work of the poets, rather than their lives, although biographical studies of other women writers are still very much in evidence. The Pre-Raphaelites are arraigned for their exploitation of women, and Charlotte Brontë assumes major canonical status alongside George Eliot, especially for feminist critics. 1982 marks a renewed interest in children's literature, ignored since the early years of the twentieth century, prompting one reviewer to comment that critics 'seem to have been moved by the cry of "women and children first"'.[26] Novelists and poets dominate, with prominence given to women writers from the centre and the margins, and impassioned claims made for other neglected areas of literatures and the 'minor' works of canonical authors.

The canon undergoes a serious crisis during this decade. No longer an acknowledged group of 'responsibly chosen classics' but a bewildering maze, the democratic openness of the field is undermined by theory and the perceived reification of English studies.[27] Feminist criticism ensures both the visibility of women writers and the continued reassessment of their male counterparts, and the map of women's literary history is substantially altered by the publication of new anthologies of women's poetry featuring lost or forgotten writers and reprints of the work of neglected women writers by The Women's Press and Virago.

Period boundaries become increasingly permeable as critical studies group writers thematically, or according to their class or gender, positing links between literary practitioners separated by half a century. Author-centred studies cede place to the analysis of genres, subgenres and liminal groups such as orphans, martyrs, scapegoats, bohemians and non-conformists, as the notion of literary and aesthetic value becomes increasingly contentious. Braddon and the sensation novel in general assume canonical status while feminist criticism and Foucauldian theory bring detective fiction, *Dracula* and the novels of Wilkie Collins back into view.

Apparently unassailably canonical writers such as Dickens and Hardy are read in the light of new critical and theoretical approaches, but Thackeray, Trollope, Meredith and Morris all but disappear. Gaskell moves from the centre of the 'social problem' debate and *Cranford* is praised for way it privileges 'women's language' and 'women's values'.[28] The social problem novel loses prominence despite attempts to enhance the genre by adding Frances Trollope, Charlotte Elizabeth Tonna, Julia Kavanagh, Charlotte Yonge, and Geraldine Jewsbury alongside Charlotte Brontë, Eliot and Gaskell. Brontë's *Villette* slips into the canon, although there seems to be little interest in Eliot's early fiction. Barrett Browning's position is strengthened by the debate concerning her feminist credentials and the aesthetic value of her poetry, and Christina Rossetti begins to displace her more famous brother. Feminist literary criticism itself undergoes a shift in emphasis away from the politics of oppression and towards ideas of resistance, subversion and agency.

In 1985 a spate of substantial anthologies creates what amounts to a separate canon of women writers to be studied alongside the existing one, or in isolation from it, although in 1987 Deidre David calls for them to be reintegrated 'into the complexity of a total culture as complicit and resistant to the powers generating their authority to speak'.[29] Children's literature gains status with the publication of the *Children's Literature Review* in 1982, as do fairy tales, and the work of Carroll, Kingsley and MacDonald.

History, Theory and the Canon

During the 1980s the canon appears to undergo a significant change in that poststructuralism, discourse theory, narratology, materialist criticism, postmodernism and attention to the relationship between literature and other forms of discourse dominate discussion. The *Cambridge Guide to Literature in English* (1988) is praised for giving historical and critical space to marginalized writers, including women. This is also true of the *Oxford Anthology of English Poetry, Volume Two: Blake to Heaney* (1990), where both Elizabeth Barrett Browning and Christina Rossetti command almost as much space as Dante Gabriel Rossetti and Robert Browning.

If the 1970s is the 'Age or Reconstruction', the 1980s demonstrate what Joseph Litvak calls the 'Return to History or the Referrant'.[30] By the end of the decade divisions between genres and disciplines break down, and journals once devoted to studies of single authors now feature articles on the wider cultural context of the period, as attention is given to the material conditions of its production. The canon remains essentially unchanged, although its authors become a battleground for competing reading strategies and women writers are more securely placed within it. Canonical and marginalized writers of both gender are re-situated within sub-genres, and both benefit greatly from the association. The trend towards placing 'prose' writing in the larger categories of discourse and genre initiates a move away from studies of the 'sages' – a term that no longer has much currency. Queer theory flourishes, giving new prominence to male writers such as Ruskin, Hopkins, Stoker and Stevenson and 'masculinity studies' is developed by Eve Kosovsky Sedgwick.

Other canonical innovations include the cultural dissemination of Victorian literature, periodicals and intertextual experiments with unfinished novels, sequels and pastiches.[31] These 'experiments' acquire a new term: 'historiographic metafiction', coined by Linda Hutcheon in 1988 to signify writing 'that refutes the natural or common-sense methods of distinguishing between historical fact and fiction'.[32] Interestingly this 'new' development echoes the Victorians' own less self-conscious fascination with history, in fact and fiction, and the challenges to historical realism that such work presents in terms of reconstruction and period authenticity.

John Sutherland's *Longman Companion to Victorian Fiction* (1991) contains entries on around 7,000 Victorian novelists but Dickens, the Brontës, Eliot and Hardy still have major canonical status, supported by Thackeray, Trollope, Collins, Meredith and Gissing, Barrett Browning and Christina Rossetti. Sheridan Le Fanu, Margaret Oliphant, Stoker and Stevenson variously appear and disappear although colonial studies give additional prominence to Stevenson's South Sea Island tales and the novels of H. Rider Haggard and Stoker, and there is some attempt to revive interest in Kingsley in the context of nationalistic and imperialist discourse. Victorian periodicals and advertising become part of the contextual background – especially for their representations of colonial England and colonized India. By 1993 the establishment of the imperial archive at the centre of Victorian representation is hailed as the 'key to mythologies of Victorian life'.[33] Colonial studies focus on national identity as it affected England and Scotland and the complication of attitudes to Ireland.

The 1990s clearly show the impact of literary and cultural theory on the formation of the canon, as interdisciplinary analyses and innovative readings of the privileged and marginalized alike undermine the singular authority of individual writers and texts and dissolve divisions between discipline boundaries such as literature and law, and between 'high' and 'popular' forms and literary and cultural artefacts, while also challenging the notion of periodicity. Litvak's call is heeded and history becomes the lens through which Victorian literature is read. The individual writer as subject is revealed as a complex intersection of overlapping or antagonistic discursive moments, sometimes appearing as little more than the subjective space in which these cohere.

In 1992 the *Year's Work in English Studies* devotes a new section entirely to 'Cultural Studies and Prose' to reflect these new developments and the lively debates over the boundaries or 'spaces' of English and cultural studies. The emergence of 'influence studies' helps push the period boundary, sometimes even beyond the 'long nineteenth-century' (1789–1914), and a growing interest in publishing history demonstrates the relationship of texts to the marketplace. The burgeoning interest in women's poetry peaks with the publication of Leighton and Reynold's seminal *Victorian Women Poets: An Anthology* (1995), which persuasively argues for a return to a scholarly and theoretical approach to women writers, particularly the now canonically central Rossetti and Barrett Browning, and gives impetus to the major work of canon reconstruction initiated by feminist criticism in the late 1960s. There is a marked emphasis on women as participators in nineteenth-century cultural practices as readers and writers, rather than victims, and a growing interest in women anti-feminists. Women's poetry is also seen to transcend the period boundary between Victorian and Romantic.

Bakhtinian dialogics in the 1990s initiates a move to redefine 'sage' writing, as discourse: 'a dialogue between a speaker and a contemporaneous audience' and to link it to all forms of writing engaged in the process of cultural construction and exchange, prompting a revival of interest in the work of Carlyle, Newman, Ruskin, Arnold, Pater and Mill.[34] Pater also features strongly in masculinity studies developed by Regenia Gagnier and Richard Dellamora alongside Sedgwick. Autobiography is interrogated for its 'masculine narrative' and biography for its relation to the 'master narratives' of 'literature' and 'history'. There is also a move to construct a 'working class' canon consisting of poetry, fiction, autobiography and journalism from the period. The 1990s demonstrates the potential power of the anthology to reshape the canon while at the same time the anthology itself is interrogated for its inclusions and exclusions.

The '1890s' is extended to include work by Corelli, Doyle, Kipling, Mary Kingsley and Joseph Conrad and merits a special edition of *Victorian Poetry*, although here again the definition of the *fin-de-siècle* is repeatedly challenged and its chronological boundaries pushed.

The centrality of poetry and particularly the novel has traditionally masked the importance of drama. This oversight is vigorously addressed in the 1990s with attention to such topics as theatre history, Charles Keane's revivals of Shakespeare, melodrama, farce, musical comedy, cross-dressing and transgression, acting careers, actor managers, women as performers, playwrights and feminist icons in their own time, 'closet drama' and 'toga plays'. The work of Shaw, women's suffrage drama and socialist theatre become increasingly important in relation to debates on class, gender and economic status and plays by J. M. Barrie, Henry Arthur Jones, Stirling Coyne, G. H. Lewes and G. R. Sims supplement the readily available work of Wilde, Shaw, Boucicault, Pinero and Sullivan. The increasing marginalization of Victorian poetry in general is noted and its corresponding lack of theorization, although there is some interest in the Victorian 'long' poem by Tennyson, Browning, Barrett Browning and Hopkins as constituting a significant challenge to genre boundaries.

Literature as Culture: The Expanding Canon

The end of the twentieth century is dominated by the perception of texts as cultural objects ranging from the novels of Dickens to Valentines, hymns, advertisements and the *Illustrated London News*, and critical attention is diverted to the study of how texts are produced and read and the interaction between words and images. The turn towards the cultural significance of photographs, paintings and illustrations revives the Pre-Raphaelites whose 'brotherhood' now includes women artists and craftspersons. Periodicals become significant for their 'cultural meaning' and for the close interaction between editor, journal and audience. Art, photography and illustration also come into view as forms of cultural production. Interest in the *fin-de-siècle* grows as the 1990s approaches its own millennial cultural moment, prompting a re-evaluation of the dialectical relationship between the past and the present, although a more sanguine outcome is predicted at the end of the century than by Lytton Strachey at the beginning. The late twentieth century privileges Oscar Wilde who will go on to gain iconic status in the twenty-first century.[25] The emphasis on Wilde's sexuality gives way to his Irishness, his fascination with Jesse James, his Catholicism and, most interestingly of all perhaps, the way in which he anticipates the 'cult of the celebrity' that has become the hallmark of the first decade of the twenty-first century.

Attention is focused on how we read and construct the Victorians, especially through film and television which are criticized for presenting 'nostalgic cultural fantasies' rather than representations of the social world. Ironically there is heightened critical interest in erstwhile canonical writers now perceived as languishing in the margins, including Patmore, Arnold, Morris and Robert Browning.

Queen Victoria and the impact of her reign on Britain become increasingly significant to critical evaluations of Victorianism, and British literary culture is placed in an ever-widening national context which includes India, Anglophone Caribbean women's writing, the opening up of China and Japan to British markets, the Boer War, Transylvania, New Zealand and East Africa.

Victorian studies in the twenty-first century is dominated by a sense that the field has become almost too vast for meaningful cultivation. The undeniable impact of developments in literary theory and cultural studies has highlighted gains and losses, insights and blind spots generated by shifts in methodology and focus as scholars negotiate the move away from the individual author as the generator of cultural meaning, eagerly colonize the so-called 'margins' and embrace the dissolution of problematic boundaries between 'high' and low' art. The idea of national identity is scrutinized as well as those conventions and institutions that form its keynotes: the domestic ideal, colonial expansionism, the nostalgic invention of the past and the anxious imagining of the future, social order and the nature of the urban. Commendably self-conscious new millennial studies, inflected by postmodernism, investigate the afterlife of the Victorians in blockbuster films, television adaptations and consumer culture exemplifying what we might call the *début-de-siècle* impulse to seek self-awareness in the present by reworking or 'othering' the past. Studies in national security seemingly anticipate our own post-9/11 consciousness and the rise of cinematic theory helps to map out the area of visual studies in the still-dominant genre of the novel.

The notion of the canon has been revised to signify a cultural edifice of Victorian writers under erosion in favour of something more open, inclusive and expansive. Technology and the internet have revolutionized the field reviving lost and forgotten texts and materials and making others more accessible. Pedagogic initiatives such as modularization, syllabus shrinkage and concomitant changes in student reading habits have been seen as threatening the dominance of the long Victorian novel, opening up the potential of poetry, drama and eventually the short story to provide equally valuable ways of reading the period. Perhaps then, the most significant change in the canon is its gradual dissolution or, conversely, its contrived ossification into a target for scholarly iconoclasts and a new generation of intellectual debunkers. As Lytton Strachey reminded his readers, 'ignorance is the first requisite of the historian' and, we might add of the canonizer, 'ignorance which simplifies and clarifies, which selects and omits, with a placid perfection unattainable by the highest art'.[36] Over half a century later Michel Foucault observed that we can learn most about a period from what we don't know: from what is hidden, ignored or simply invisible. In the process, however, perhaps we risk losing sight of what we know already. Some form of map or blueprint is a useful starting point in our understanding of the past, providing we keep in mind who drew the map and why. As Philip Davis, citing Newman, suggests: '"there is no one aspect deep enough to exhaust the contents of the real idea, no one term or proposition which will serve to define it". The "real idea" in every sense of that phrase, goes beyond the closures of history or scholarship'.[37]

8 Changes in Critical Approaches

Martin Willis

Reading Criticism and Theory

In the first decade of the twenty-first century we are reading different Victorian literature from our predecessors. As the last chapter has shown, there are many reasons for this changing canon of texts. We are also, however, reading the *same* texts as our predecessors differently; and this difference is due to another canon and its evolution – the canon of Victorian literary criticism. Victorian literary criticism can mean two distinct bodies of work: the enormous volume of analysis and opinion that the Victorians contributed on their own literary culture and the even larger volume of scholarly work on Victorian literature written after the Victorian period. This chapter concentrates exclusively on the latter, taking Victorian literary criticism to refer to the academic writing on the fiction, poetry and drama of the Victorian period that has emerged since the 1950s. Focusing on Victorian literary criticism appears to be taking one step further away from the principal concern of the study of Victorian literature – the literary text. Reflecting on the critical work that reflects on the literature is, in some senses, a meta-critical activity, and perhaps simply a further obstruction in the difficult journey towards producing first-class literary analysis. Whatever decisions an individual scholar might make in terms of their own practice, becoming familiar with the extant criticism of Victorian literature is a central part of becoming a competent, even skilful, critic of that literature. Indeed it is an understanding of the critical apparatus brought to bear on the literary text – and its methods, perspectives and politics – that makes Victorian literature an object of study as well as an object of reading pleasure.

Understanding the shifts and changes of critical opinion is one of the hardest tasks for any student of Victorian literature. Dealing with the literature itself, and with the critical views on any given text, seems enough to manage without having to take account of how these views have evolved over the last half century of scholarship. Yet it is certainly desirable to know something of this critical evolution and it is undoubtedly necessary for advanced work on Victorian literature to understand it a good deal more thoroughly. This chapter offers a framework for beginning to see more clearly the structures of the Victorian critical canon. One of the most useful elements of a chapter like this (or at least what a chapter like this should aim to achieve) is to provide a working knowledge of the critical canon so that the opinion of any given piece of critical writing within the broad spectrum of 50 years can be recognized as belonging to a particular school of thought, or to a specific time period.

To do this, one has to understand that changes in critical perspective are not taken up equally across the academic community of Victorian literary scholars. Indeed, there is often as much resistance (explicit or otherwise) to new methods and approaches as there is a determination to investigate and expand on innovation. This leads to a complex evolution of Victorian literary criticism, rather than to distinct paradigm shifts that can be readily and clearly dated. Any cross-section of criticism for a specific period of years, therefore, will be a mixed bag of new and traditional critical positions, some consciously seeking to invigorate the field with distinct and original methods, some continuing to mine a methodological vein that has been in place for some time, and some explicitly revisionist work that demands a return to older traditions that are, perhaps, on the wane. It is important to be able to recognize these different critical voices and to differentiate between the new, the commonplace and the traditional. Without such knowledge it is increasingly difficult to discover a distinct critical position from which to comment on the literature and culture of the Victorians. Equally, without an understanding of the different methods and perspectives taken by critics, seemingly contradictory analyses might all potentially be 'right', and an explication of the literary text can become a confusing melange of opposing and conflicting opinion.

One answer to this might be never to read any critical material at all and attend only to the literary text (although this in itself is a methodological stance with its own particular history). Another is to engage with the history of the canon of Victorian literary criticism in order to be able to make judgements based upon the perspectives and approaches taken by individual scholars. An understanding of these perspectives, and more particularly their place within the history of Victorian literary criticism, makes more realizable the discovery of preferences within one's own work, which can lead in turn to greater critical focus, as well as clarity of purpose, and to an engagement with the literary work of the Victorians as it impacts upon one's own history, culture and politics. In order to do this – and to reach the point of recognizing that even this last statement betrays the influence of the changing critical canon of Victorian literary criticism – it is important to provide some suitable structure within which the key elements in the evolution of Victorian literary criticism can be clearly demarcated. This, unavoidably, tends both towards some simplification and a certain subjectivity. It is to be hoped, however, that in reaching the end of the chapter its own critical preferences will have become apparent (and can be critiqued) and that some further reading will allow for a reflection on its necessarily reduced complexity in its role as introductory guide.

Part of that reduced complexity comes in the organization of the remainder of the chapter. For the sake of temporal clarity and ease of future consultation what follows is divided into five sections, each roughly occupying the space of a single decade, so beginning with 1950 to 1960 and ending with 1990 to the present (which is, clearly, the longest time period). The limited overlap of a single year between each section hints at the fact that these decade delineations are not hard and fast in terms of subject matter. As one should expect from a process that is evolutionary rather than revolutionary, change occurs over extended periods of time that cannot be neatly circumscribed within discrete decades. Nevertheless, the most important changes in Victorian literary criticism, as well as those perspectives that maintain an influential position, are still illuminated by dealing in turn with the past five decades of critical endeavour.

1950–60: Liberal Humanism and Cultural History

Victorian literary criticism as defined within this chapter did not begin in the 1950s. It began as soon as the Victorian period had come to an end. Yet it was only in the 1950s that the literature and culture of the Victorians came under such productive critical scrutiny that Victorian literary criticism claimed a place in the academic firmament. Although literature (and perhaps its literary criticism) has come to be the dominant scholarly discipline that deals with the Victorian period, it is both the literary critic and the historian that we must credit with bringing the excitement and sophistication of the Victorians (and their literature) to the attention of the scholarly community. The publication of a series of important literary and historical studies of the Victorian period – among them Jerome Buckley's *The Victorian Temper* (1951), John Holloway's *The Victorian Sage* (1953), Asa Briggs's *Victorian People* (1954) and Walter Houghton's The *Victorian Frame of Mind* (1957) – energized the field of Victorian studies by revealing first the vitality of Victorian literature, culture and society and, second, making clear the potential for future research in the period. Such promotion of the Victorians coincided with the promotion of the study of literature as a whole, which had begun towards the end of the 1940s under the leadership of the Cambridge critic F. R. Leavis. His important 1948 work, *The Great Tradition*, which privileged literature as the most civilizing of all artistic activities, focused largely on the nineteenth-century novel and thereby valued Victorian fiction above all other periods and genres. Leavis was arguably the most influential critic of his own and succeeding generations, and the principles of his version of literary criticism continue to be discussed in the twenty-first century.

What has become known as Leavisite literary criticism (or alternatively liberal humanism) had as its foundation the belief that the 'greatness' of great literature lay in its morality, and in the ability of its writer to instil the same moral sensibility in the reader. The purpose of literary criticism was to help the reader recognize and understand such moral greatness, and in the process learn both important human truths and the methods by which writers construct their works so as to lay bare the essential aspects of the human condition. Leavis's literary criticism was not new in arguing for literature's importance on these grounds. In fact, he was taking a lead from the Victorian educationalist Matthew Arnold, who had argued over a century before that education (including a literary education) should teach only those things that would uphold and celebrate proper moral values. Problematic in this type of literary criticism was any defining notion of moral value; for Arnold and Leavis it was self-evident (and therefore undefined), a belief that their liberal upper-middle-class 'truth' was universally accepted and understood.

In the important Victorian literary studies of the 1950s Leavisite liberal humanism dominated. Victorian literary criticism dealt predominantly with the formal aesthetics of the fiction and poetry, seeking to uncover the moral compass of the age in the language and techniques of its literary masters. These notions of 'the age' and 'literary mastery' go some way towards illuminating the type of unconscious ideological assumptions the liberal humanist Victorian critics were making. There was little or no attention being paid to the actual and specific historical moments within which the Victorians lived. Rather there was a vague understanding of the age: that long period defined by Victoria's reign but given little other definition beyond that. Like their New Critical colleagues in the United States, Victorian literary critics, such as

Buckley, paid attention to the text without the addition of extensive supplementary contexts. The specific literary texts under consideration were also limited to those written by accepted masters of Victorian prose, poetry and, to a lesser extent, drama. There was no room for popular writers (often called 'lesser' or 'minor' writers) who did not, in the view of the critics themselves, offer the innovative and dynamic forms revealing of the best investigation of moral questions. The criticism tended, therefore, to focus on a limited canon of eminent Victorian writers: primarily Arnold, Dickens, Thackeray, Trollope, the Brontës, Gaskell, Eliot, Hardy, Tennyson, Browning and Hopkins.

However in 1957 a new journal, *Victorian Studies*, led by Michael Wolff and edited from Indiana University, and with a different remit from the scholarly work of the liberal humanist Victorian critics, began to shape an alternative critical methodology. *Victorian Studies* was not exclusively literary in its interests (as the title suggests) but it was dominated by literary critics, Wolff among them. The journal's editorial team had become frustrated by the lack of attention paid to other disciplines by the literary critic; disciplines such as history which clearly had a lot to offer in any investigation of the past. *Victorian Studies* aimed to publish essays that dealt with at least two disciplines (for example, literature *and* history) rather than focusing entirely on one. Although the journal was not entirely successful in this aim it did engender within Victorian literary criticism an increased attention to context as well as text, an emergent, if still very much nascent, interdisciplinarity.

In the same year, Raymond Williams, a young Welsh Marxist critic, published his *Culture and Society*, which was equally sympathetic to the importance of the contexts of social and cultural history when commenting on Victorian literature. Together with other publications, such as Richard Altick's *The English Common Reader* (1957), the work of Williams and Wolff began to shift Victorian literary criticism away from its Leavisite traditions and towards a different methodology: one open to engagement with other disciplines such as history, keen to see Victorian literature as part of larger Victorian culture and society and determined to uncover the political influences of Victorian writers and readers.

1960–70: Marxism and New Criticism

By the middle of the 1960s Michael Wolff was calling the methodology proposed by *Victorian Studies* (and performed by himself and others) a form of 'cultural history'. In an article in 1965 Wolff reiterated the importance of context in Victorian literary criticism, by which he meant an engagement with the history of the Victorian period as well as its literary culture.[1] Although this might be seen as an early attempt at the interdisciplinarity that *Victorian Studies* had called for it is more accurately a version of historicism in which history is used to elucidate the literary text. While this formulation of cultural history allowed the literary text to remain the dominant subject of inquiry, and was therefore much valued by Victorian literary critics, other forms of cultural history were being written that had as great an influence on the canon of Victorian literary criticism. With the same ideological engagement as Raymond Williams was revealing in his own work, historians of Victorian society, such as E. P. Thompson and Eric Hobsbawm, were investigating lesser-known individuals, groups and movements who had been as important in creating Victorian Britain as the artistic and social figureheads that were prominent in previous histories and literary scholarship.

For the first time, then, there was a sustained academic interest in Victorian class positions: articulated predominantly from a Marxist perspective, it sought to argue for the importance of analysing the ideologies inherent in Victorian Britain that were borne out of economic and political inequality. Victorian literary critics soon followed the lead of their colleagues in history in writing this form of cultural history. In part, this was a challenge to the assumptions of liberal humanist or Leavisite critics, whose pursuit of essential human truths in Victorian literature had universalized a set of values that were not, in actual fact, universally held (either by critics or by the Victorians themselves). However, Marxist cultural history of the literary variety was more confrontationally in opposition to New Criticism, which entirely disregarded the influence on the literary text of society and culture in favour of a strictly formalist aesthetic of literary language and structure.

To some extent, therefore, 1960s Victorian literary criticism can be seen as a conflict between formalist New Criticism and Marxist cultural history. It may even be argued that formalism was the more dominant mode of criticism at this time, exemplified by works such as Barbara Hardy's *The Novels of George Eliot*. Still, the use of context championed by *Victorian Studies* and the abiding influence of Raymond Williams's cultural criticism did offer Victorian literary criticism a scholarly method that looked beyond the language of the text and into the complexity of Victorian society and culture. This infant cultural materialism – a politically engaged criticism that made manifest both the unconscious ideology of liberal humanism and the ideological structures of the Victorian period itself – drew a certain dynamism from its ability to disrupt the categories within which Victorian literature had been placed and examined. Its most important contribution to Victorian literary criticism was to give prominence for the first time to one side of the triangle of class, gender and race that came to dominate in the 1980s and 1990s. Class was the vital ingredient for Marxist literary critics, and their attention to ideologies of class in the Victorian period shed new light on its literary culture as well as its society and politics. The importance of the new knowledge that Marxist critics uncovered was not lost on the more astute critics of the period, even those who had been working within more traditional paradigms. Jerome Buckley, for example, whose *The Victorian Temper* had been so important in the 1950s, commented in the introduction to the revised edition of this book in 1969, that were he to have written his book in the 1960s he would have paid 'more attention to social culture and not just literary culture'.[2]

Nevertheless, more traditional liberal humanist criticism remained an essential aspect of Victorian literary criticism throughout the 1960s. In Britain, and despite the emergence of Wolff's cultural history and Marxist perspectives on class, Leavisite critics such as Geoffrey and Kathleen Tillotson were major influences on the critical canon. Geoffrey Tillotson, for example, had been engaged to write a volume on the Victorians for the *Oxford History of English Literature* series (although he died before its completion) while Kathleen Tillotson's work on Dickens was at the forefront of its field. Their liberal humanist approach can be exemplified by Geoffrey Tillotson's comment in *A View of Victorian Literature* (published posthumously in the 1970s from his research for the *Oxford History*) that 'at any time literature that is popular expresses and represents the primary human emotions, but not always worthily'.[3] Tillotson's value of what he believes to be 'great' literature over more popular work, and his privileging of individual humanity, places him in a continuum of Victorian literary criticism that traces its history back through Leavis. It would, then, have been possible, indeed easily so, for the inexperienced scholar or student of Victorian literature, and perhaps especially in Britain, to be unaware of the emerging conflicts in the canon of Victorian literary criticism.

1970–80: Feminism and Poststructuralism

It is worth pausing to explain how this might have been the case in the 1960s, and to show that it remained so throughout the 1970s. One of the central methods of disseminating knowledge to new students of Victorian literature was through the extensive published surveys of literature and literary history. These surveys hold some power; they are often produced by leading academic publishers (Oxford and Cambridge are obvious choices), or by publishers whose name is familiar and trusted by the reading public (such as Penguin). By the 1970s Victorian literature had become a central component of the academic study of English literature, thanks in no small part to those critics of the 1950s and 1960s of every methodological persuasion, who had shown its instrumentalism for our consideration of modernity. There was, then, an increasing number of surveys of Victorian literature (as there was of surveys of literature as a whole) designed to offer new students a general map of the field.

In the main these surveys failed to engage with the most recent changes in the canon of Victorian literary criticism. The volumes dedicated to the

Victorians in the *Cambridge History of English Literature* were republished in the 1970s entirely unchanged from their initial publication in the 1910s. The prefatory note to these republished volumes hoped that they made Victorian literature 'easily available to a wider circle of students and other readers who wish to have on their shelves the full story of English literature'.[4] No mention is made of the half-century and more of scholarly work dedicated to enhancing that story for the student of the 1970s. Similarly, the relatively new *Penguin History of Literature* series published a volume on *The Victorians* in 1970, edited by Arthur Pollard, contained only two writers (Reade and Hardy) and one topic (the *fin-de-siècle*) that differed from the *Cambridge History* and was on the whole dominated by a Leavisite agenda. Perhaps most surprisingly, one of the volumes dealing with Victorian literature in the *Oxford History of English Literature*, which was originally to have been completed by Geoffrey Tillotson, appeared only in 1990, relied almost exclusively on Tillotson's own bibliographic research conducted in the 1960s, and precisely followed his liberal humanist methodology.

Clearly it is not only surveys of literary history that the student of Victorian literature is likely to read. Yet both their apparent authoritative status and their breadth of coverage does lend itself to a potential inequality of influence when compared with other critical works. The survey's slower process of publication combined with their relative longevity within the field of literary criticism (as witnessed by the surfeit of reprints) makes it difficult for this particular form of criticism to keep in step with changes to the critical canon. It is, perhaps, this dual problem of limited responsiveness to changing perspectives allied to a position of authority that leads to the unintended continuation of rather dated critical methodologies (as opposed to those conscious rejections of new critical ideas). This was most marked in the 1970s, not only because of the proliferation of the survey of Victorian literature but also because the 1970s witnessed the rapid emergence of a new critical perspective: feminism.

Victorian literature became one of the key testing grounds for feminist literary criticism in the 1970s. Once again the journal *Victorian Studies* led the way. When Michael Wolff handed on the editorship to Martha Vicinus in 1971 the journal's remit began to privilege feminist work. Vicinus herself edited an important work of feminist literary scholarship that grew out of the journal's change of direction, *Suffer and Be Still: Women in the Victorian Age*, in 1972. It is not surprising, given the role of *Victorian Studies*, that feminist work on Victorian literature was sympathetic to the methods of cultural history that Wolff had promoted. For feminist scholars of Victorian literature and culture the role of the woman writer was not the only consideration. Rather, it was the ideological positioning of women, both in literature and in society, that demanded reconsideration and re-evaluation.

Moreover, this early feminism also sought to uncover female literary traditions, illuminating the particularly female power of the woman novelist that they felt had been undeveloped and ignored within Victorian literary criticism. This was not to say that writing by Victorian women had gone without representation, but that gender had not played a significant enough role in the criticism that dealt with them. Most influential in this celebratory and emasculating feminism was the work of Elaine Showalter, whose *Literature of their Own* was published in 1977, and Sandra Gilbert and Susan Gubar, who cowrote what was to become a feminist classic, *The Madwoman in the Attic* (1979). While feminist literary criticism was to undergo a number of changes of its own in the 1980s and 1990s, it was in the 1970s that its powerful new voice within Victorian literary criticism gave it the foundation from which it became the second side of the triangle of literary critical preoccupations with class, gender and race.

Feminism was not the only new methodology to come to prominence in the 1970s. Poststructuralism, an inheritor (and subvertor) of the tradition of formalist and structuralist poetics that had been influential alongside Marxist cultural history in the 1960s, was also emerging as a new force in Victorian literary criticism, led by J. Hillis Miller, whose *The Form of Victorian Fiction* had actually appeared in 1968. The poststructuralist technique of deconstruction upheld the new critical belief in the primacy of the text, but directly opposed it in believing the text to be a complex web of disunity and contradiction rather than an organic and complete object of art. Where Marxist cultural history and New Criticism had been in conflict in the 1960s over the relative importance of text and context, in the 1970s feminism and poststructuralism vehemently disagreed about the role of the author and the representative nature of the Victorian literary text. For feminism the Victorian woman author acted as the author-God of her texts, constructing a female and feminine world of the imagination that subverted patriarchal authority. Poststructuralist critics argued that no such authorial presence existed within Victorian literature and that the texts themselves revealed a decided lack of omnipotent design and intention.

In part the divisions between firstly New Criticism and Marxist cultural history and, later, feminism and poststructuralism were made a virtue in a new type of critical endeavour, a 'blending of textualism and historicism', as George Levine has put it, that became known as the new historicism.[5] If feminism had invigorated the Victorian literary criticism in the 1970s, when the field was at a lower ebb than it had been previously, new historicism brought about a renaissance in the study of Victorian literature in the 1980s that made critics ponder the very nature of the literary text as a separate object of study.

1980–90: New Historicism and Postcolonialism

New historicism arose first in studies of Renaissance literature, primarily in the work of Stephen Greenblatt. But by the mid-1980s – with Catherine Gallagher's book *The Industrial Reformation of English Fiction* (1985) – it had taken root in Victorian literary criticism. New historicism brought together the textual approaches of previous critical methodologies with the contextual analysis of cultural history by arguing that the literary text was a form of discourse similar to many other discourses of the Victorian period, from parliamentary debates to scientific theses. All the discourses that might relate to a certain event or topic (for Gallagher this was industrialization) could be considered alongside one another, thereby illuminating both the language of the literary text and the contexts out of which it had arisen.

To a significant number of scholars, this seemed an ideal solution to the conflicts between text and context that had been a consistent part of Victorian literary criticism through the 1960s and 1970s. Marxist literary critics took up the methods of the new historicist project and added to them a more explicit political dimension. Their version of new historicism became known as cultural materialism and was, in Britain if not in the USA or elsewhere, the dominant form of new historicist criticism. Michael Wolff's methodology for cultural history in the pages of *Victorian Studies* in the mid-1960s could now also be seen as a measured and limited cultural materialism, with its interest in discovering how Victorian literature and culture connected to present socio-political concerns.

In historical rather than literary criticism, the 1980s also witnessed what many historians now refer to as the linguistic turn: an increasing interest in language and its structures and meanings that had not previously been at the forefront of historical scholarship. This also brought the literary and the historical closer together, as Victorian literary critics increasingly paid attention to historical documents at the same time as historians began to address questions of language. This 'space for dialogue with other disciplines', as the historian Rohan McWilliam has characterized it, both reinforced the legitimacy of new historicism and cultural materialism as methods and raised the possibility that the interdisciplinarity that *Victorian Studies* had aimed for in 1957 might now have reached maturity.[6] Certainly some of the new historicist work in the 1980s appeared to make manifest the thoroughly interdisciplinary nature of new historicism, drawing on a wide range of discourses and subjects to paint new pictures of Victorian literature and culture. Mary Poovey's *Uneven Developments* (1989) was one such work, combining women's history with Victorian economics and literary fiction (which Poovey extended to take account of broader notions of society in her later book, *The Making of a Social Body* (1995)).

Despite new historicism's dominance, and its usefulness as a method for those critics placed within other critical paradigms such as feminism, it did not have a monopoly on Victorian literary criticism throughout the 1980s. In fact, one of the most important present interests of Victorian literary critics first made its mark in this decade. What has become known as postcolonial studies – an area of literary studies concerned with the literature by, and about, the subjects of formerly colonized nations – partly developed out of critical interest in the Victorians' own relationship with empire. Postcolonial critics exposed Victorian literature's often implicit recognition of the marginalized subjects of the British empire just as, before them, Marxist critics had 'discovered' distinct ideologies of class and feminist critics had illuminated a Victorian obsession with gender. In a landmark essay in 1985, for example, Gayatri Chakravorty Spivak, offered an innovative reading of *Jane Eyre* that focused attention on the character of Bertha Mason, Rochester's Creole wife, and argued that Jane Eyre's emergence as the (white British) heroine of Brontë's novel was dependent upon the destruction of the oppressed racial other, Bertha Mason. Attaching importance to race and ethnicity in Victorian literature for the first time, criticism like Spivak's opened a wholly new area of study for Victorian literary criticism. Moreover, it added the third and final side of the triangle of class, gender and race that have become the most common interests of Victorian literary critics at the end of the twentieth century.

Postcolonial criticism developed only moderately quickly in Victorian literary criticism in the 1980s, but it was significantly bolstered by the publication of one of the first book-length studies of the ideologies of empire at the end of the decade. Patrick Brantlinger's influential *Rule of Darkness* (1988), explored not only Victorian literature's responses to imperialism but also the political, social and cultural contexts for colonial oppression that the Victorians had constructed for themselves. Brantlinger's methodology, then, was one familiar to Victorian literary criticism; he performed at the same time a kind of cultural history of literature and also a highly politicized new historicism (or cultural materialism). The currency of this methodological approach within Victorian literary criticism gave Brantlinger's work added significance and led to an increase in postcolonial analyses of Victorian literature in the 1990s.

1990–Present: Combining or Coming Full Circle?

The continued significance of cultural history from its origins in the 1950s and the emergence of the linguistic turn in the 1980s gave a new character to Victorian literary criticism in the last decade and a half. The characterization of literature not only as an imaginative form but as a discourse similar to any other mode of writing can be argued to reach its inevitable conclusion in the 1990s turn towards interdisciplinary cultural studies in Victorian literary criticism (as well as across the humanities). For many critics of Victorian literature in the late twentieth and early twenty-first centuries, the literary text was no longer the single object of study. Indeed, the literary text had become one document (among many) that gave access to the culture of the Victorian period. Culture, rather than literature, therefore, was the true focus of scholarly work. While it may seem strange, and it would be too crude an analysis, to suggest that literature no longer held the interest of literary critics, it was the case that Victorian literary critics were increasingly engaging with disciplines, and therefore texts, other than the literary.

One of the key reasons for this was the freedom felt by literary critics to explore other disciplines and subjects using the tools of literary criticism (such as close textual analysis). After all, if, as certain philosophers of history, for example, were arguing, the past was only recoverable through a palimpsest of existent texts, then the Victorian literary critic could say as much about Victorian society and culture as about Victorian literature. As George Levine perceptively argued in the early 1990s, 'Victorian *literature* as a category has been put to the question . . . The subject has imperceptibly shifted from the great writers to the complicity of all texts in the hegemonic discourse of a Victorian culture'.[7] One of the outcomes of this has been an extension of the interdisciplinary methodology that *Victorian Studies* – in a less sophisticated way – aimed to achieve from 1957. The interdisciplinary projects of the 1990s argued that they offered a more productive scholarship because they maintained a balance between the different disciplines under investigation rather than privileging the literary text. The aim of the new interdisciplinarity was not to elucidate the literary text alone, but to offer an equal analysis of several different (and perhaps disparate) discourses, discovering new truths about the Victorians by the very fact of that equality of analysis. Most successful in this attempt was the work of scholars of Victorian literature and science, such as Sally Shuttleworth's *Charlotte Brontë and Victorian Psychology* (1996) or William Greenslade's *Degeneration, Culture and the Novel 1880–1940* (1994).

The interconnectedness of disciplines was being further reinforced in Victorian literary criticism in the cross-correspondences that began to be drawn between the three sides of the canonical triangle of class, gender and race. Literary critical work in each of these areas became more sophisticated in the 1990s and 2000s, and part of that sophistication came out of an increasing tendency to view them together rather than separately. Postcolonial criticism, the latest addition, was the first to recognize the potential in drawing on issues of gender for further exploration of Victorian literature. Indeed, it criticized some feminist approaches for failing to take account of the many different women involved in literary production and representation. Class, too, became a defining feature of some feminist work leading to a rise in interest in, for example, the working-class woman writer. It is unsurprising that Marxist, feminist and postcolonial methodologies found common ground: each can lay claim to a dominant interest in the ideologies of power relations between differently positioned individuals and groups, whether organized by class, gender or race.

Overall, what the Victorian literary criticism of the 1990s and 2000s has recognized, and explicitly investigated is the influence of both the present historical moment and the individual critic on the criticism it was producing and had produced in the last 50 years. The changing culture of Britain since 1950 had shaped the concerns of those entering the academy and embarking on their own literary criticism. Put crudely, many more women, many more from the working classes and a much more ethnically diverse body of literary critics were attending to Victorian literature in the 1990s than had been in the 1950s. This is not to suggest that it was only feminism, Marxism or postcolonialism that interested these scholars, but there was an effect on the range of experiences and interests being brought to bear on the Victorian literary text. Likewise, fundamental changes both in British society, and across the globe, also had an influence on what Victorian literary critics sought out in the Victorian period. Undoubtedly the breakdown of the Soviet empire and the enhanced global position of the one remaining superpower, the USA, led a number of critics to return with renewed interest to the empire over which Queen Victoria reigned. Similarly, Britain's central role in the global political economy of the last decade has seen increased attention given to Victorian political economy and the role of the writer within it.

The moral dimension to many political events in the 2000s might also be one of the contexts for recent critical interest in the liberal humanism of the 1950s. The ethical foundations of the work of Leavis (and of Matthew Arnold) have been given much more consideration since the turn of the millennium than they had been in the previous decades, despite the fact that liberal humanism had continued to exist alongside, if somewhat marginalized from, more mainstream literary critical methods. This may seem as though we have come full circle, as some critics suggest, but it is much more likely that ethical criticism will be produced from other, contemporary methodologies, such as ecocriticism, than from a turn back towards the liberal humanist critiques with which Victorian studies began. Indeed, those liberal humanist critics that were so influential in arguing for Victorian literature's important place in our literary and cultural history were also determined to highlight its significance in enabling us to understand our own present.

9 Interdisciplinarity in Victorian Studies

Laurie Garrison

Chapter Overview

It happened that I had now, and commencing with my first introduction to Latin studies, a large weekly allowance of pocket-money, too large for my age, but safely entrusted to myself, who never spent or desired to spend one fraction of it upon any thing but books. But all proved too little for my colossal schemes. Had the Vatican, the Bodleian, and the Bibliothèque du Roi been all emptied into one collection for my private gratification, little progress would have been made towards my content in this particular craving. Very soon I had run ahead of my allowance, and was about three guineas in debt . . . With respect to the debt, I was not so ignorant as to think it of much danger by the mere amount: my own allowance furnished a scale for preventing *that* mistake . . . But this other case was a ground for anxiety even as regarded the amount; not really; but under the jesting representation made to me, which I (as ever before and after) swallowed in perfect faith. Amongst the books which I had bought, all English, was a history of Great Britain, commencing of course with Brutus and a thousand years of impossibilities; these fables being generously thrown in as a little gratuitous *extra* to the mass of truths which were to follow. This was to be completed in sixty or eighty parts, I believe. But there was another work left more indefinite as to its ultimate extent, and which from its nature seemed to imply a far wider range. It was a general history of navigation, supported by a vast body of voyages. Now, when I considered with myself what a huge thing the sea was, and that so many thousands of captains, commodores, admirals, were eternally running up and down it, and scoring lines upon its face so rankly, that in some of the main 'streets' and 'squares' as one might call them) their tracks would blend into one undistinguishable blot, – I began to fear that such a work tended to infinity. What was England to the universal sea?[1]

So writes Thomas de Quincey of his childhood experience of collecting a library. A figure whose work spans the traditional divisions between the Romantic and Victorian eras and who therefore witnessed their cultural shifts, de Quincey in this anecdote captures one of the central concerns of Victorian thinkers and twenty-first century critics of Victorian culture. How does one confront such a vast and ever more quickly expanding collection of print matter? This question is one of the central problems in approaching the study of Victorian culture. De Quincey also articulates several other concerns that are characteristic of Victorian thought here. Being rather politically conservative, de Quincey implicitly expresses anxiety over the expansion of literacy to lower and lower classes facilitated by the growing availability and affordability of such print matter. The masses of print matter thus take on a threatening air in the same way that educated masses of a politically discontent working class might. However, de Quincey was also interested in the ways this expanse of print matter shaped middle-class identity, which Josephine McDonagh has argued 'provoked a state of insanity' in de Quincey's eyes. A paradoxically miserly gluttony drove the consumer to hoard continually but also to desire continually what was potentially outside his or her economic limitations, inciting a constant urge to spend.[2] Ideas about political economy, illness and print culture combine in de Quincey's thought in a way that for the late twentieth-century reader necessitates the investigation of how these fields were conceived when he was writing in the early 1840s.

Furthermore, the fear of the ever-expanding narrative of the history of Britain as well as the reluctant fascination with the potentially infinite narrative of global navigation are emblematic of de Quincey's imperialist thought. In this passage, the history of the British Empire is overwhelmingly long, illustrious and connected at least tentatively with classicism. Though de Quincey does not explicitly state this, the implication of bringing together the history of Britain with the more international history of navigation is to suggest that British history, or British thought, might travel along the 'lines' scored in the globe by navigators, presenting further and further reaches of the world with Britain's achievements. But de Quincey's characteristic paranoia insistently returns: the navigators' 'tracks would blend into one undistinguishable blot'. Dropped within a vast assortment of other imperial activities, Britain may lose its unique importance and identity ('What was England to the universal sea?').

Perhaps not so coincidentally, similar concerns again face twenty-first-century scholars as markets, publishing patterns and student recruitment become ever more influenced by global economics and networks. Readings of de Quincey's work as imperialist writing produced within a colonial culture account for many of his idiosyncrasies, but we might also place his thought and style within a number of other historical trends. We might examine his economic concerns as part of the discourse of political economy,[3] his struggles with opium addiction as medical or psychological history[4] or his obsession with print culture of the early nineteenth century as emblematic of a Victorian cultural moment. This variety of approaches is the result of the current critical turn toward interdisciplinarity.

The term 'interdisciplinarity' is a complex one because it refers to so many different forms of critical practice. Interdisciplinary work can employ the methods of other disciplines, examine materials traditionally studied by other disciplines, place the ideas of a writer into histories other than the literary, or it may rely on any combination of these practices. This has resulted in a rich field of criticism where texts such as novels, poems, plays and non-literary prose are read against paintings, objects and institutions. One may seek to document the cultural history of glass through readings of literary and visual materials as does Isobel Armstrong.[5] Or one may read Darwin's *On the Origin of Species* as a prose text that employs literary technique to articulate its theory as does Gillian Beer.[6] Victorian literature classrooms in turn tend to be amply supplemented with discussion of visual materials such as paintings, engravings and photographs or highly influential non-literary, prose texts such as de Quincey's work, J. S. Mill's *The Subjection of Women* or Ruskin's *Sesame and Lilies*.

The various forms of literature that were established, evolved and transformed during the period we call Victorian are particularly well suited to interdisciplinary approaches. Victorian literature differs from that of other periods in its lack of a set of central, organizing figures and works. The two literary periods that border the Victorian era, the Romantic and the Modern, are both titled with terms that easily translate into '–isms'; they are characterized by experimental work, generally in the highest literary form – poetry – that loosely forms part of a larger movement. Victorian literature, however, consists of a number of amorphous movements such as decadence and aestheticism of the 1890s or difficult to define genres such as spasmodic poetry and sensation novels of the 1850s and 1860s. Indeed any genres we might identify in the Victorian era are usually the products of relatively short-lived cultural moments. Furthermore, the evolution of literary styles and cultural concerns over the seven or so decades that make up the Victorian era at times is astounding. The formation of a canon of major works and authors of this period has necessarily been troubled at best and thus the period seems to invite methods of interrogation that do not rely on questions of literary aesthetics. This chapter will examine the politics that surround some of the interdisciplinary initiatives in the study of Victorian literature and summarize some of the important interdisciplinary developments in the field.

Politics

Interdisciplinarity is a current trend that holds much cultural weight in the field of Victorian studies; it is simultaneously a method of yielding up new and innovative histories and criticisms as well as a mode of further dissemination of work. However, the history of Victorian studies as an academic endeavour was influenced by the idea of interdisciplinarity well before the trend achieved its current hold. The leading journal of the field, *Victorian Studies*, founded in 1957, proposed a form of study of the Victorian era that was 'more likely to be realized through the coordination of academic disciplines than in departmental isolation. It is the tradition for journals to devote themselves to particular disciplines, but *Victorian Studies* will publish work addressed to all students of the Victorian age' (3).[7] This relationship with interdisciplinarity is generally a forgotten one, sidelined by other developments in the wider view of the history of literary criticism in general.

The middle decades of the twentieth century are usually considered to be the years where New Criticism held dominance in the field. The year 1946 saw the publication of 'The Intentional Fallacy' by William K. Wimsatt and Monroe C. Beardsley, which argued for the erasure of consideration of authorial intention. In 1948 F. R. Leavis published *The Great Tradition*, which effectively solidified the thought behind the canon formation that so much energy is now devoted to undoing. This movement sought to isolate the text, distancing it from the personal, historical and material conditions under which it was written. This approach has been long repudiated by literary critics, but its legacy haunts us in the forms of close reading we conduct in combination with other forms of reading. Thus the interdisciplinary commitment of Victorian studies, widespread and accepted enough to incite the founding of what has become one of the most important journals in the field, is a curious one to have arisen in the theoretical landscape of New Criticism. In the very age that the likes of Wimsatt, Beardsley and Leavis had – very successfully – set up a form of criticism that was intentionally apolitical, refusing consideration of social and cultural circumstances, proponents of the new field of Victorian studies sought to study these very relationships.

At the same time that these two movements were forming, a third that is still crucially influential in shaping the thought behind contemporary interdisciplinary work was brewing. Cultural studies – probably the most important influence in the development of the current interest in interdisciplinarity –

to a large extent brought the triumvirate of gender, class and race to literary studies, and this model continues to dominate the field. Furthermore, the texts and history of the nineteenth century were important sites for carrying out this shift in critical thought. Two important early books that helped shape cultural studies as a critical approach largely took nineteenth century texts and history as their subject: *Culture and Society* by Raymond Williams (1958) and *The Making of the English Working Class* by E. P. Thompson (1963). Thompson's book examines its subject – class – as a process (11). For him, class is more like an event or a series of events than a 'structure' or a 'category', because it is perpetually changing. As in Williams's understanding of culture, we need to question our understanding of class continually not only because it is so overwhelmingly complex, but also because it reveals some of the deep-seated cultural anxieties that powerfully influence our personal, political and international relations.

Indeed, the idea that class is a process – and even more so that culture is a process – remain highly influential in the field of Victorian studies. For literary critics, the significance of looking at these terms as social processes is that the boundaries between texts can be eradicated. While New Critics looked at literature, particularly poetry, as a form of art, cultural studies places literary forms within a number of social complexes like 'culture' and 'class'. If, as Williams argues, 'culture' is the overarching control that we might look to in order to understand changes in the meanings of 'industry', 'democracy', and 'class', then virtually any material produced by a society can function as evidence of such changes. Literature, prose writing, periodicals, advertising, visual culture in any of its forms, letters, manuscripts and even historical events all might hold equal importance.

A movement that has been even more directly influential in Victorian studies is poststructuralism and in particular the work of Michel Foucault. Poststructuralism is itself an interdisciplinary movement, comprised of work from disciplines as disparate as philosophy, linguistics, literary criticism and psychoanalysis. While cultural studies eradicated the boundaries between literary and non-literary texts, poststructuralism seemed to widen the arena of context that might be relevant in a particular reading and argued for the legitimacy of each of these readings. Indeed, the test of Foucault's influence lies in its infiltration of disciplines other than the one within which he was working. Foucault's work has moved from philosophy to literary criticism, history, art history, history of science, sociology and psychology. Furthermore, the reaction against Foucauldian theory is in full force; we have not moved on even though the mode of discussing Foucault has shifted from employment of his theory to railings against his limitations.[8] Stefan Collini, for example, has argued that 'post-structuralist ideas have led to a concentration on the figural nature of all writing and hence to the assertion of the equally "fictional" status of discursive and novelistic prose' (21). And the key term here is 'fictional', as fiction and other literary forms so often represent the site of resistance to and transgression of dominant discursive modes.

Although the interdisciplinary turn of Victorian studies has yielded much important, fascinating work, one of the major pitfalls of the practice is a tendency toward decentred generality. Teaching and research staff as well as university administrations often see interdisciplinarity as the future of English studies, but the perspectives of each do not necessarily coincide. As Regenia Gagnier points out in a recent essay, the future of Victorian studies and British academics in general will be dependent on 'our embeddedness in market society' (465). Now that British education is a major income-generating industry, everything depends on how money will be raised and spent. Unfortunately, generic appeal and more extensive dissemination can appear to represent reliable investments.[9] In a recent debate on the future of the theoretical journal, *Critical Inquiry*, interdisciplinarity was also seen to be an integral part of the future of the journal and the field. Sander Gilman embraces globalization, and what seems to only be describable as an eradication of the boundaries between certain institutions rather than collaboration between them, arguing that we might 'think of the university as part of a world of education and the production of knowledge that is better integrated with other such institutions such as museums, adult education structures, public television and radio' (390). James Chandler seems to embrace globalization in the guise of interdisciplinarity, viewing the founding of centres for interdisciplinary study of the humanities as a trend commencing in the United States, which has now 'spread around the world' (357). The cultural and political moment no longer seems to require theoretical investigations but rather investigations into maintaining academic and ethical integrity in commodity based education. The dilemma critics practising interdisciplinarity now face is whether to maintain independence in this system or to allow themselves to be tempted by globalization's promises of ample funding.

Practice

Once cultural studies and literary theory began to eradicate the boundaries between the literary and the non-literary text, critics became and continue to be fascinated with a number of areas within the larger field of Victorian studies. Victorian science in all of its legitimate and illegitimate forms has become perhaps the most popular subfield for literary critics. Partly arising from the interest in science, studies of race and imperialism, particularly of the very late nineteenth century, are growing in number. Visual culture in various forms has become a very popular subfield with a large number of well-established critics working in this area. Print culture and the study of

Victorian entertainment also necessitate interdisciplinary approaches, though more work in these areas is needed. Such interests within the field have facilitated the development of approaches that take into account of a vast array of other disciplines, including history, history of science, postcolonial studies, history of art, media studies and theatre studies.

The most natural of disciplinary partners with criticism of Victorian literature is history. With the shift in focus and method inspired by cultural studies and the literary theory revolution of the 1980s, this partnership has become so commonplace it hardly seems to warrant noting. Virtually all criticism of nineteenth-century literature takes into account the historical events surrounding its production, if not the material conditions of the era, author and method of publication as well. The pairing of the history of science with Victorian literature, however, has proved a particularly fruitful combination in recent years. Not surprisingly, the single most influential scientific book published in the nineteenth century, *On the Origin of Species*, has often been the subject of these studies. Two influential critics, Gillian Beer and Sally Shuttleworth, dominate this sub-field of literary criticism with Gillian Beer's *Darwin's Plots* (1983) standing as the first in a wave of studies of science and literature by Victorianists. *Darwin's Plots* provides a foundation for so much future work by arguing that scientific writing has literary qualities, that such writing can be placed in a literary tradition[10] and that literature comprises an important component of the cultural reaction to scientific discoveries and theories. The literariness of scientific writing, for Beer, is symptomatic of the problem of representing something that there is yet no language to represent. In order to negotiate this problem, Darwin 'sought to appropriate and to recast inherited mythologies, discourses, and narrative orders' (3). Literary language and technique is thus transformed into scientific theory.

But Darwinian theory also held implications for the manner in which the Victorians thought about life, death and 'development'. It was a theory that resisted inclusion into the tradition of development theory from which it arose because it suggested uncertainty. The development of species was uncertain; in a sense 'ascent' or 'descent' of an organism was equally possible. Evidence to support positivism and degeneration at once existed in this single, complex text. As Beer argues: 'Darwinian theory will not resolve it a single significance nor yield a single pattern. It is essentially multivalent. It renounces a Descartian clarity, or univocality' (6). This discursive messiness continues to make Darwinian theory fascinating to literary critics and many have studied in particular the literary reaction to it. Following from the methods established by Gillian Beer and others, less prominent evolutionary texts have also come to the attention of Victorianists. The historian of science, James Secord, has written a massive work on the popular and scientific impact of Robert Chambers' early nineteenth-century evolutionary theory titled, *Victorian*

Sensation: The Extraordinary Publication, Reception, and Secret Authorship of Vestiges of the Natural History of Creation. Isobel Armstrong's work on Victorian poetry notably reads Tennyson's writing against Charles Lyell's *Principles of Geology,* a text that maintained a troubled relationship with early nineteenth-century creationist theories.[11]

The interest in Victorian science sparked by the work of Beer has inspired work on so many different facets of the subject that it would be impossible to list them all here. Instead, I will describe a few examples and trends. Much interest has been devoted to Victorian psychology, for example, in part because the discipline of psychology in the Victorian era was generalist, assuming knowledge of what we would consider disparate disciplines such as philosophy and literature. Helen Small's *Love's Madness* and Rick Rylance's *Victorian Psychology and British Culture, 1850–1880* delve into the intricacies of nineteenth-century psychology. Small, for example, traces the way major figures in the field thought about literature in their work, arguing that literary reference was often a strategy for flaunting the author's wide-ranging knowledge. *In the Secret Theatre of Home: Wilkie Collins, Sensation Narrative and Nineteenth-Century Psychology* and *Charlotte Brontë and Victorian Psychology,* by Jenny Bourne Taylor and Sally Shuttleworth respectively, each examine a single author's engagement with psychology, but they take opposing approaches of the social system in which these theories and novels function. Taylor argues that 'an ideology always contains a trace of resistance to its dominant meanings' and seeks to 'focus on the more equivocal aspects of nineteenth-century psychology' and 'to see it as articulating those points of dissonance' (30). Shuttleworth is more interested in thinking about psychology as an institution of power and employs a staunchly feminist approach in thinking about the ways that nineteenth-century sciences read the female body.

A number of less legitimate fringe sciences, united with each other and with psychology by their self-conscious and deliberate efforts to achieve legitimacy, have also come to the attention of literary critics. Mesmerism, spiritualism and telepathy, which in some ways engage directly with psychology, have received much attention in recent years. Two books on these subjects have very recently been published: *Literature, Technology and Magical Thinking* by Pamela Thurschwell and *The Invention of Telepathy* by Roger Luckhurst. Thurschwell argues that far from simply being marginalized forms of science, parapsychology and psychical research influenced the formulation of modern psychoanalysis. Luckhurst uses the fields of spiritualism and telepathy quite differently; the manner in which the conglomerate of discourses produced in these fields functions in disparate locations: colonial encounters, the late nineteenth-century Gothic and early twentieth century modernism. Another fringe science critics have recently become interested in is economics. Not surprisingly given that nearly every nineteenth-century fictional text deals with incomes and economy, some important critics have addressed this topic. Regenia Gagnier examines economic theory in *The Insatiability of Human Wants*, identifying a major shift in thought from concern with property, ownership and landlord–tenant relations to concern 'with the individual's subjective demand for goods' that occurs around 1871 (4). In other words, the psychology of the consumer became the central concern of economics. In *The Body Economic*, Catherine Gallagher examines political economy of the earlier nineteenth century, arguing that medical and physiological science were the source of some of the descriptive modes of political economists and, further-more, that such discourses were interrogated in novels by Charles Dickens and George Eliot.

Not much to Darwin's credit, it is an easy transition from the discussion of science in the Victorian era to imperialism in the Victorian era. Darwin's work inspired Spencer as well as many other social theorists who applied versions of evolutionary theory to cultures, societies and peoples, a practice that not-so-coincidentally reached its zenith at the height of Britain's imperial power at the end of the nineteenth century. The study of race and imperialism is an emerging sub-field that seems to have been reinvigorated by the current abundance of interest in postcolonial studies, and indeed work published on nineteenth-century imperialism is intended to appeal to this audience as well as critics of Victorian literature. One of the most important studies of imperialism in literature is Patrick Brantlinger's *Rule of Darkness*, which attempts to extend the definition of imperialism beyond the implementation of militaristic and economic domination of certain regions. Anne McClintock's *Imperial Leather*, a study of degeneration theory, sexuality and popular culture in an imperialist context, is also one of the more important studies to date.

In addition to focusing on these decades, the subject of studies of Victorian imperialism tends to be a range of male authors including Conrad, Kipling, Haggard, Stevenson with the occasional look back to Dickens. Taking H. Rider Haggard as an example, a range of approaches is evident. Wendy Katz in *Rider Haggard and the Fiction of Empire* examines Haggard's novels as romances and looks at the effect of positioning certain subjects such as science in Haggard's literature of imperial fantasy. Gail Ching-Liang Low's study of Haggard and Kipling is concerned with the manner in which the colonial citizen under-stands him- or herself in opposition to the racial other, at once distancing and desiring the other. Joseph Bristow's *Empire Boys* looks at homoerotic desire in Haggard's fiction where desire is manifested as a unity against dangerous native femininity. It is also worth noting here that a trend of looking at the New Woman in an imperial context has also recently developed. *New Woman and Colonial Adventure Fiction* by Lee Anne Richardson compares New Woman fiction of the 1890s with male-orientated adventure fiction, arguing that New

Woman novels were influential in the formation of 1890s imperialism. *The New Woman and the Empire* by Iveta Jusová explores the manner in which authors of New Woman novels 'constructed the New Woman project in relation to the late-Victorian colonial contest' (7), devoting particular attention to the significance of evolutionary theory in the work of these authors and their conceptions of imperialism.

The current interest in Victorian science is also evident in the large amount of work recently produced on visual culture, though this field holds much more affinity with art history. The single most influential book in the study of Victorian visual culture is *Techniques of the Observer*, written not by a literary critic, but by the art historian, Jonathan Crary. As Kate Flint notes, '[f]or us, as for the Victorians, the topic of seeing is one which breaks down disciplinary divisions' (39), and Crary sets out to do just this, arguing that 'concepts of subjective vision . . . pervaded not only areas of art and literature but were present in philosophical, scientific, and technological discourses' (9). *Techniques of the Observer* indeed addresses each of these areas, engaging with painting, literary writing, scientific and philosophical texts as well as optical technologies. In doing so, Crary creates a framework that we continue to engage in critical debate, setting out several important concepts. Taking his cue from the work of Michel Foucault, Crary begins with the idea that the grooming of human beings by institutions of power, such as governments, prisons, schools, becomes internalized in the modern era (commencing roughly in the mid- to late eighteenth century) and that this internalization coincides with the development of mass production and the rise of the capitalist system. He then investigates the particular implications for vision and seeing in light of these rising systems and the self-policing implied with the internalization of discipline. Perhaps the most obvious result of these changes is the 'standardization' of visual images, a process that creates and reinforces the use of particular modes of perception and for Crary results in 'the normalization and subjection of the observer' (17). The observer becomes subject to the will of institutions of power. A sort of 'visual nihilism' is created in the observer, who, as a result of this standardization, will fail to recognize the manner in which institutions influence thought and behaviour (14).

In addition, the internalization of discipline was accompanied by a shift in the study of optics 'from the geometrical optics of the seventeenth and eighteenth centuries to physiological optics, which dominated scientific and philosophical discussion of vision in the nineteenth century' (16). For Crary, 'subjective vision . . . had been taken out of the incorporeal relations of the camera obscura and relocated in the human body' (16). The manner in which an individual sees became an object of study, not merely in the sense of the manner in which an organ like the eye might function, but also in the sense that one's thoughts and emotions might be trained to view an object in a certain manner with deviation representing error or illness. Finally, one of the qualities of vision in the nineteenth century that Crary identifies and that other critics have often addressed is the disorientation associated with modern vision. The 'industrial remapping of the body in the nineteenth century' for Crary results in a 'separation of the senses' where each sense might be studied and exploited in industrial production or as a stimulus to consumption. However, not only did this system allow institutions to learn better how to exploit the observer, it also inspired commodity fetishism. The isolation of the visual sense 'enabled the new objects of vision (whether commodities, photographs, or the act of perception itself) to assume a mystified and abstract identity, sundered from any relation to the observer's position within a cognitively unified field' (19). Disorientating the viewer also might allow institutions to exploit more effectively, but one of the more subtle points of Crary's work is that the eradication of overt discipline of the eye of the seventeenth and eighteenth centuries results not only in a new, internalized means of discipline, but that this means of discipline:

> required a notion of visual experience as instrumental, modifiable, and essentially abstract, and that never allowed a real world to acquire solidity or permanence. Once vision became located in the empirical immediacy of the observer's body, it belonged to time, to flux, to death. The guarantees of authority, identity, and universality supplied by the camera obscura are of another epoch. (24)

As in the work of Michel Foucault, resistance – facilitated by this system's utter precariousness and lack of 'guarantees' of the success of power – is implied within.

It is this very plurality, first extensively explored by Crary, that has inspired much fascinating work on Victorian visual culture, often by well-known critics. Isobel Armstrong's long-awaited book on the mass production of glass and its aesthetic implications has become something of a legend.[12] Presumably first conceived in approximately the same years that Crary's work was being written and published, Armstrong provides a more sustained critique of Crary than others researching visual culture. In a recent article, Armstrong argues that Crary's 'model produces a monolithic account of technologies of vision in the nineteenth century that ignores the degree of conflict and ideological challenge created by rival epistemologies of seeing' ('Microscope' 35). Armstrong here suggests that the discursive field surrounding the act of seeing is more complex than Crary allows and that his lack of attention to the interest in mediation in nineteenth century writing is an oversight ('Microscope' 35). In seeking to capture this complexity, Armstrong describes 'the mediation of glass' as:

troubling because, as with the eye, you cannot see yourself seeing, is also troubling because you *can* see *it*, the fragile interposing sheet of almost nothingness with a sheen to it . . . Glass is a transitive material . . . a material which made one intensely aware that, in the movement between one state and another, there is a third term. ('Transparency' 131)

For Armstrong, it is the existence as well as the transitory/intransitory nature of this third term that plagued the thoughts of the Victorians and inspired them to provide so many fascinating accounts of glass and seeing in general. Armstrong resists Crary's assertion that a much more narrow understanding of vision dominates, celebrating instead the multiplicity of reactions to kalei-doscopes, microscopes and telescopes. Others inspired by these debates include Kate Flint, whose massive study, *The Victorians and the Visual Imagina-tion*, self-consciously seeks to move beyond Crary by 'considering the act of viewing in the light of other current practices employed in the interpretation of culture, dependent upon, and reinforcing, the hidden, invisible, interwoven threads of ideology' (22). Like Kate Flint, Lindsay Smith is also largely con-cerned with the implications of the unseen as well as the seen in her more specific study, *Victorian Photography, Painting and Poetry*.

The most obvious interdisciplinary path for criticism in light of the integra-tion of non-literary texts into the canon of readable material is the study of mass print culture, though this subject remains rather understudied by literary critics. The field is dominated by the study of the Victorian periodical press, which in reality functioned as a primary method of disseminating literary texts. The Victorians would have received their literary texts via a lens of advertising, reviewing, illustration and other material components of the popular press. The field we have come to call print culture therefore incorpo-rates these material elements and draws on the disciplines of literary criticism, media studies, design, history and potentially others. Laurel Brake's work in this area is perhaps more extensive and more influential than that of any other critic. Her first book on the subject, *Subjugated Knowledges*, seeks to break down the barriers between literature and journalism, arguing that the separation of these two forms of print is symptomatic of the institutionalization of the study of literature within the university. In order for literature – particularly litera-ture in English – to be a subject justifiably suitable for university study, it needed to be separated from its more mundane relatives like journalism. As Brake shows, however, this is a false dichotomy; these two forms of writing were much more closely intermingled in the nineteenth century than critics have previously allowed.

Other important work in this area includes Brake's second book, *Print in Transition, 1850–1910*, a focused look at the intermingled material histories of the book and the serial, as well as Linda K. Hughes and Michael Lund's *The*

Victorian Serial, which looks at the serialization of various forms of literature. Most recently, *Gender and the Victorian Periodical* by Hilary Fraser, Stephanie Green and Judith Johnston examines Victorian journalism published in over 120 periodicals, producing a massive work on an as yet understudied topic that will surely be referred to by scholars of the periodical press for many years to come. It is also important to note that a whole sub-genre of reading Victorian science through periodicals has developed with three recent, virtually simultaneous publications: *Science Serialized: Representations of the Sciences in Nineteenth-Century Periodicals, Science in the Nineteenth-Century Periodical: Reading the Magazine of Nature* and *Culture and Science in the Nineteenth-Century Media.*

Another sub-area of Victorian studies that necessitates interdisciplinary inquiry is the study of Victorian entertainment. The interdisciplinary turn of nineteenth-century literary studies has led scholars to think about material culture in addition to print culture. Thus the theatre with all its rich materiality – in the form of stage design, settings, costumes, theatrical spaces – would appear to be an obvious subject for interdisciplinary investigation. However, the material culture of the theatre remains understudied. As Jacky Bratton shows, Victorian theatre is plagued by the dual problem of being an ephemeral field with little primary material to study as well as a field that lacks literary aesthetics within the texts that are available for study.[13] The melodrama that is so popular throughout the Victorian era is 'bad drama', writes Bratton, 'it is the word used whenever a critic, trained or untrained, wishes to indicate that they think poorly of the art of the enacted fiction they are discussing, to deny it the universally praiseworthy character of being "realistic", "true to life"' (12). Melodrama, it seems, is still too aesthetically unrefined even after all of the breaking down of boundaries between types of texts inspired by Williams, Thompson, Barthes and Foucault. Even studies of melodrama tend to be more concerned with melodrama in more traditionally literary texts than in the drama, and this lack of literary aesthetics in dramatic texts has led scholars in the field to seek connections with the 'real' literature of the Victorian period.[14] Indeed, two recent studies about Victorian theatre quite clearly span the fields of literature and drama. Deborah Vlock's *Dickens, Novel Reading and the Victorian Popular Theatre* examines exchanges between Dickens's novels and the stage while Katherine Newey's *Women's Theatre Writing in Victorian Britain* looks at the position of the female playwright in Victorian culture. Jacky Bratton's work, however, offers a contrasting and unique approach in her *New Readings in Theatre History* and *The Victorian Clown,* taking account of the materiality of the texts we study as well as the material conditions of various figures that are often sidelined: from librarians and prompters to clowns, and acrobats to nineteenth-century biographers and historians. Given the lack of primary material available, studies of Victorian entertainment must necessarily rely on materiality and innovative approaches to studying it.[15]

Even though Victorian literature is difficult to characterize as a whole, a frequent and common interest in political and social engagement makes Victorian literature particularly appropriate to interdisciplinary readings. Some of the most widely read and disseminated work in the field draws on combinations of literary analysis and the placement of texts within histories other than the literary. Given the increasing interest in global education and the dissemination of work to more and more distant markets, the interdisciplinary turn in criticism will presumably continue to expand over the next couple of decades.

10 Mapping the Future of Victorian Studies

Ruth Robbins

Introduction

> I am sure that the study of portions of the best English authors, and com-
> position, might with advantage, be made a part of [elementary school
> pupils'] regular course of instruction to a much greater degree than it is at
> present. Such a training would tend to elevate and humanize a number of
> young men, who at present, notwithstanding the vast amount of raw infor-
> mation they have amassed, are wholly uncultivated; and it would have the
> great social advantage of tending to bring them into intellectual sympathy
> with the educated of the upper classes.[1]

As the old joke has it, like nostalgia, Victorian literary studies are not what
they used to be, and we certainly do not read literary texts these days in the
hope of producing social cohesion in a top–down model in which the upper
classes influence the lower, nor in the hope of 'elevating and humanizing'
students and readers. We are not even sure that we know in absolute terms
who the 'best' English authors (or writers in English) are. It has never been the
case that the study of Victorian literature was entirely limited by the kind of
narrow canon that F. R. Leavis announced in 1948 with magisterial and

anti-geographical authority: '[t]he great English novelists are Jane Austen, George Eliot, Henry James and Joseph Conrad',[2] with Emily Brontë as marginal example of an alternative 'greatness'. In almost any incarnation of the Victorian curriculum, the limitations on the study of the Victorian canon of fiction (and, indeed, poetry) have always been much broader than Arnoldian or Leavisite notions of value would suggest. George Eliot might be the 'great' Victorian novelist, but Dickens has always been the most studied figure of the period. Emily Brontë might be a peculiar example, but the Brontë sisters as a whole have always had an audience.

Victorian Studies Now

Over the last 25 years or so, the canon has been vastly expanded, not to say exploded. It is not just that the names of the writers studied in undergraduate courses have overspilled the limits of the greatness that Leavis declared; in the wake of the theoretical preoccupations of the last 30 years or so, the very questions that critics ask of literary texts and periods have also changed. 'Greatness' is a word we scarcely use and we rarely apportion 'value', whether aesthetic or moral, to the poems, plays and fictions of the period. Periodicity itself has become problematic since the arbitrary dates of Victoria's reign do not necessarily map neatly onto the developments of the period. It has long been observed for instance that the early poetry of Tennyson owes much to Keats and the Romantic traditions of Wordsworth; we can also easily see that the later productions of nineteenth-century fiction (in Hardy for, example), both belong to an earlier tradition and predict future developments. The beginnings and endpoints of 'the Victorian' are now much more permeable. We read different books from our predecessors because we begin and end in different places. We also read for different purposes and focus less on the great Realist tradition of moral seriousness to be found in *Middlemarch*, and more on the sensational pleasures and thrills that the Victorians loved and feared, and that the present locates in *Lady Audley's Secret* or *East Lynne*.

Any brief survey of publications aimed at undergraduate students to enable them to 'get into' the Victorian period, and of the curricula by which they do so, demonstrates immediately that what we mean by Victorian literature and how we study it is the subject of constant revision. The contemporary critic's focus is resolutely double: context as well as text, sometimes with texts offering only a pretext for a critical discussion that is also about historical moments and movements. The recent plethora of surveys of the Victorian period's literary production is testament to a shift in the location of what Victorian literature and its study are. In publication terms, the focus is strongly slanted towards the novel, a preference which speaks (ironically perhaps) to Leavis's continued influence, for as Francis O'Gorman has noted, 'the

increased standing of the novel and the willingness of the critical community
to consider it as a significant genre . . . owed much . . . to F. R. Leavis's critical
endeavours'.[3] But the novels that are studied now belong to very different
traditions than did those on which the critical past focused.

O'Gorman's own survey of Victorian criticism of the Victorian novel offers
a history of its criticism during the twentieth century, with substantial extracts
from major critical works. The chapter titles and subheadings show how
developments in critical practice are produced by theoretical thinking. The
introduction briefly covers topics such as feminism and masculinity studies,
arguing that these were essential to the new formations (from the 1980s
onwards) of the Victorian literary canon, which included forms such as
popular sensation form and the Gothic. At the far end of the nineteenth
century, it also helps to explain the rise of the New Woman fiction of first-wave
feminism which refocuses the politics of fiction. Individual chapters are
devoted to the early twentieth-century criticism of the novel via George
Saintsbury, David Cecil, E. M. Forster and Leavis, the effects of feminist criticism, the focus on realism as a form and the related nineteenth-century genre
of social-problem fiction (particularly the industrial novel), questions of
language and form which preoccupy the whole century, and it ends with
substantial sections on the relatively new disciplines of the 'history of the
book' (literary production and its effects on fiction) and of postcolonial
approaches to the novel.

O'Gorman makes the case – widely accepted by contemporary critics,
though not advocated by Leavis – that any critique of the Victorian novel form
must take proper note of the contexts of production that made the novel.
Contemporary criticism is 'embedded' in its period, and extensive discussion
of context is required for any comprehension of text. That this is the new
critical orthodoxy is evidenced by multiple other books and text books that
seek to enable students to negotiate the complexities of Victorian culture.
Herbert Tucker's *Companion to Victorian Literature and Culture* (1999), has
chapters which name firstly important dates (1832, 1848, 1870 and 1897, the
years of the first Reform Act, of Chartist agitation and European revolution, of
the declaration of the British Empire and the conferment of Victoria's title as
Empress of India and of her Diamond Jubilee respectively), and thereafter
which name contexts and concepts rather than individual texts. The single
word chapter titles (for instance, in the 'Walks of Life' section, the chapter titles
include 'Clerical', 'Medical', 'Legal', 'Educational' and so on) focus attention
primarily on the way that the Victorians lived rather than on what they wrote,
which comes to the forefront only in Part 4, though the majority of
contributors would certainly be identified primarily with literary rather than
historical studies.

Similarly, Deirdre David's *Cambridge Companion to the Victorian Novel* (2001) has more extensive chapter titles, but it also demonstrates the extent to which issues that most concern us now (race, sexuality, gender – though class is sadly absent, an omission that says something rather worrying about the nature of contemporary social critique) inflect what we seek in nineteenth-century fiction: this history of literature is very much about the present. The collection opens, however, with essays on the Victorian reading public and on the *business* of Victorian publishing – the history of the book itself is the keynote for the collection. Moreover, David also commissioned essays on the sensation novel and on detection in the Victorian novel, choices which suggest the extent to which the *Cambridge Companion* was responding to changes in modern university curricula, themselves altered by the new foci of contemporary criticism. Indeed, the volume speaks of the extent to which the detective novel and the sensation novel are unproblematically included in those curricula, and thus it signals a broader interest in the popular forms of the period as opposed to or alongside its more 'highbrow' literary products.

These large major collections of essays are supplemented in contemporary publishing by texts much more clearly marketed towards the undergraduate student market. Sean Purchase's *Key Concepts in Victorian Literature* (2006) gives an alphabetical plethora of concepts and contexts for the period, from the age of Victoria and architecture to violence and war, before turning to the major genres to offer a brief historical survey of several of them (concentrating mostly on prose and mostly on fiction), and finally he offers an overview of a variety of critical and theoretical approaches to the period and its texts. In a slightly different way, Maureen Moran's *Victorian Literature and Culture* (2006) spends just under a half of its length giving its readers a 'Historical, Cultural and Intellectual Context' for the period, before turning to genres and movements and theories and methods. Perhaps because the Victorian period is now more than a century away from us in time, and thus is no longer within living memory, and perhaps, too, because the teaching of narrative history has been largely excised from the British national history curriculum (and British history may have always been less significant in non-British contexts which still nonetheless read Victorian literature), in these student texts there is a real necessity to provide very basic information about what was happening politically and culturally in nineteenth-century Britain.

Comparing this small part of the contemporary collections on the Victorian period with works published 30 or more years ago, there is, in some ways, less difference than one might assume. Volume VI of Boris Ford's *Pelican History of English Literature*, entitled *From Dickens to Hardy* (1958) is clearly a different kind of production than is to be found in contemporary publishing, not least because it names two 'great' novelists in its title with the clear presumption that these are major writers who mark out the period's meaning, a presumption that is more difficult to sustain in contemporary criticism. But, like contemporary reformulations of the period, there is an emphasis on context in this volume; it is just that the nature of the context that is being asserted is rather different. The text opens with G. D. Klingopulos's 'Notes on the Victorian Scene': but here, rather than focusing on 'way of life' issues as Tucker does, the scene that is sketched out is one based on philosophical and political thought – for instance, the expansion of democracy following the various Reform Acts of the nineteenth century, and the examination of such broad concepts as utilitarianism, liberty, anarchy and religion. The original educated reader of this text, it could be taken for granted, knew the basic history in terms of the various Acts and reforms that marked the period. What she or he needed help with was reconstructing the impact of new ideas on the century, and although there are essays on magazine culture and the Victorian reading public, the vast majority of the space of the text is given over to named novelists and poets, often insisting on the primacy of a particular work (*Wuthering Heights* or *Middlemarch*, for example). Similarly, Arthur Pollard's *The Victorians* (1969) is resolutely focused on texts and authors. There are two contextual essays by A. O. J. Cockshut on Victorian thought and Victorian religion, suggesting a similar concern about the history of ideas rather than social factors. Thereafter, every chapter is about a novelist or poet, with a nod to the *fin-de-siècle* period and to Victorian theatre in two chapters at the end.

This chapter seeks to stand as both a commentary on some recent developments in the Victorian literary field and a speculation on where such developments may lead in the future. As I suggest above, because of canon revision, and because the Victorian period itself was very long, the field is vast, and I cannot do it all justice in the available space, not least because one of the shifts that has occurred in boundaries is the very one of period. The Queen's long reign has been rendered longer by a move towards the study of 'the long nineteenth century', which often begins as early as 1760 and ends sometime around the First World War, 1914 to 1918. Victorian literature, as it is understood in the academy, has already become something that perhaps the Victorians themselves would not have recognized. What might it yet become? The discussion that follows discusses both pedagogic and critical practices (common university courses and the research which supports them) since the curricula we construct now are the product of recent research and define what 'Victorian Studies' means to a generation of students who will be the next providers of the research which forms the curriculum for the future.

The Way We Read Now?

In his recent book *English in Practice* (2003), Peter Barry offers a lively and accessible introduction to the way we read now, in Victorian studies and elsewhere in the literary academy. As well as offering a history of English studies, including the traditions of close reading of the text in isolation, the moves towards contextualization and the effects of literary theory on reading practices, Barry makes a strong case for a mode of interpretation which is appropriately reflective and thereby which is able to take account of a variety of textual possibilities. As well as reading the words on the page with close attention, readers should also carefully consider the context in which the text was first produced and read, the history of its reception (what the original readers and subsequently the critics have said about it) and the concerns of the present. As he puts it, in the course of an exemplary (in all senses of the word) reading of 'The Lady of Shallott': 'however we read . . . our reading will be *partial*, in both senses; firstly it will not be able to take account of every element . . . and secondly it will be the product of a personal predisposition or prejudice.'[4] The key to an intelligent reading is to be as aware as possible of the forces which shape the readings one undertakes, to read the words of the text and the multiple contexts of those words with close attention. Barry's solution to the problem of reading is to suggest a 'combination' method that he calls 'total textuality' in which readers are alive to a series of possibilities. The reader needs to be alert to the following elements (and as lecturers, tutors need to train students in these various forms of attention). Readers can justifiably focus on some (and even all) of the following:

1. Textuality (also known as 'the words on the page')
2. Intertextuality (roughly, the words on related pages)
3. Contextuality (the social, cultural and historical context of the work)
4. Multitextuality (the textual variants of the work itself . . .)
5. Peritextuality (also known as literary criticism – the words alongside the text).[5]

The choice about which of these elements one focuses most attention on is an issue that depends on the kind of study one undertakes. In genre studies or in special author studies, for instance, textuality and intertextuality are probably most important, though contextuality will also have its place. Multitextuality is probably mostly significant for the reading of poetry, particularly where multiple variants of the same poem exist. Peritextuality, the process of finding critical resources and their evaluation, is central to critical endeavour, and is a key skill for English graduates.

The recent history of Victorian literary studies is the story of how Barry (and others) came to this view of the methods for reading literature; it is also the history of literary theory in the academy. The way we read now is marked by the concerns of theory even when theory is not always at the forefront of the discussion. The shift from primarily textual studies to contextual studies of the Victorian period was a response to and reaction against the close

reading/practical criticism emphasis of the kind of literary criticism advocated by Leavis and his contemporary, I. A. Richards. Leavis's 'great tradition',
like Matthew Arnold's 'touchstone' before it, was an assertion of timeless
value, of the continuity of 'human nature' and of the social responsibilities of
the individual writer and reader, as Chris Baldick's *The Social Mission of English
Criticism* (1983) has thoroughly demonstrated. Period studies, however, necessitate an understanding of period itself. If the critic sets out to write a kind of
literary history, to see connections between contemporary texts and to track
the tensions and difficulties of a period in the texts it produced, there is
no escape from historical context which becomes embedded in the process of
constructing criticism. Moreover, the detailed study of period always
demonstrates the strangeness and distinctiveness of the past at least as much
as it offers any consolatory sense of continuity.

The kinds of contexts that we now reconstruct for the Victorian period are
clearly inflected by the concerns of the present. Like the reconstruction of
history, literary studies that focus on period cannot simply remake the past as
it actually was: we remake the past through the lens of our own interests. In
the twentieth century and beyond, those interests have recently included a
very strong focus on gender and its politics born out of second-wave
feminism, a fascination with Victorian sexual morality and mores that in part
arises from our own post-Freudian sensibilities, an ongoing excavation of the
meaning of empire to the Victorians which in part is an intellectual response to
the contemporary world's immersion in new kinds of globalization and an
interest in print culture itself as a material medium that stands as the Victorian
equivalent of our own multi-media culture.

The single most important incursion of theory into Victorian literary studies
has been the intervention of feminist scholarship. The difference it has made is
immeasurable, leading to a radical reformation of the curriculum and, in the
1980s, to a revolution in publishing as the expanded canon required the
support of good editions of the 'new' books for students to read. Despite this
transformation, which was both welcome and necessary, it could be suggested
that the feminist literary-critical project has stalled, at least in nineteenth-
century studies. There are problems with potentially insufficiently critical
readings of women writers, both by students and by critics. Because of the
complexity of creating a context for reading – the difficulties of reconstructing
not the facts of the legal or social constraints on women or the ideological
weight brought to bear on forms of idealized behaviour, but that of working
out what women may have really felt about these constraints – too much
emphasis is placed on the binary constructions of the angel and the whore,
and too little of student and/or critical energy is spent in close attention to
what women writers actually did with these figures (their often subversive
treatments of them are subtle and therefore easily ignored). On the other hand,

the Victorian period was particularly rich in print culture, much of which has been reproduced in accessible forms. The field of feminism in the Victorian academy still has much to offer. There is still much to do in recovering some of the lost voices, not simply in terms of reproducing the texts, but also in terms of finding ways of reading them which do not do them violence. And along-side uncovering what Mary Poovey has called 'the ideological work of gender' for women, a consequence of the attention on women's writing within the context of the 'woman question' has been an explosion of interest in the way that men (real men, characters in texts and male writers) responded to the constraints of gender that logically, since gender is a cultural construction, must also have affected male lives. The 'man question' has only just begun to be asked by writers like James Eli Adams, Richard Dellamora, Herbert Sussmann and Eve Kosofsky Sedgwick, among others.

Where Next?

If a 'third wave' of feminist (and masculinist) still remains to happen, what are the other areas that might form the future of Victorian studies? The discussion of interdisciplinarity in Chapter 9 shows in detail the extent to which the boundaries between the literary and the non-literary text have been broken down and how literary studies now are a facet of a wider study of culture. Although this seems certain to continue to be the case, the question is which are the fields of culture that might offer such productive analyses as there have been in literature and science. One possible such field is economics, under-stood in its wider sense, where money is seen as a social form and indeed as the dominant social form. In this kind of analysis, a more subtly inflected version of Marx's proposition that material life determines consciouness is possible. Regenia Gagnier's *The Insatiability of Human Wants: Economics and Aesthetics in Market Society* (2000) is a good example of this kind of reading, as is Catherine Gallagher, *The Body Economic: Life, Death, and Sensation in Political Economy and the Victorian Novel* (2006). Interest in materiality is also manifest in the growing numbers of studies of leisure and the commodity. Although in its weakest form such studies can be little more than a rehearsal of the unthinking hypnosis that the commodity exerts in our own time, in some recent work this has been revealingly combined with questions of gender and imperialism: a development which is to be welcomed.

Of course, all the works of literature that we read have a very material history. This is a significant new field in the old subject area, though in some senses an interest in print culture *as print* is as old as Richard D. Altick's *The English Common Reader*, first published in 1958, and therefore not especially 'new' at all. The suggestions that Altick's methods offered, however, for evalu-ating the commercial and practical considerations relating to the words on the page (whose words they were, if they were signed, how much did the words cost for the publisher and for the reader, whose words surrounded them in a periodical printing of a novel text, what adverts there were, who could read, how reading took place – as private activity or as social process and so on), did not get taken up especially quickly. Individual exceptions, such as Guinevere Griest's study of Mudie's Select Circulating Library (1970) and John Sutherland's and Gaye Tuchman's very differently slanted studies of the relationship between publishers and writers, offered some provocative directions for future study. Sutherland's comment that there was 'no Victorian novel . . . which was not materially affected by the publishing system'[6] is a very important corrective to any view that writers are the unaided producers of works of genius. Moreover, he reminds us that the experience of reading was very different indeed in the nineteenth century from the way we actually read Victorian writing now. Because large numbers of fictional works were published in part formats, reading fiction was often a serial process, taking place over months, rather than one which offered immediate gratification. The novelists and other writers whose works are reprinted today in good quality paperback editions for students to use, with scholarly apparatus and the reassurance of quality that the 'classic' series title gives to the work, are 'canonized' by that imprimatur. Many of the formats in which those works were originally read – as borrowed copies from Mudie's, as part works in ephemeral publications – suggested something rather different about their meaning for their first audiences.

The questions that insights such as these raise for the project of understanding Victorian literary production are manifold. There are methodological and theoretical problems attached to interpreting the textuality of the texts in relation to contextuality and peritextuality. We cannot, for example, reconstruct the audiences in all their multiplicity – the knowledge we have is necessarily partial. Nonetheless, as recent discussions of the field have suggested, the fact that we cannot tell the *whole* story does not mean that we cannot tell any stories at all. The works of Altick, Griest, Sutherland and Tuchman offer important signposts for thinking about books as material objects, commodities (with a cost and a consumer) and about audiences. The history of print culture also overlaps in interesting ways with other approaches to literary studies. Important texts such as Kate Flint's *The Woman Reader, 1837–1914* (1993) or Joseph Bristow's *Empire Boys: Adventures in a Man's World* (1991), for instance, signal that there is a relationship between the product and its market which is usually strongly gendered. Texts also went out as trade commodities to the empire, and one has to assume that they were not necessarily read in the same ways 'over there' as they were 'over here'. The history of shifts in publishing culture is thus also a history of shifts in attitudes and anxieties about gender and/or empire. The peritextual discussions of what is 'permitted' copy in a periodical or Mudie's novel aimed at a family audience with a price tag which reflects what kind of family is implied also has important implications for the interpretations we make and the choices that authors made in their own time. A recent collection like Laurel Brake, Bill Bell and David Finkelstein's *Nineteenth-Century Media and the Construction of Identities* (2000) contains essays which place Dickens's serial fiction, for example, firmly in the context of a wider print culture with various audiences and publishers both of whom had different agendas. Simon Eliot's *Some Patterns and Trends in British Publishing, 1800–1919* (1994) makes a strong case for the importance of seeing that the really popular writings of the Victorian period were not the novels which had circulations in excess of 100,000, but pamphlet publications such as broadsheets, aimed squarely at working-class audiences, which could occasionally beat the million-seller mark. The history of that reading public is harder to excavate – the ephemeral nature of the publications aimed at them is one bar to a full discussion; the relative silence in print culture of their audiences is another. Nonetheless, Eliot's argument is that we must try to take account of the labouring poor in our estimation of who was reading what, since this group made up by far the largest reading public of the period. More still needs to be done.

Another material condition of our own time also seems likely to influence the future direction of Victorian studies. The bodies that fund research in the humanities have in recent years increasingly favoured large collaborative projects, many of which are centred on the digitization and production of searchable databases of printed material such as periodicals. The greater availability of these resources in electronic form has made work on the material very much easier in practical terms, and has opened archives and collections in virtual form to many more widely dispersed scholars. Some of the products arising from the work have already been published, especially in the area of science which is, as we have seen, itself one of the distinctive developments of the renewed impulse towards interdisciplinary study. As periodicals represent a relatively under-researched field they are an attractive resource for new (and old) scholars, and a greater volume of publication emerging from this material is to be expected. As the Victorian periodical is such a heterogeneous production it is likely to offer rich resources to many areas, including questions of democratization of knowledge, formation of intellectual communities and the organization of consensus on political and social issues. The presence of women as writers, often anonymously, has been noted in Laurel Brake's pioneering work and further work here may be a way of developing the more nuanced understanding of gender that I argued for earlier.

It also may also be a way back into some questions of form. As suggested above, the knowledge of how a work was first read can have profound implications and issues of form are among these. Victorian studies, and arguably literary studies in general, suffer an asymmetry produced by the perceived attractiveness of content and the perceived difficulty of form, the result of which is a relative neglect of formal questions on the part of both students and published scholars. There needs to be a rehabilitation of 'close reading', a practice unfortunately tainted by its association with the Leavisite literary studies that were challenged by the theoretical approaches of the 1980s. The obvious beneficiary of a renewed practice of close reading would be poetry, the genre that was important to the Victorians themselves, but which has been overshadowed by the attention paid to the novel.

In thinking about what we do now, I have been very struck by the relative indifference of much contemporary criticism and of many contemporary students to questions about class. At one time, when Victorian literary studies were clearly something else, there was a burning interest in this key concept, signalled by the centrality of the 'condition of England novel' in the university curriculum. Sometimes this interest in class was naïve; often it was inflected by a politics that is perhaps no longer fashionable. But it existed and it was discussed. At precisely this moment in history, when students are least aware of the ways in which class operates on them, the academy needs to return to one of its roots, and to find ways of communicating an intelligible theory of class to a student body which has been interpellated into disavowing that there is any such thing. Simon Eliot's book, or work like that of Gagnier discussed briefly above, offer possible ways forward into that terrain. Signs of a return to such issues are already apparent. Over the last decade or so, Victorian studies have been dominated by interest in the latter part of the period, an interest driven largely by the widening of the canon discussed above, in which contemporary concerns with gender, race and sexuality have found productive texts in such late nineteenth-century forms as sensation fiction or the Gothic and in 'minor' works. This interest has been so pronounced that the *fin-de-siècle* no longer appears, as used to be the case, in the curriculum as a short section of a longer course, or as the final chapter of a book. It now occupies a space of its own and has become a large and distinct field in its own right, somewhat to the detriment of the study of the earlier decades. The Romantics, mostly conveniently dead before Victoria's accession, are seen as belonging to the end of the eighteenth century and the critical vigour of the Romantic studies has itself tended to dissuade the Victorianist from incursion into it.

In the last few years, however, it has been apparent at conferences and from journal articles (where 'new' scholarship tends to be published more quickly than in book form) that focus is shifting to the other end of the century, to the earlier part of Victoria's reign, and indeed to the period preceding it – the *fin-de-siècle* of the eighteenth century, rather than the nineteenth. Although questions of politics and economics are obviously not limited to any particular period, the very raw effects of industrialization and the complex debates about reform in the first decades of the nineteenth century arguably provoke sharper analysis of those questions. The condition of England novel and its contexts may again become central, albeit read in new and different ways.

Finally, then, combination methods of reading are very likely to continue into the future: textuality, and its various prefixes, alongside a rigorous post-theoretical perspective (in which theory is not 'over' but continues to inform interpretation) are a way forward. They offer a complexity of interpretation that has the benefits of being intellectually satisfying and which also gets us nearer to some partial truths. But alongside them, we need to reinvigorate some big concepts, and especially the concept of class, and we need to do so with a strong emphasis on the materiality of the Victorian world of print culture.

Further Reading

This list of further reading has been organized by topic to enable the student to follow up particular areas of interest. It begins with general texts on the period, followed by groups listed alphabetically by topic.

General Introductions to Victorian Literature and Culture

As well as being introductory, these texts also show the chronological development and changes in thinking about Victorian studies. Buckley and Houghton were written in the 1950s when Victorianism was not fashionable, and thus represent something like a defence of the subject as worthy of study. As with Lerner, Kumar and Pollard from the 1960s, Buckley and Houghton are informative and useful texts, but do not explicitly examine more recent areas of critical interest such as race or gender. In Stonyk, Gilmour and Davis it is possible to recognize contemporary Victorian studies in their greater emphasis on these issues. Kucich et al. is an interesting examination of the re-presentation and adaptations of Victorianism in the twentieth century (see also: Victorian Studies).

Buckley, Jerome Hamilton, *The Victorian Temper: A Study In Literary Culture*, Cambridge, MA: Harvard University Press, 1951.
Bullen, J. B., *Writing and Victorianism*, London: Longman, 1997.
Davis, Philip, *The Victorians: 1830–1880*, Oxford: Oxford University Press, 2002.
Gilmour, Robin, *The Victorian Period: The Intellectual and Cultural Context of English Literature 1830–1890*, London: Longman, 1993.
Hillis Miller, J., *Victorian Subjects*, Durham: Duke University Press, 1991.
Houghton, Walter, *The Victorian Frame of Mind, 1830–1870*, New Haven: Yale University Press, 1957.
Kucich, John and Dianne F. Saddoff (eds), *The Victorian Afterlife: Postmodern Culture Rewrites the Nineteenth Century*, Minnesota: University of Minnesota Press, 2000.
Kumar, Shiv. K., *British Victorian Literature: Recent Revaluations*, New York: New York University Press, 1969.
Lerner, Laurence (ed.), *The Victorians*, London: Methuen, 1978.
Newsome, David, *The Victorian World Picture: Perceptions and Introspections in an Age of Change*, New York: Rutgers University Press, 1997.
Pollard, Arthur, *The Victorians*, Harmondsworth: Penguin, 1970.
Schad, John, *Victorians in Theory: from Derrida to Browning*, Manchester: Manchester University Press, 1999.

Stonyk, Margaret (ed.), *Nineteenth-Century English Literature*, London: Macmillan, 1983.
Wheeler, Michael, *English Fiction of the Victorian Period, 1830–1890*, London: Longman, 1985.

Children and Childhood

Coveney is the classic study, published in 1967 but still a good introduction. Mitchell and Bristow look at gender and the child, and Sanders is a collection of accounts of the lives of real children. Children were a popular subject for photography: Brown examines visual representations, as does Robson. Robson also takes childhood as a metaphorical and symbolic condition not simply confined to children, and this approach is shared by Peters and Berry.

Berry, Laura C., *The Child, the State and the Victorian Novel*, Charlottesville: University Press of Virginia, 1999.
Bristow, Joseph, *Empire Boys: Adventures in a Man's World*, London: HarperCollins, 1991.
Brown, Marylin (ed.), *Picturing Children*, Aldershot: Ashgate, 2001.
Coveney, Peter, *The Image of Childhood*, London: Penguin, 1967.
Kincaid, James R., *Child-Loving: The Erotic Child and Victorian Culture*, London: Routledge, 1992.
Mitchell, Sally, *The New Girl: Girls' Culture in England 1880–1913*, New York: Columbia University Press, 1997.
Peters, Lara, *Orphan Texts: Victorian Orphans, Culture and Empire*, Manchester: Manchester University Press, 2000.
Robson, Catherine, *Men in Wonderland: The Lost Girlhood of the Victorian Gentleman*, New Jersey: Princeton University Press, 2001.
Sanders, Valerie (ed.), *Records of Girlhood: Nineteenth Century Childhoods*, Aldershot: Ashgate, 2000.

The City

Critical work on the city, also known as urban studies, has expanded considerably since the 1980s. Williams is an important early work which takes a Marxist perspective, and Briggs is historical with a great deal of factual detail. Dyos and Wolff is historical and sociological in approach. Victorian London, because of its unprecedented size and complexity, has attracted much attention: Nead is on visual representation and is highly illustrated. Koven and Walkowitz both focus on gender and the effects of class and poverty, while McLaughlin and Wolfreys include substantial analyses of literary material (see also: Degeneration, Crime).

Briggs, Asa, *Victorian Cities*, Harmondsworth: Penguin, 1963.
Dyos, H. J. and Michael Wolff, *The Victorian City: Images and Realities*, London: Routledge and Kegan Paul, 1973, 2 vols.
Hall, Catherine, *Civilizing Subjects: Metropole and Colony in the English Imagination 1830–1867*, Chicago: Chicago University Press, 2002.
Koven, Seth, *Slumming: Sexual and Social Politics in Victorian London*, Princeton: Princeton University Press, 2004.

McLaughlin, Joseph, *Writing the Urban Jungle*, Virginia: University Press of Virginia, 2000.

Nead, Lynda, *Victorian Babylon: People, Streets and Images in Nineteenth-century London*, New Haven and London: Yale University Press, 1995.

Walkowitz, Judith, *City of Dreadful Delight: Narratives of Sexual Danger in Late-Victorian London*, London: Virago, 1992.

Williams, Raymond, *The Country and the City*, London: Penguin, 1973.

Wolfreys, Julian, *Writing London*, London: Palgrave, 1999.

Bailey, Peter, *Popular Culture and Performance in the Victorian City*, Cambridge: Cambridge University Press, 1998.

Class

The question of class was an important driver of the revitalization of Victorian studies and Thompson, Williams and Stedman Jones are among the leading texts in this respect. Most of the works listed here are from an historical perspective, focusing on gender (Tosh, Clark) or the middle class (Tosh, Davidoff, Hall). Young specifically relates these issues to the novel (see also: Politics and Economics).

Baldick, Chris, *The Social Mission of English Criticism: 1848–1932*, Oxford: Oxford University Press, 1983.

Clark, Anna, *The Struggle for the Breeches: Gender and the Making of the British Working Class*, Berkeley: University of California Press, 1995.

Davidoff, Leonore and Catherine Hall, *Family Fortunes: Men and Women of the English Middle Class, 1780–1850*. Chicago: University of Chicago Press, 1994.

Gallagher, Catherine, *The Industrial Reformation of English Fiction: Social Discourse and Narrative Form 1832–1867*, Chicago: University of Chicago Press, 1985.

Himmelfarb, Gertrude, *The Idea of Poverty*, New York: Knopf, 1983.

Joyce, Patrick, *Democratic Subjects: The Self and the Social in Nineteenth-Century Britain*, Cambridge: Cambridge University Press, 1996.

Keating, P. J., *The Working Classes in Victorian Fiction*, London: Routlege Kegan Paul, 1971.

Phillips, K. C., *Language and Class in Victorian Britain*, Oxford: Blackwell, 1984.

Rose, J., *The Intellectual Life of the British Working Classes*, New Haven and London: Yale University Press, 2001.

Stedman Jones, Gareth, *Languages of Class: Studies In English Working Class History 1832–1982*, Cambridge: Cambridge University Press, 1983.

Thompson, E. P., *The Making of the English Working Classes*, New York: Vintage, 1966.

Thompson, F. M. L., *The Rise of Respectable Society: A Social History of Victorian Britain, 1830–1900*, Cambridge, MA: Harvard University Press, 1988.

Tosh, John, *A Man's Place: Masculinity and the Middle Class Home in Victorian England*, London: Yale University Press, 1999.

Williams, Raymond, *Culture and Society: Coleridge to Orwell*, London: The Hogarth Press, 1987.

Young, Arlene, *Culture, Class and Gender in the Victorian Novel*, Basingstoke: Macmillan, 1999.

Colonialism, Imperialism and Race

The impact of postcolonial thought on Victorian studies has been significant. Two foundational texts are Said and Spivak, establishing critical ideas of orientalism and the subaltern respectively. The contribution of travel writing and photography to ideas of imperialism is explored in Franey, McEwan, Ridley and Ryan. The new genre of adventure fiction is seen as a product and a contributor to imperialism in Green and Katz, and there are gendered perspectives in Iveta, Meyer, Kitzan and Richardson. Brantlinger has been of particular importance in establishing an idea of imperial Gothic.

Bivona, Daniel, *British Imperial Literature*, Cambridge: Cambridge University Press, 1998.

Brantlinger, Patrick, *Rule of Darkness: British Literature and Imperialism, 1830–1914*, London: Cornell University Press, 1988.

Dawson, Graham, *Soldier Heroes: British Empire and Images of Masculinity*, London: Routledge, 1994.

David, Deirdre, *Rule Britannia: Women, Empire and Victorian Writing*, Ithaca: Cornell University Press, 1996.

Franey, Laura E., *Victorian Travel Writers and Imperial Violence*, Basingstoke: Palgrave, 2003.

Green, Martin, *Dreams of Adventure, Deeds of Empire*, New York: Basic Books, 1979.

Iveta, Jusová, *The New Woman and the Empire*, Columbus: Ohio State University Press, 2005.

Katz, Wendy, *Rider Haggard and the Fiction of Empire*, Cambridge: Cambridge University Press, 1987.

Kitzan, Laurence, *Victorian Writers and the Image of Empire*, Westport: Greenwood Press, 2001.

Low, Gail Ching-Liang, *White Skins/Black Masks: Representation and Colonialism*, London: Routledge, 1996.

Macdonald, Robert H., *The Language of Empire: Myths and Metaphors of Popular Imperialism 1880–1914*, Manchester: Manchester University Press, 1994.

McClintock, Anne, *Imperial Leather: Race, Gender and Sexuality in the Colonial Contest*, London: Routledge, 1995.

McEwan, Cheryl, *Gender, Geography and Empire*, Aldershot: Ashgate, 2000.

Meyer, Susan, *Imperialism at Home: Race and Victorian Women's Fiction*, Cornell University Press, 1996.

Phillips, Richard, *Mapping Men and Empire*, London: Routledge, 1997.

Pratt, Mary Louise, *Imperial Eyes: Travel Writing and Transculturation*, London: Routledge, 1992.

Richardson, Lee Anne M., *New Woman and Colonial Adventure Fiction in Victorian Britain*, Gainesville: University Press of Florida, 2006.

Ridley, Hugh, *Images of Imperial Rule*, Kent: Croom Helm, 1983.

Ryan, James R., *Picturing Empire: Photography and the Visualisation of the British Empire*, London: Reaktion, 1997.

Said, Edward, *Orientalism*, London: Routledge, 1978.

—— *Culture and Imperialism*, New York: Vintage, 1993.

Spivak, Gayatri Chakravorty, 'Three women's texts and a critique of imperialism', *Critical Inquiry*, 12:1 (Autumn 1985), 235–61.

Thomas, Nicholas, *Colonialism's Culture: Anthropology, Travel and Government*, Oxford: Polity Press, 1994.

Crime, Underworlds and Detective Fiction

Leps and Maunder and Moore discuss the crucial ways in which the criminal and criminality are re-defined in the period. Trodd focuses on a particular aspect: 'domestic' crime within the family and household. The social and literary effects of drugs are examined in Milligan and Berridge and Edwards, as is the emergence of underworlds related to narcotics. Detective fiction is another new genre formed in the late nineteenth century; Frank and Thomas are complex and wide-ranging treatments of the genre and its relationship to the contexts of science. Warwick and Willis takes one of the defining crimes of the Victorian period and examines it from different literary and cultural perspectives (see also: The City, Degeneration).

Berridge, Virginia and Griffith Edwards, *Opium and the People: Opiate Use in Nineteenth-century England*, New Haven and London: Yale University Press, 1987.

Frank, Lawrence, *Victorian Detective Fiction and the Nature of Evidence*, Basingstoke: Palgrave, 2003.

Leps, Marie-Christine, *Apprehending the Criminal: The Production of Deviance in Nineteenth-Century Discourse*, Durham: Duke University Press, 1992.

Maunder, Andrew and Grace Moore (eds), *Victorian Crime, Madness and Sensation*, Aldershot: Ashgate, 2004.

Milligan, Barry, *Pleasures and Pains: Opium and the Orient in Nineteenth-Century British Culture*, London: University Press of Virginia, 1995.

Thomas, Ronald R., *Detective Fiction and the Rise of Forensic Science*, Cambridge: Cambridge University Press, 1999.

Trodd, Anthea, *Domestic Crime and the Victorian Novel*, Basingstoke: Palgrave Macmillan, 1989.

Warwick, Alexandra and Martin Willis, *Jack the Ripper: Media, Culture, History*, Manchester: Manchester University Press, 2007.

Darwinism

Beer (first published 1983) is the groundbreaking text which opened new areas of inquiry into the place of science within Victorian literature and culture. Young is also an important early work in the field. Texts listed here concentrate on Darwin's theory of evolution through natural selection. Beer, Bernstein and Levine focus particularly on literature's relationship to Darwin's ideas, while Richards and Young look more widely at the metaphorical applications of the theory in Victorian culture (see also: Science and Technology, Degeneration).

Amigoni, David and Jeff Wallace, *Charles Darwin's The Origin of Species: New Interdisciplinary Essays*, Manchester: Manchester University Press, 1995.

Beer, Gillian, *Darwin's Plots: Evolutionary Narrative in Darwin, George Eliot and Nineteenth-Century Fiction* (second edition), Cambridge: Cambridge University Press, 2000.

Bernstein, Susan D., 'Ape anxiety: sensation fiction, evolution, and the genre question', *Journal of Victorian Culture* 6.2 (2001), 250–71.

Jones, Greta, *Social Darwinism and Victorian Thought: The Interaction between Biological and Social Theory*, Brighton: Harvester, 1980.
Levine, George, *Darwin and the Novelists: Patterns of Science in Victorian Fiction*, Cambridge, Mass.: Harvard University Press, 1988.
Richards, R. J., *The Meaning of Evolution: The Morphological Construction and Ideological Reconstruction of Darwin's Theory*, Chicago: University of Chicago Press, 1992.
Young, Robert, *Darwin's Metaphor: Nature's Place in Victorian Culture*, Cambridge: Cambridge University Press, 1985.

Degeneration and the Fin de Siècle

Nordau is a contemporary text (published in English in 1895), and a long and dense 'proof' of the existence of degenerates and degeneration in European society and the arts. Luckhurst and Ledger is a good selection of primary material from the period with short introductory essays; Pykett a similarly good selection of significant critical essays on the fin de siècle. Dijkstra focuses on the visual arts with a large number of striking and unfamiliar examples. Greenslade and Pick are both strong readings of the idea and depictions of degeneration – Greenslade in the novel and Pick in European culture more widely (see also: Darwinism, Gothic and Sensation, Gender and Sexuality).

Bergonzi, Bernard, *The Turn of the Century*, London: Macmillan, 1973.
Dijkstra, Bram, *Idols of Perversity: Fantasies of Feminine Evil in Fin de Siècle Culture*, Oxford: Oxford University Press, 1986.
Greenslade, William, *Degeneration, Culture and the Novel 1880–1914*, Cambridge: Cambridge University Press, 1994.
Hill, Tracey, *Decadence and Danger: Writing, History and the Fin de Siècle*, Bath: Sulis Press, 1997.
Ledger, Sally and Scott McCracken, *Cultural Politics at the Fin de Siècle*, Cambridge: Cambridge University Press, 1995.
Luckhurst, Roger and Sally Ledger (eds), *A Fin de Siècle Reader*, London: Routledge, 2002.
Mix, Katherine L., *A Study in the Yellow Book and its Contributors*, Kansas: Kansas University Press, 1960.
Nordau, Max, *Degeneration*, Lincoln and London: University of Nebraska Press, 1993.
Pick, Daniel, *Faces of Degeneration*, Cambridge: Cambridge University Press, 1989.
Pykett, Lynn (ed.), *Reading Fin de Siècle Fictions*, London: Longman, 1996.

Drama and Theatre

Critical work on Victorian drama and theatre, except on individual dramatists such as Oscar Wilde and Bernard Shaw, has been relatively sparse. The main texts in this field have been theatre histories such as Booth, but work is now developing more widely, particularly on women as writers, audience and actors (Gardner and Rutherford, Newey, Powell) and on the cross-relations of theatre and other social and literary forms such as political protest (Hadley) and the novel (Vlock).

Booth, Michael R., *Theatre in the Victorian Age*, Cambridge: Cambridge University Press, 1991.

Bratton, Jacky and Ann Featherstone, *The Victorian Clown*, Cambridge: Cambridge University Press, 2006.

Bratton, Jacky, *New Readings in Theatre History*, Cambridge: Cambridge University Press, 2003.

Foulkes, Richard (ed.), *British Theatre in the 1890s: Essays on Drama and the Stage*, Cambridge: Cambridge University Press, 1992.

Gardner, Vivien and Susan Rutherford (eds), *The New Woman and Her Sisters: Feminism and Theatre 1850–1914*, Ann Arbor: University of Michigan Press, 1992.

Hadley, Elaine, *Melodramatic Tactics: Theatricalized Dissent and the Marketplace, 1800–1885*, Stanford University Press, 1995.

Jenkins, Anthony, *The Making of Victorian Drama*, Cambridge: Cambridge University Press, 1991.

Newey, Katherine, *Women's Theatre Writing in Victorian Britain*, Basingstoke: Palgrave, 2005.

Powell, Kerry, *Women and Victorian Theatre*, Cambridge: Cambridge University Press, 1997.

Vlock, Deborah, *Dickens, Novel Reading and the Victorian Popular Theatre*, Cambridge: Cambridge University Press, 1998.

Gender and Sexuality

Feminist criticism had an early impact on Victorian studies: notable texts here are Beer, Gilbert and Gubar, Showalter and Vicinus. Nead too has been important on the question of visual representations of women. Equally significant in the study of masculinity and male homosexuality is Sedgwick, whose influence can be seen in Craft and Dellamora. Faderman provides a parallel establishment of a field of lesbian studies. Bland is a primarily historical text – thorough and detailed on Victorian feminism – and Flint is a good treatment of the place of women as readers and writers in literary culture. The New Woman has been a topic of recent critical interest, and Pykett, Richardson and Willis and Ledger are all strong works on the subject.

Adams, James Eli, *Dandies and Desert Saints: Styles of Victorian Masculinity*, Ithaca and London: Cornell University Press, 1995.

Ardis, Ann, *New Women, New Novels: Feminism and Early Modernism*, New Brunswick: Rutgers University Press, 1990.

Beer, Patricia, *Reader, I Married Him: A Study of the Women Characters of Jane Austen, Charlotte Brontë, Elizabeth Gaskell and Jane Austen*, London: Macmillan, 1974.

Bland, Lucy, *Banishing the Beast: English Feminism and Sexual Morality 1885–1914*, London: Penguin, 1995.

Cohen, William, *Sex Scandal: The Private Parts of Victorian Fiction*, Durham, NC: Duke University Press, 1996.

Craft, Christopher, *Another Kind of Love. Male Homosexual Desire in English Discourse 1850–1920*, Berkeley: University of California Press, 1994.

Dellamorra, Richard, *Masculine Desire: The Sexual Politics of Victorian Aestheticism*, London and Chapel Hill: University of North Carolina Press, 1990.

Faderman, Lillian, *Surpassing the Love of Men*, New York: William Morrow, 1981.

Flint, Kate, *The Woman Reader, 1837–1914*, Oxford: Clarendon Press, 1993.

Fraser, Hilary, Stephanie Green and Judith Johnston, *Gender and the Victorian Periodical*, Cambridge: Cambridge University Press, 2003.

Gilbert, Sandra and Susan Gubar, *The Madwoman in the Attic: The Woman Writer and the Nineteenth Century Literary Imagination*, New Haven: Yale University Press, 1979.

Heilmann, Ann, *New Woman Fiction: Women Writing First-Wave Feminism*, Basingstoke: Macmillan, 2000.

Ledger, Sally, *The New Woman, Fiction and Feminism at the Fin de Siècle*, Manchester: Manchester University Press, 1997.

Lootens, Tricia, *Lost Saints: Silence, Gender, and Victorian Literary Canonizations*, Charlottesville: University Press of Virginia, 1996.

Mason, Michael, *The Making of Victorian Sexuality*, Oxford: Oxford University Press, 1995.

Miller, Andrew and James Eli Adams (eds), *Sexualities in Victorian Britain*, Bloomington: Indiana University Press, 1996.

Nead, Lynda, *Myths of Sexuality: Representations of Women in Victorian Britain*, Oxford: Blackwell, 1988.

Poovey, Mary, *Uneven Developments: The Ideological Work of Gender in Mid-Victorian England*, Chicago: Chicago University Press, 1988.

Pykett, Lyn, *The Improper Feminine: The Women's Sensation Novel and the New Woman Writing*, London: Routledge, 1992.

Richardson, Angelique and Chris Willis, *The New Woman in Fiction and Fact*, Basingstoke: Palgrave, 2002.

Russett, Cynthia Eagle, *Sexual Science: The Victorian Construction of Womanhood*, Cambridge, MA: Harvard University Press, 1989.

Sanders, Valerie, *Eve's Renegades: Victorian Anti-Feminist Women Novelists*, London and New York: St Martin's Press, 1996.

Sedgwick, Eve Kosofsky, *Between Men: English Literature and Male Homosocial Desire*, New York: Columbia, 1985.

Showalter, Elaine, *A Literature of their Own: Women Writers from Brontë to Lessing*, London: Virago, 1977.

Sussmann, Herbert, *Victorian Masculinities: Manhood and Masculine Poetics in Early Victorian Literature and Art*, Cambridge: Cambridge University Press, 1995.

Vicinus, Martha, *Suffer and Be Still: Women in the Victorian Age*, Bloomington: Indiana University Press, 1972.

Gothic and Sensation

Punter is the standard work on Gothic (first published 1980) and the expanded second edition is a sound survey. Punter's psychologically inclined approach is productively countered by Baldick's political reading which is excellent on monsters and monstrosity, and by Mighall's historicizing of the Gothic. A third strand of Gothic criticism is influenced by Derrida's ideas of haunting and spectrality: this can be seen in Wolfreys and Wolfreys and Robbins. Malchow examines the Gothicization of race through literary texts. Hurley proposes that the metamorphic human body is the centre of the fin de siècle Gothic literary revival (see also: Degeneration, Science and Technology, Spiritualism and the Supernatural).

Baldick, Chris, *In Frankenstein's Shadow: Myth, Monstrosity and Nineteenth-century Writing*, Oxford: Clarendon, 1987.

Hughes, Winifred, *The Maniac in the Cellar: Sensation Novels of the 1860s*, Princeton:

Princeton University Press, 1980.

Hurley, Kelly, *The Gothic Body: Sexuality, Materialism and Degeneration at the Fin de Siècle*, Cambridge: Cambridge University Press, 1996.

Malchow, H. L., *Gothic Images of Race in Nineteenth-century Britain*, Stanford, CA: Stanford University Press, 1996.

Millbank, Alison, *Daughters of the House: Modes of Gothic in Victorian Fiction*, Basingstoke: Macmillan, 1982.

Mighall, Robert, *A Geography of Victorian Gothic Fiction*, Oxford: Oxford University Press, 1999.

Punter, David, *The Literature of Terror* (revised edition, 2 vols), London: Longman, 1996.

Robbins, Ruth and Julian Wolfreys, *Victorian Gothic*, Basingstoke: Palgrave, 2000.

Smith, Andrew, *Medicine, Masculinity and the Gothic at the Fin de Siècle*, Manchester: Manchester University Press, 2004.

Wolfreys, Julian, *Victorian Hauntings*, Basingstoke: Palgrave, 2002.

The Novel

Leavis is foundational of English literature as a subject and of studies of the novel. His three major examples of the 'great tradition' are all Victorian authors. The novel dominates Victorian literature and its characteristic attention to the contemporary world means that many studies, including Guy, Altick and Flint, look at representations of society and class/social relations. Franklin and Horsman pay attention to the form of the novel and Griest and Keating especially to its function as social currency. O'Gorman and David are good collections of essays on the novel in relation to a range of topics such as the visual arts, philosophy, sexuality and empire (see also: Class, Politics and Economics, Realism).

Altick, Richard, *The Presence of the Present: Topics of the Day in the Victorian Novel*, Ohio: Ohio State University Press, 1991.

David, Deirdre (ed.), *The Cambridge Companion to the Victorian Novel*, Cambridge: Cambridge University Press, 2001.

Flint, Kate (ed.), *The Victorian Novelist: Social Problems and Social Change*, London: Croom Helm, 1987.

Franklin, J. Jeffrey, *Serious Play: The Cultural Form of the Nineteenth-Century Realist Novel*, Philadelphia: University of Pennsylvania Press, 1999.

Griest, Guinevere, *Mudie's Circulating Library and the Victorian Novel*, Bloomington: Indiana University Press, 1970.

Guy, Josephine M., *The Victorian Social-Problem Novel: The Market, the Individual and Communal Life*, Basingstoke: Palgrave, 1996.

Horsman, Alan, *The Victorian Novel*, Oxford: Oxford University Press, 1990.

Johnson, Edgar, 'Bleak House: the anatomy of society', *Nineteenth-Century Fiction*, 7.2, September 1952, 73–85.

Keating, Peter, *The Haunted Study: A Social History of the English Novel 1875–1914*, London: Secker and Warburg, 1989.

Leavis, F. R., *The Great Tradition: George Eliot, Henry James, Joseph Conrad*, London: Chatto and Windus, 1948.

O'Gorman, Francis (ed.), *The Victorian Novel*, Oxford: Blackwell, 2002.

Periodicals, Serials and Publishing Culture

This group of texts examines different areas of the enormous and ever-growing Victorian publishing industry. Publishers were influential, and Sutherland and Tuchman demonstrate the effects that they could have on literary careers and on society itself. Many Victorian novels appeared first in serial form: Hughes and Lund and Law explore the reasons and effects of this in both literary and cultural terms. Periodicals had huge readerships, but large-scale study of them is relatively recent: Brake is crucial in this field.

Altick, Richard D., *The English Common Reader: A Social History of the Mass Reading Public, 1800–1900*, Chicago and London: Chicago University Press, 1957.

Brake, Laurel, *Print in Transition, 1850–1910*, Basingstoke: Palgrave, 2001.

——, *Subjugated Knowledges: Journalism, Gender and Literature in the Nineteenth Century*, Basingstoke: Macmillan, 1994.

Eliot, Simon, *Some Patterns and Trends in British Publishing, 1800–1919*, London: The Bibliographical Society, 1994.

Feltes, N. N., *Modes of Production of Victorian Novels*, Chicago: University of Chicago Press, 1986.

Hughes, Linda K. and Michael Lund, *The Victorian Serial*, University of Virginia Press, 1991.

Law, Graham, *Serializing Fiction in the Victorian Press*, Basingstoke: Palgrave, 2000.

Shuttleworth, Sally and Jonathan R. Topham, *Science in the Nineteenth-Century Periodical: Reading the Magazine of Nature*, Cambridge: Cambridge University Press, 2004.

Sutherland, John, *Victorian Novelists and Publishers*, Chicago: University of Chicago Press, 1976.

——, *Victorian Fiction: Writers, Publishers, Readers*, Basingstoke: Macmillan, 1995.

Tuchman, Gaye with Nina Fortin, *Edging Women Out: Victorian Novelists, Publishers and Social Change*, New York and London: Routledge, 1989.

Poetry

Armstrong is an influential Victorian scholar and her 1993 work on poetry is an important standard text. Bristow's well-chosen collection of essays ranges widely across issues of form, content and context. Najaran foregrounds the debate about the canon of poetry and the relative values ascribed to 'major' and 'minor' writers. Other studies examine more closely aspects of poetry and poetics: the influence of the Romantics (Harrison), gender and love (Blair, Leighton), form (Langbaum) and different published editions (Griffiths).

Armstrong, Isobel, *Victorian Scrutinies: Reviews of Poetry 1830–1870*, London: Athlone, 1972.

——, *Language as Living Form in Nineteenth-Century Poetry*, Sussex: Harvester, 1982.

——, *Victorian Poetry: Poetry, Poetics and Politics*, London: Routledge, 1993.

Blair, Kirstie, *Victorian Poetry and the Culture of the Heart*, Oxford: Clarendon Press, 2006.

Bristow, Joseph (ed.), *The Cambridge Companion to Victorian Poetry*, Cambridge: Cambridge University Press, 2000.

Griffiths, Eric, *The Printed Voice of Victorian Poetry*, Oxford: Clarendon Press, 1987.

Harrison, Anthony H., *Victorian Poets and Romantic Poems: Intertextuality and Ideology*, Charlottesville: University Press of Virginia, 1990.

——, *Victorian Poets and the Politics of Culture*, Charlottesville: University Press of Virginia, 1998.

Langbaum, Robert, *The Poetry of Experience: The Dramatic Monologue in Modern Literary Tradition*, London: Chatto & Windus, 1956.

Leighton, Angela, *Victorian Woman Poets: Writing Against the Heart*, Virginia: University of Virginia Press, 1992.

Najarian, James, 'Canonicity, Marginality and the Celebration of the Minor', *Victorian Poetry*, 41:4, 2003, 570–4.

Politics and Economics

Early studies (Lucas) tend to focus only on the straightforward depiction of political events and figures in fiction or on the political allegiances of authors. Later texts produce more complex arguments about the relations of public politics to individual subjectivity and social relations. Likewise, economics has come to be understood more widely than just the circulation of money and rather as a critical force in shaping society and the public and private imagination: Searle looks at morality and market forces, Gallagher at romantic relationships and criminal activity and Gagnier at aesthetics (see also: Class, The City).

Armstrong, Nancy, *Desire and Domestic Fiction: A Political History of the Novel*, Oxford: Oxford University Press, 1987.

Brantlinger, Patrick, *The Spirit of Reform: British Literature and Politics, 1832–1867*, Cambridge, MA; Harvard University Press, 1977.

Collini, Stefan, *Public Moralists: Political Thought and Intellectual Life in Britain 1850–1930*, Oxford: Clarendon, 1991.

Gagnier, Regenia, *The Insatiability of Human Wants: Economics and Aesthetics in Market Society*, London: University of Chicago Press, 2000.

Gallagher, Catherine, *The Body Economic: Life, Death, and Sensation in Political Economy and the Victorian Novel*, Princeton: Princeton University Press, 2006.

Lucas, John (ed.), *Literature and Politics in the Nineteenth Century*, London: Methuen, 1971.

Miller, Andrew H., *Novels Behind Glass: Commodity Culture and Victorian Narrative*, Cambridge: Cambridge University Press, 1995.

Poovey, Mary, *The Making of a Social Body: British Cultural Formation 1830–1864*, Chicago: University of Chicago Press, 1995.

Searle, George, *Morality and the Market in Victorian Britain*, Oxford: Clarendon, 1998.

Weiss, Barbara, *The Hell of the English: Bankruptcy and the Victorian Novel*, London: Associated University Presses, 1986.

Psychology and the Mind

The latter part of the nineteenth century saw increasing interest in the human mind, its pathologies and potential. It is another relatively recent area of critical interest, and although it might appear to be divided into studies of medical/scientific work on the mind and brain (Rylance, Scull, Reed) and those of more disreputable psychological practices (Luckhurst, Winter, Pick, Willis and Wynne), these books show that such distinctions are not easily made. Logan, Taylor and Small all examine the literary manifestations of the new Victorian interest in the powers of the mind (see also: Science and Technology, Spiritualism and the Supernatural).

Harrington, Anne, *Medicine, Mind and the Double Brain: A Study in Nineteenth-Century Thought*, Princeton: Princeton University Press, 1987.
Hartley, Lucy, *Physiognomy and the Meaning of Expression in Nineteenth-Century Culture*, Cambridge: Cambridge University Press, 2001.
Logan, Peter Melville, *Nerves and Narratives: A Cultural History of Hysteria in Nineteenth-Century British Prose*, Berkeley: University of California Press, 1997.
Luckhurst, Roger, *The Invention of Telepathy*, Cambridge: Cambridge University Press, 2002.
Pick, Daniel, *Svengali's Web: The Alien Enchanter in Modern Culture*, Cambridge: Cambridge University Press, 2000.
Reed, Edward, *From Soul to Mind: The Emergence of Psychology from Erasmus Darwin to William James*, New Haven: Yale University Press, 1997.
Rylance, Rick, *Victorian Psychology and British Culture 1850–1880*, Oxford: Oxford University Press, 2000.
Scull, Andrew, *Madhouses, Mad-doctors and Madmen: A Social History of Psychiatry in the Victorian Era*, Philadelphia: University of Pennsylvania Press, 1981.
Shuttleworth, Sally, *Charlotte Brontë and Victorian Psychology*, Cambridge: Cambridge University Press, 1996.
Small, Helen, *Love's Madness: Medicine, the Novel and Female Insanity, 1800–1865*, Oxford: Clarendon, 1996.
Taylor, Jenny Bourne, *In the Secret Theatre of Home: Wilkie Collins, Sensation Narrative and Nineteenth-Century Psychology*, London: Routledge, 1988.
Taylor, Jenny Bourne and Sally Shuttleworth, *Embodied Selves: An Anthology of Psychological Texts, 1830–1890*, Oxford: Clarendon Press, 1998.
Winter, Alison, *Mesmerised: Powers of Mind in Victorian Britain*, Chicago: University of Chicago Press, 1998.
Willis, Martin and Catherine Wynne (eds), *Victorian Literary Mesmerism*, Amsterdam: Rodopi Press, 2006.

Realism

Realism is a highly contested critical term, and the association of it with nineteenth-century literary and art forms has meant that a number of studies of Realism include extensive discussions of the Victorian novel: Walder, Levine and Furst for example. Morris is a good brief introduction to the term. The relationship of Realism to Naturalism is clearly explored in Lehan, while several texts (C. Levine, G. Levine and Franklin) emphasize the potential and actual uses of Realist narratives in ways more often associated with non-Realist and other experimental writing strategies (see also: The Novel).

Beaumont, Matthew, *Adventures in Realism*, Oxford: Blackwell, 2007.
Brooks, Chris, *Signs for the Times: Symbolic Realism in the Mid-Victorian World*, London: George Allen and Unwin, 1978.
Byerly, Alison, *Realism, Representation, and the Arts in Nineteenth-Century Literature*, Cambridge: Cambridge University Press, 1998.

Furst, Lillian, *All is True: the Claims and Strategies of Realist Fiction*, Durham: Duke University Press, 1995.

Hillis Miller, J., 'The Fiction of Realism', in Lilian Furst (ed.), *Realism*, London: Longman, 1992, pp. 85–126.

Franklin, J. Jeffrey, *Serious Play: The Cultural Form of the Nineteenth-Century Realist Novel*, Philadelphia, PA: University of Pennsylvania Press, 1999.

Lehan, Richard, *Realism and Naturalism: The Novel in an Age of Transition*, Wisconsin: University of Wisconsin Press, 2005.

Levine, Caroline, *The Serious Pleasures of Suspense: Victorian Realism and Narrative Doubt*, Virginia: University of Virginia Press, 2004.

Levine, George, *The Realistic Imagination*, Chicago: University of Chicago Press, 1981.

Morris, Pam, *Realism*, London: Routledge, 2003.

Walder, Dennis (ed.), *The Realist Novel*, London: Routledge, 1995.

Science and Technology

The cross-disciplinary study of science and literature is now a large field. Cosslett is a useful collection of contemporary primary texts on religion and science. Clifford et al. and Lightman are collections discussing ways in which science itself developed and the different sciences became established or fell out of the mainstream. Cooter takes one such now-discredited practice – phrenology – and indicates how its uses were more than simply scientific. Like Cooter, Luckhurst and McDonagh examines the cultural, social and political functions of science in 'non-scientific' contexts. Armstrong, Morton and Shuttleworth see ways in which new scientific and technological discoveries were used figuratively in Victorian fiction and culture (see also: Darwinism, Psychology and the Mind, Science Fiction).

Armstrong, Isobel, 'Tennyson in the 1850s: from geology to pathology', *In Memoriam* (1850) to *Maud* (1855)', in Philip Collins (ed.), *Tennyson: Seven Essays*, New York: St Martin's, 1992, pp. 102–40.

——, 'Transparency: towards a poetics of glass in the nineteenth century', in Francis Spufford and Jenny Uglow (eds), *Cultural Babbage: Technology, Time and Invention*, London: Faber and Faber, 1996, pp. 123–48.

Cantor Geoffrey, Gowan Dawson, Graeme Gooday, Richard Noakes, and Sally Shuttleworth (eds), *Science Serialized: Representations of the Sciences in Nineteenth-Century Periodicals*, London: MIT Press, 2004.

Clifford, David, Elisabeth Wadge, Alexandra Warwick and Martin Willis (eds), *Repositioning Victorian Sciences: Shifting Centres in Nineteenth Century Scientific Thinking*, London: Anthem Press, 2006.

Cooter, Roger, *The Cultural Meaning of Popular Science: Phrenology and the Organization of Consent in Nineteenth-century Britain*, Cambridge: Cambridge University Press, 1984.

Cosslett, Tess (ed.), *Science and Religion in the Nineteenth Century*, Cambridge: Cambridge University Press, 1984.

Henson, Louise, Geoffrey Cantor, Gowan Dawson, Richard Noakes, Sally Shuttleworth and Jonathan R. Topham, *Culture and Science in the Nineteenth-Century Media*, Aldershot: Ashgate, 2004.

Lightman, Bernard, *Victorian Science in Context*, Chicago: Chicago University Press, 1997.

Luckhurst, Roger and Josephine McDonagh (eds), *Transactions and Encounters: Science and Culture in the Nineteenth Century*, Manchester: Manchester University Press, 2002.

Morton, Peter, *The Vital Science: Biology and the Literary Imagination*, Cambridge, MA: Harvard University Press, 1989.

Ritvo, Harriet, *The Platypus and the Mermaid*, Cambridge, MA: Harvard University Press, 1997.

Rowold, Katharina (ed.), *Gender and Science: Nineteenth-Century Debates on the Female Mind and Body*, Bristol: Thoemmes, 1996.

Secord, James, *Victorian Sensation: The Extraordinary Publication, Reception, and Secret Authorship of Vestiges of the Natural History of Creation*, Chicago: University of Chicago Press, 2000.

Shuttleworth, Sally, *George Eliot and Nineteenth-Century Science: The Make Believe of a Beginning*, Cambridge: Cambridge University Press, 1984.

Science Fiction

As with the detective story, science fiction emerges as a genre in the Victorian period. Aldiss is the standard account and the 2001 edition is expanded and updated. Most work on science fiction concentrates on twentieth-century texts, but Seed and Alkon give good accounts of the emergence of the form before 1900. Suvin and Willis discuss the contexts of science and scientific cultures in relation to the fiction, while Ellis is useful in indicating possible critical and theoretical approaches (see also: Science and Technology).

Aldiss, Brian, *Trillion Year Spree: The History of Science Fiction*, Thirsk: House of Stratus, 2001.

Alkon, Paul, *Science Fiction Before 1900: Imagination Discovers Technology*, New York: Routledge, 2002.

Ellis, R. J., *Science Fiction Roots and Branches: Contemporary Critical Approaches*, New York: St Martin's Press, 1990.

James, Edward and Farah Mendlesohn (eds), *The Cambridge Companion to Science Fiction*, Cambridge: Cambridge University Press, 2003.

Seed, David (ed.), *Anticipations: Essays on Early Science Fiction and Its Precursors*, New York: Syracuse University Press, 1995.

Suvin, Darko, *Victorian Science Fiction in the UK: The Discourses of Knowledge and Power*, Boston: G. K. Hall, 1983.

Willis, Martin, *Mesmerists, Monsters and Machines: Science Fiction and the Cultures of Science in the Nineteenth Century*, Ohio: Kent State University Press, 2006.

Spiritualism and the Supernatural

Pearsall is an accessible general introduction to the topic of Victorian occultism. Wheeler is informative on the range and development of Christian beliefs regarding the afterlife. Owen, Oppenheim and Barrow are essential studies of the movement, beliefs and impact of spiritualism. Barrow focuses particularly on issues of class and the democratizing effects of spiritualism, while Owen argues for similar effects in relation to women. Bown et al. is a good collection on various different aspects of the supernatural and Thurschwell a strong and detailed argument that forms of 'magical thought' can be identified throughout the literature and culture of the turn of the century (see also: Psychology and the Mind, Gothic and Sensation).

Barrow, L., *Independent Spirits: Spiritualism and English Plebeians 1850–1910*, London: Routledge and Kegan Paul, 1986.

Bown, Nicola, Carolyn Burdett and Pamela Thurschwell (eds), *The Victorian Supernatural*, Cambridge: Cambridge University Press, 2004.

Oppenheim, Janet, *The Other World: Spiritualism and Psychical Research in England 1850–1914*, Cambridge: Cambridge University Press, 1985.

Owen, Alex, *The Darkened Room: Women; Power and Spiritualism in Late-Victorian England*, London: Virago, 1989.

——, *The Place of Enchantment: British Occultism and the Culture of the Modern*, London and Chicago: University of Chicago Press, 2004.

Pearsall, Ronald, *The Table Rappers: The Victorians and the Occult*, London; Sutton Publishing, 2000.

Poovey, Mary, 'Mediums, media, mediation: response', *Victorian Studies* 48.2, 2005, 248–55.

Thurschwell, Pamela, *Literature, Technology and Magical Thinking, 1880–1920*, Cambridge: Cambridge University Press, 2001.

Wheeler, Michael, *Heaven, Hell and the Victorians*, Cambridge: Cambridge University Press, 1994.

Willburn, Sarah A., *Possessed Victorians: Extra Spheres in Nineteenth-Century Mystical Writings*, Aldershot: Ashgate, 2006.

Victorian Studies

This section represents the debates about Victorian studies itself, showing scholars thinking about the nature of the field in which they work and arguing both about what constitutes the 'Victorian' and the proper study of it. All the work listed here is in article form and each piece has a strong central thesis. Students interested in this question should read the articles as a debate and think about how this kind of discussion has influenced the ways in which they study the Victorians (see also: Introductions to Victorian Studies).

Anderson, Amanda, 'Victorian Studies and the Two Modernities', *Victorian Studies* 47.2, 2005, 195–203.

Armstrong, Isobel, 'Victorian Studies and Cultural Studies: A False Dichotomy', *Victorian Literature and Culture* 27.2, 1999, 513–16.

Collini, Stefan, 'From "Non-Fiction Prose" to "Cultural Criticism": genre and disciplinarity in Victorian studies', in Juliet John and Alice Jenkins (eds), *Rethinking Victorian Culture*, Basingstoke: Macmillan, 2000, pp. 13–28.

Gallagher, Catherine. 'Theoretical Answers to Interdisciplinary Questions or Interdisciplinary Answers to Theoretical Questions?', *Victorian Studies* 47.2, 2005, 253–9.

Hewitt, Martin, 'Victorian Studies: problems and prospects?', *Journal of Victorian Culture* 6:1, 2001, 137–61.

Levine, George, 'Victorian Studies' in Stephen Greenblatt and Giles Gunn (eds), *Redrawing the Boundaries: The Transformation of English and American Literary Studies*, New York: MLA, 1992, pp. 130–53.

McWilliam, Rohan, 'What is Interdisciplinary about Victorian History Today?', *19:*

Interdisciplinary Studies in the Long Nineteenth Century, 1, 2005, www.19.bbk.ac.uk, pp. 1–29.

Rogers, Helen, 'Victorian Studies in the UK', in Miles Taylor and Michael Wolff (eds), *The Victorians Since 1901: Histories, Representations and Revisions*, Manchester: Manchester University Press, 2004, pp. 244–59.

Rowlinson, Matthew, 'Theory of Victorian Studies: Anachronism and Self–Reflexivity', *Victorian Studies* 47.2, 2005, 241–52.

Vernon, James, 'Historians and the Victorian Studies Question', *Victorian Studies* 47.2, 2005, 272–9.

Wolff, Michael, 'The Use of Context: Aspects of the 1860s', *Victorian Studies* 9, 1965, 47–63.

Visual Culture

Visual culture was important in Victorian society in many forms, from fine art to newspaper illustration and from the diorama to the microscope. Flint is good on the range and variety to be found, on the lack of strict separation between high and low art and between scientific work and popular entertainment. Crary and Foster are theorizers of nature and place of visuality, but are not introductory texts. Photography and cinema are both Victorian inventions, A. Armstrong and Smith are good treatments of the relations of fiction and photography. Roston, Christ and Jordan also discuss photography and its effects on literature, but include also painting, newspaper illustration and optical entertainments.

Armstrong, Isobel, 'The Microscope: mediations of the sub-visible world', in Roger Luckhurst and Josephine McDonagh (eds), *Transactions and Encounters: Science and Culture in the Nineteenth Century*, Manchester: Manchester University Press, 2002, pp. 30–54.

Armstrong, Nancy, *Fiction in the Age of Photography: The Legacy of British Realism*, Cambridge, MA: Harvard University Press, 1991.

Christ, Carol and John O. Jordan (eds), *Victorian Literature and the Victorian Visual Imagination*, Berkeley: University of California Press, 1995.

Crary, Jonathan, *Techniques of the Observer: On Vision and Modernity in the Nineteenth Century*, London: MIT Press, 1990.

Flint, Kate, *The Victorians and the Visual Imagination*, Cambridge: Cambridge University Press, 2000.

Foster, Hal (ed.), *Vision and Visuality*, Seattle: Bay Press, 1988.

Green-Lewis, Jennifer, *Framing the Victorians: Photography and the Culture of Realism*, Ithaca: Cornell University Press, 1996.

Lalvani, Suren, *Photography, Vision and the Production of Modern Bodies*, New York: SUNY Press, 1996.

Plunkett, John, 'Optical recreations and Victorian literature', *Essays and Studies* 58, 2005, 1–28.

Roston, Murray, *Victorian Contexts: Literature and the Visual Arts*, New York: New York University Press, 1996.

Smith, Lindsay, *Victorian Photography, Painting and Poetry: The Enigma of Visibility in Ruskin, Morris and the Pre-Raphaelites*, Cambridge: Cambridge University Press, 1995.

Appendix: A Survey of Victorian Literature Curricula

Mark Bennett

A Note on the Survey

This analysis is based on data collected through a survey of individual courses on Victorian literary topics at 50 different universities, divided evenly between British and American institutions. The majority of the information gathered was taken from institutions' own publicly available descriptions of courses and reading lists. All modules offered by a given institution and deemed relevant to the survey were included but, in order to streamline the data, the presence of an author or text was only noted once for each institution. The resulting statistics are by no means intended to offer an exhaustive representation of current curricula. Instead it is to be hoped that the survey and its analysis provides a representative snapshot of current pedagogical trends and practices.

Novels and Novelists

Unsurprisingly, the novel represents one of the most integral forms within modules dealing with Victorian literature; even the few courses that completely eschew long prose work usually form part of a wider syllabus within which a dedicated module on the Victorian novel makes up the difference. There is, however, an impressive variety of approaches to teaching the novel, and specialist courses dealing with this form often represent some of the most interesting higher level modules offered in the field of Victorian literature. The five most popular authors within this article's survey are, in the following order: Charles Dickens, George Eliot, Charlotte Brontë, Thomas Hardy and Elizabeth Gaskell.[1] Dickens leads by a healthy margin, perhaps reflecting the fact that, in spite of considerable recent expansion of the canon to include a number of hitherto sidelined forms, texts and writers, study of the Victorian novel is still more or less inextricable from that of its most famous exponent. This is reflected more broadly in pedagogical approaches wherein the study of traditionally major authors is enhanced, rather than replaced, by a growing interest in rediscovered authors and new methodological approaches.

The five leading authors' most popular novels appear as follows: Dickens's *Bleak House* and *Great Expectations* are jointly the most popular of his works, closely followed by *Hard Times*.[2] Eliot's *Middlemarch* and *The Mill on the Floss* were equally popular within the institutions surveyed, while her other novels appear to be taught much more infrequently.[3] Unsurprisingly, *Jane Eyre* is the most popular of Charlotte Brontë's four novels, though *Villette* is close behind its more famous predecessor.[4] *Tess of the d'Urbervilles, Jude the Obscure* and *The Return of the Native* respectively represent the most popular of Hardy's longer fictions.[5] Finally, Gaskell's *North and South* is the most popular of her novels, followed by *Mary Barton*, after which figures for her other works decline rather steeply.[6]

The popularity of these authors and texts perhaps reflects their broad pedagogical utility. The period stretching from the publication of *Jane Eyre* in 1847 to that of *Jude the Obscure*, Hardy's final novel, in 1895 covers almost the entirety of the Victorian period itself. This alone perhaps explains the popularity of these authors on broad survey modules wherein they offer a useful window onto the development of the Victorian novel. The two writers chronologically stationed at either end of this 'top five' also offer inviting opportunities to modules undertaking a more fluid approach to periodization. Charlotte Brontë's novels, along with those of her sisters, are often used to reconsider the boundary between the Romantic and Victorian periods. Hardy's later work, meanwhile, is often considered within modules considering the transition from the Victorian era into the early twentieth century's emergent modernity. Of course these five authors collectively provide an arena within which a broad range of approaches to the period and its literature can be economically mobilized, either on a general survey module, or within a course picking up on a specific issue and tracing its engagement or deployment within a number of appropriate works. These require little specific enumeration here: all of these writers offer texts wherein a gendered perspective will be amply rewarded; one need look no further than *Hard Times, North and South* or even *The Mayor of Casterbridge* for evidence of the Victorian novel's interest in social critique; and an approach interested in genre and sub-genre will find plenty to occupy it in *Great Expectations* renegotiation of the *Bildungsroman*, *Jane Eyre* and *Villette*'s reworking of elements of the Gothic, George Eliot's pivotal renditions of domestic realism or *Bleak House*'s important early deployment of detection. These and other critical perspectives characterize a number of survey modules and a wide variety of specialist courses, rendering it hardly surprising that these canonical authors and texts are of particular utility to a range of module designs.

Other authors, both canonical and otherwise, are also well represented on the survey but their comparatively poor performance therein perhaps reflects some interesting trends within current teaching of the period. To anyone familiar with the canonical writers usually associated with the Victorian novel, Thackeray and Trollope are perhaps conspicuous by their absence thus far. Indeed, Emily Brontë's *Wuthering Heights* might also have been expected to approach the popularity enjoyed by her elder sister's novels. As it happens none of these three authors comes particularly close to the five already discussed.[7] This is largely due to most survey modules overlooking Thackeray and Trollope completely, and relatively few teaching *Wuthering Heights*. Outside the necessarily proscriptive boundaries of the broad survey course, however, these authors do occur within some interesting specialist contexts. Modules focused on the novel's development during the first few decades of Victoria's reign tend to teach both *Vanity Fair* and *Wuthering Heights* alongside a selection of Dickens's early work. Teaching of Trollope is spread across a fairly disparate selection of his work, his 'Chronicles of Barsetshire' being his most popular novels; often within modules focusing specifically upon the nature and development of literary realism. Emily Brontë's work, both her novel and her poetry, is often present on modules considering the early Victorians' Romantic heritage, as well as on courses reflecting emergent interest in Victorian Gothic.[8] Broadly speaking, it is perhaps possible to account for Thackeray and Trollope's relative absence in current teaching through reference to spatial constraints: the length of many of these authors' canonical texts perhaps precludes their being economically taught within survey modules already having to cope with a number of longer works. Across the survey as a whole, the ten most popular novels are now listed.[9] *Jane Eyre* enjoys a marginal lead over Dickens's and Eliot's most popular novels, despite these authors enjoying a greater overall presence on the courses surveyed. Second and third place is jointly occupied by Dickens's *Bleak House* and *Great Expectations*, perhaps suggesting the mutual popularity of two broad approaches to teaching Dickens: either through the use of a shorter, more accessible novel, or through recourse to a longer, formally complex work.

The novels occupying the fourth, fifth, sixth, seventh and eighth spots on the survey's top ten all score equally with 13 instances of each, reflecting the established popularity of a number of these texts and the emergent success of others. Dickens's *Hard Times* arguably succeeds due to its brevity and the ease with which it can be annexed to modules concerned with a range of obvious contextual issues. That Eliot's *Middlemarch* and *The Mill on the Floss*, two of her longest novels, are her most popular is perhaps initially surprising, though the former's utility as a central touchstone within several survey modules perhaps accounts for its high placement.

The other fictions taught with this level of frequency are also surprising. The popularity of *Villette* is initially unexpected, but further consideration might explain the text's success in light of the growing number of gendered perspectives applied to Victorian novels as well as the text's playful deployment of certain Gothic devices. Mary Elizabeth Braddon's *Lady Audley's Secret* similarly benefits from the growth of interest in the Victorian Gothic though its popularity largely reflects the number of modules specifically dealing with Victorian sensation fiction, for which this is a key text.

The final two positions on the survey's top ten are jointly filled by Thomas Hardy's *Tess of the d'Urbervilles* and Robert Louis Stevenson's *The Strange Case of Dr Jekyll and Mr Hyde*. The former's popularity is perhaps as unsurprising as that of *Jane Eyre*: both novels enjoy a relatively high cultural profile and both particularly reward the large number of teaching approaches interested in exploring the Victorian's literary engagement with concepts and depictions of gender and femininity. The success of Stevenson's novella within curricula (it incidentally manages to push Gaskell's work out of the top ten) is arguably reflective of an established interest in *fin-de-siècle* topics and a burgeoning interest in the Victorian Gothic.

Poetry and Poets

Due to the specific difficulties experienced when collecting data for poetry, the decision was made early in the surveying process to record this information in the form of selections by author, rather than references to individual poems. However, the recourse, by several important writers, to longer poetic forms, arguably represents one of the most interesting aspects of Victorian poetics; in many cases serving to represent several of the period's most distinctive poetic characteristics and developments. The survey therefore attempted to record data for long poems separately and as accurately as possible, in the belief that current teaching of these texts offers a window onto a number of issues characteristic of current pedagogical approaches to the period.

The survey gives the top five Victorian poets as follows: Tennyson leads by a fair margin, followed by Christina Rossetti, Elizabeth Barrett Browning, Robert Browning and Matthew Arnold, in that order.[10] What is perhaps most interesting about this sequence is the statistical proximity of the bulk of these writers: with the exception of Tennyson, the remaining poets are each separated by a single point. Tennyson's lead is interesting, but perhaps as ultimately unsurprising as that of Dickens elsewhere: both writers enjoy high cultural profiles, both offer a number of important and accessible texts and both are popular representative choices on those modules wherein space is limited and a broader selection of writers is difficult to achieve.[11]

These five major poets are generally the most likely to be included on survey modules as broadly representative of Victorian poetry in general and their success within the survey is reflective of this tendency along with their obvious utility within courses devoted exclusively to poetry. A number of other poets are also routinely taught. Each of Gerard Manley Hopkins, Algernon Charles Swinburne and Dante Gabriel Rossetti only narrowly miss the top five and these in turn are joined on a number of courses by a host of other writers, many of them traditionally neglected.[12]

The general pattern on a survey module is to surround generous selections from the work of five or six major poets with a small number of poems by less canonical writers.[13] Such a strategy enables a module designer to combine traditional approaches with the broadening of the canon enabled and inspired by recent critical developments, particularly the ongoing scholarly reclamation of a number of marginalized women poets. Approaches to poetry within module design are impressively varied and offer a real opportunity to reflect both the research interests of a course convenor or students' own anticipated areas of interest. The comparative brevity of the bulk of poetic material, coupled with the sheer number of writers and texts available and the relative economy with which they can be procured means that even a survey module allows for a degree of innovation with regard to the specific authors and texts studied. This choice of material itself often reflects a module's broader approach to periodization. While a core survey module will usually undertake a chronological survey of the period's major poets, a number of specialist courses focus on the transition into and out of the Victorian era. These approaches allow for an interesting emphasis to be placed upon both marginal writers and major poets' marginal texts. Modules focusing upon the transition from romantic to Victorian, for example, allow for material such as Emily Brontë's poetry, or the early work of Tennyson or E. B. Browning to take on an unprecedented significance. Similarly, modules dealing with late Victorian or *fin-de-siècle* poetry emphasize the poetry and aesthetic theory of writers such as Oscar Wilde while also juxtaposing these texts with an emergent modernist aesthetic located in the early work of poets such as W. B. Yeats. It is perhaps interesting to note that poetry takes on a particular significance within specialist courses actively reconsidering periodical distinctions, and often constitutes a central thread running through those very broad survey modules that take in a range of texts from across the nineteenth century. Again the economy, with which a large number of poetic texts can be mobilized and addressed, allows for a unique amount of flexibility within module design; a flexibility that extends to questions of periodization.

Of course a significant factor with regard to the teaching of Victorian poetry is the availability of the texts themselves. The vast majority of modules teach poetry through recourse to a readily available scholarly anthology yet, due to obvious spatial constraints, few anthologies include longer works in their entirety. Moreover, while some selections from major canonical works such as *In Memoriam* are to be expected in an anthology, relatively few are willing to devote space to traditionally minor long poems such as Rossetti's *Monna Innominata*.[14] Though some modules utilize handouts or e-texts to supplement a given anthology's selection criteria, supplying a long poem in this manner can be difficult or uneconomical. These factors clearly present something of a stumbling block to a course designer looking to devote time to longer poems and no one solution entirely negates the problem. There are, however, a number of newer anthologies being produced, many of which reflect increasing demand both for the reproduction of major long poems in their entirety and for the provision of more marginal texts.[15] This trend in itself perhaps indicates the widening field available to the student and teacher of Victorian poetry.

Drama and Dramatists

There is little to be said regarding the teaching of drama on most of the courses surveyed. Very few survey modules appear to teach dramatic texts and there exists a similar dearth of modules specializing in the form. The *fin-de-siècle* period is sometimes represented in survey contexts through recourse to one or more of Oscar Wilde or George Bernard Shaw's plays, though it is far more likely that a novel such as *The Picture of Dorian Gray* or *The Strange Case of Dr Jekyll and Mr Hyde* will perform this function.[16] The survey's examination of modules on sensation fiction, meanwhile, recorded a single reference to a selection of Dion Boucicault's sensation melodramas. Both of these sub-periods represent interesting areas of development as regards the provision of specialist modules, with their inclusion of drama representing one particular facet of this interest. It is with a necessarily compact analysis of these and other popular candidates for module specialization that this appendix will now proceed, in part with the belief that these specialist courses and periods in fact represent interesting potential sites for the re-emergence of currently marginalized texts and forms, such as Victorian drama itself.

Specialist Modules

The scope of the Victorian period and its literature is amply indicated by the diverse range of specialist modules currently offered by universities. These range from focused analysis of a specific author or sub-period to the application of complex theoretical approaches and methodologies, to texts both canonical and otherwise. Perhaps the most interesting aspect of these modules is the degree to which they offer an insight into the process whereby developments in research and criticism gradually influence teaching approaches at an undergraduate level, and a means by which a scholar working in these areas can share their own research interests with their students. The majority of these modules are offered at later stages in a university's undergraduate degree programme, usually after students have already had the chance to familiarize themselves with the period through a survey module offered in previous years.

A relatively high number of modules now focus exclusively on sensation fiction, perhaps indicative of the extent to which its texts are particularly conducive to a number of theoretical perspectives. The sensation novel's fondness for the depiction of transgressive heroines, villainesses and those feminine characters who inextricably blur the two, renders it a fruitful subject for any approach considering the development of female characterisation and authorship within the Victorian period.

Those sensation novels studied, both on specialist modules and as representative texts within surveys, effectively equate to a small canon of now well-established works. Mary Elizabeth Braddon's *Lady Audley's Secret* is the most popular, followed by Wilkie Collins's *The Woman in White*, then Ellen Wood's *East Lynne*. Other popular choices include Braddon's *Aurora Floyd* and Collins's *The Moonstone*.[17]

Courses on the *fin-de-siècle* are perhaps the most established of those dealing with a specific Victorian sub-period. These courses also represent something of a mainstay for the study of the Victorian Gothic, many of the texts associated with which are covered by this sub-period. The popularity of these modules, along with a smaller number dealing exclusively with the topic, are largely responsible for the fairly high incidence of texts such as *Dracula* and *The Strange Case of Dr Jekyll and Mr Hyde* within the survey.[18]

In contrast to those modules dealing with sensation fiction wherein the canon of texts is as yet still limited, modules focusing on the *fin-de-siècle* appear to offer a potentially bewildering array of texts and a significant degree of liberty for innovative course design. Of particular interest is the degree to which these specialist courses are able to engage students with compact, accessible and stimulating literary texts, while simultaneously introducing them to a range of potentially complex interdisciplinary methodologies.

Single author modules represent one of the most established options within specialist module design. They are also, however, surprisingly varied, with courses on specific authors being tailored to a wide range of purposes and theoretical approaches. Even the choice of author upon whom to specialize offers a module designer a number of options. Many courses undertake extensive exploration of a canonical author, either as a means of introducing students to the period or in order to demonstrate the application or utility of a particular theoretical approach within a familiar context. Others instead address more marginal writers with the kind of depth impossible on a survey module.

Dickens is, unsurprisingly, the most popular candidate by far for such specialization, yet the variety of modules focusing upon his work illustrates a range of very different approaches. Some are clearly intended to introduce first-year students to the study of the novel, the Victorian period or both. Others, meanwhile, use Dickens as a familiar authorial microcosm within which to apply advanced theoretical perspectives. The survey recorded a number of approaches of this kind, ranging from the intensive formal study of Dickens's plots to the historicizing of his position within a wider cultural milieu. These latter modules paid particular attention to Dickens's role as an editor, even going as far as to consider fiction produced under his 'influence' by writers such as Gaskell and Collins, thereby offering an interesting example of the manner in which the single author course format can be intriguingly renegotiated to explore the personal and literary relationships between writers within a tightly focused context.

As has perhaps been evident throughout the foregoing discussion, a large number of modules of all varieties are characterized by the introduction and application of a range of different theoretical perspectives and methodological practices. In many cases these approaches are implicitly embodied within the choices made regarding the design of a specific module or its reading list. In other situations, particularly within higher level modules, students' engagement and application of specific theoretical material is an explicit expectation and a stated learning outcome.

Gendered readings and approaches now characterize to some degree almost all the modules offered on syllabi: the majority of survey modules list gender as an area of interest and a large number of specialist modules devote themselves to the study of gendered writing, representation and characterization. The critical and theoretical texts typically invoked to support and inform gendered approaches are, in several cases, now stalwarts of the secondary reading lists supplied by modules more generally. Indeed, the frequency of references to works such as Sandra Gilbert and Susan Gubar's influential *The Madwoman in the Attic* testifies to the manner in which gendered approaches now implicitly inform a vast number of modules.

The influence of another methodological approach, of more recent scholarly provenance, is indicated by the vast number of modules approaching texts from a new historicist perspective. Few modules explicitly avow such a theoretical affiliation, yet the influence of associated approaches is arguably apparent within the large number of other cultural documents now offered for study alongside literary texts. This in turn links closely with a burgeoning pedagogical interest in interdisciplinarity. Approaches that dialogize scientific and literary documents are perhaps some of the most established, both in criticism and teaching, yet even these evince a wide variety of strategies and specific areas of interest.[19] The majority of survey modules now consider the influence and importance of evolution as a nineteenth-century cultural discourse. Separate to the study of science and literature there also exist a number of highly specialized modules operating from an interdisciplinary perspective: ranging from the parallel study of literature and journalism to the comparison of literary narrative and historiography with regard to the production and viability of objective 'truths'.

Other theoretical perspectives are more diffuse and often tailored very closely to specific teaching aims and module specializations. Differences between North America and the UK are also observable to an extent within this context, with some North American courses having embraced the study of a broad range of cultural documents and discourses to a particularly impressive degree. Of course, the specific use of theoretical documents and approaches within a module is often determined by other factors, particularly a course's broader provision of secondary material and its specific expectations with regard to students' independent reading. A module's position within a wider syllabus also determines the nature and range of the theoretical perspectives it is able to employ. Survey modules are less likely to devote dedicated space to theoretical concepts while specialist courses are conversely able to build upon the presumed prior study of a survey and offer up more time to the teaching and application of theory. It is with a brief consideration of these issues, the placement of modules within broader curricula, their assessment criteria and learning outcomes, their use of secondary material and the degree to which these and other factors broadly differ between North American and UK institutions, that this appendix will now close.

Curriculum Structure, Assessment, Provision of Secondary Material and North American/UK Comparisons

Modules on Victorian topics divide broadly into those surveying the scope of the period and those specializing in a particular topic or sub-period. Within British universities Victorian survey modules are typically offered in a student's first or second year, to be followed by a range of associated special options in the final year. In some cases Victorian survey modules represent compulsory 'core' courses, functioning as part of a broad grounding in major literatures and periods. Within North American universities this structure is somewhat more flexible. This is largely due to the fact that the North American degree system allows for a different kind of student choice, with specialization and the declaration of a 'major' following an introductory course of freshman study across a number of subject areas. In addition to this, North American modules on British Victorian literature often represent an area of specialization in and of themselves. This is not to say that broad survey modules on the Victorian period are absent within North American curricula, rather that other modules often perform the task of introducing students to representative texts and authors: the role played by a British core module on Victorian literature is instead undertaken by survey courses on major British authors across a far broader period, often stretching from the eighteenth to the twentieth century. This in turn appears to have had an interesting effect on the design of those North American modules that do undertake to survey the Victorian period. Many of these eschew the inclusion of lengthy novels, instead using a far broader selection of poetry and other cultural documents as well as short stories. This interesting approach frees up space for other texts and is compensated for by the presence of specialist modules dealing exclusively with the Victorian novel or by the institutions offering a much broader survey of major British novels and novelists elsewhere on their syllabi.

Assessment also differs quite dramatically between UK and North American courses. Most modules in Britain divide assessment between essay assignments and the setting of a formal examination at the end of the academic year. A small percentage of a student's grade is also usually determined through assessment of their oral performance, dependent either upon a specific presentation task or upon course-wide monitoring of seminar participation and evidence of preparation for classes. Assessment options in North America are comparatively diverse: examinations are usually broken down into a midterm and a final, while the place of an essay is taken by a wide range of comparable tasks, often including close reading and research exercises. North American institutions are also more likely to assess a student through their production of a 'portfolio' of material across the course, consisting either of responses to small-scale questions and assignments or alternatively providing evidence of students' own independent research and study. This practice is comparatively rare in British institutions, but was utilized on a few of the courses surveyed. In both cases the weighting of individual assignments varies between specific institutions. As a general rule, a core survey module will be weighted more towards an exam, while on specialist courses the onus upon a student's own research and essay work is typically greater. North American courses also seem more disposed to set students creative writing tasks, perhaps reflecting the growth of this discipline at university level and the inter-subject flexibility allowed by the North American degree system. The use of secondary sources and the specific examples recommended or provided varies extensively from course to course. Most modules provide students with some form of secondary reading list and the material included on these is generally similar, though they range in scope from a selection of relevant overviews and influential works to a detailed bibliography, organized into entries appropriate to each author studied. Particularly prominent works, relevant to a wide number of modules, include the following: Gillian Beer, *Darwin's Plots*, Patricia Beer, *Reader, I Married Him*, Kate Flint, *The Victorian Novelist*, Sandra Gilbert and Susan Gubar, *The Madwoman in the Attic*, Robin Gilmour, *The Victorian Period*, Michael Wheeler, *English Fiction of the Victorian Period, 1830–1890* and Elaine Showalter, *A Literature of Their Own*.

The list is by no means exhaustive, instead serving as a reflection of those critical works recommended most often across a broad range of modules. The manner in which students are encouraged to engage with this material varies. In some cases little to no stipulation is made regarding use of critical material, however, several higher level modules specify the use of secondary material in general or the application and interrogation of specific perspectives. This latter scenario is typical of those modules constructed according to a specific theoretical approach. Some survey courses, particularly in the USA, teach primary material through regular reference to a selected secondary text included on the module's main reading list. As a general rule the specification and use expected of secondary material is contingent upon the level of the module in question. Survey modules supply the most extensive bibliographies but rarely make their use compulsory, while advanced courses typically expect recourse to a respectable amount of criticism, usually researched by the students themselves.

In Conclusion

The one thing definitely evident from the foregoing information and analysis is the sheer variety of teaching approaches and practices engendered by the Victorian period and its texts. To a certain extent, however, all of the modules surveyed within this appendix find themselves fulfilling a similar set of broad criteria. All need to somehow appeal to and entice prospective students. All need to balance offering an interesting range of material and meeting the demands of textual economy. Similarly, many courses need to find a means of negotiating the lack of availability of certain texts. Some of the most interesting courses also find themselves striking an interesting balance between reflecting developments in research and criticism, particularly the interests of the module designer themselves, while at the same time fitting within and complementing the broader aims and structure of a university's curriculum. It is often in the meeting of these and other challenges that some of the most innovative choices are made with regard to course design.

Anyone interested in further investigating current curricula for themselves may find the following websites useful:

Links to a range of English departments at universities worldwide can be found at:

www.nyu.edu/gsas/dept/english/links/dptsa-c.html

A large number of course descriptions, several of them included within this article's survey, are linked to a useful resource at:

http://victorianresearch.org/teaching.html#surveys

Finally, the Victorian Web offers a range of useful material, including a small number of course outlines:

www.victorianweb.org/courses/courses.html

The author would like to thank the academics and scholars of the Victoria Listserv for their helpful responses to a request for course information.

Notes on Contributors

Mark Bennett is a postgraduate student at the University of Glamorgan, currently researching for his PhD thesis on Wilkie Collins. His areas of interest are focused around the nineteenth-century Gothic, its deployment and development within genre fiction and the associated significance of Anglo-European literary exchanges and the penny blood.

Kirstie Blair is a lecturer in English literature at the University of Glasgow. She has published widely on nineteenth-century poetry and poetics and has edited a special edition of *Victorian Poetry* on Tractarian poetics. Her first monograph, *Victorian Poetry and the Culture of the Heart* was published in 2006.

Kirsty Bunting has recently completed a PhD at the University of Birmingham on late nineteenth-century women's collaborative authorship, having read for an MA in Shakespeare studies at the Shakespeare Institute, Stratford upon Avon.

Miriam Elizabeth Burstein is Associate Professor of English at the State University of New York, College at Brockport. She is author of *Narrating Women's History in Britain, 1770–1902* (2004), and is currently working on a book about the Reformation in Victorian popular culture.

Martin Danahay is Professor of English at Brock University in Canada. He is the author of *A Community of One: Masculine Autobiography and Autonomy in Nineteenth Century Britain* (1993) and *Gender at Work in Victorian Culture: Literature, Art and Masculinity* (2005). He has published numerous articles on Victorian culture and co-edited the collection *Animal Dreams: Representations of Animals in Victorian Literature and Culture* (with Deborah Denenholz Morse, 2007).

Carol Margaret Davison is Associate Professor of English Literature at the University of Windsor, Canada, where she is a specialist in Gothic and Victorian literature, African-American literature, women's writing and cultural teratology. She is the author of *British Gothic Literature, 1764–1824* (2009) and *Anti-Semitism and British Gothic Literature* (2004), which was shortlisted for the J. I. Segal Award. The author of numerous articles and book chapters, she is the editor of the award winning collection, *Bram Stoker's Dracula: Sucking Through the Century, 1897–1997* (1997). She is currently at work on *Gothic Scotland/Scottish Gothic: The Politics and Poetics of a Cultural Tradition*.

Michael Helfand is an Associate Professor of English in the University of Pittsburgh. He is co-author and co-editor of *Oscar Wilde's Oxford Notebooks* (1989) and general editor of the first series of American literary histories translated and published in China. He has also published articles and reviews on Victorian literature and contemporary British and American fiction and been a Fulbright lecturer in three countries.

Priti Joshi is Associate Professor of English at the University of Puget Sound in USA. She has published on Edwin Chadwick, Dickens, the Brontës, masculinity and industry and empire. She is currently working on two projects: a book on middle-class identity and the category of the poor and another on 're-visions' of *Jane Eyre*.

Grace Moore teaches at the University of Melbourne, Australia. She is the author of *Dickens and Empire* (2004), which was short-listed for the New South Wales Premier's Award for Literary Scholarship (2006) and the co-editor of *Victorian Crime, Madness and Sensation* (2004). She is at present editing a collection on nineteenth-century piracy (contracted to Ashgate) and writing a monograph on reinventing Victorianism.

Solveig C. Robinson is Associate Professor of English and Director of the Publishing and Printing Arts program at Pacific Lutheran University in Tacoma, Washington. She is the editor of *A Serious Occupation: Literary Criticism by Victorian Women Writers* (2003), and the author of several articles on Victorian editors. Her most recent work, on author–publisher relations in Victorian Britain, has been published in *Book History*. In addition, she is Managing Editor of *Perspectives in Biology and Medicine* and book review editor for *Victorian Periodicals Review*.

Ruth Robbins is Principal Lecturer in English at Leeds Metropolitan University. Her publications include *Literary Feminisms* (2000), *Pater to Forster, 1873–1924* (2003) and *Subjectivity* (2005). She is currently working on an edition of nineteenth-century medical advice books entitled *Medical Advice for Women, 1830–1915* to be published by Routledge in their History of Feminism series.

Jane E. Thomas lectures in English at the University of Hull. She has published widely on the work of Thomas Hardy and is the author of *Thomas Hardy: Femininity and Dissent: Reassessing the Minor Novels* (1999). She has additional research interests in nineteenth-century literature and art, twentieth-century literature, gender and women's writing and has published chapters and articles on Thomas Woolner, William Morris, Carol Anne Duffy, Caryl Churchill and Michèle Roberts. She is currently writing a monograph on *Thomas Hardy and Desire*.

Tamara S. Wagner obtained her PhD from the University of Cambridge in 2002 and is currently assistant professor at Nanyang Technological University, Singapore. Her books include *Longing: Narratives of Nostalgia in the British Novel,*

1740–1890 (2004), *Occidentalism in Novels of Malaysia and Singapore, 1819–2004* (2005) and *Financial Speculation in Victorian Fiction: Plotting Money and the Novel Genre, 1815–1901* (forthcoming). Her current projects include a study of Victorian cultural fictions of the 'shabby genteel' and a special issue on the silver-fork novel for *Women's Writing*.

Alexandra Warwick is Head of the Department of English and Linguistics at the University of Westminster. She is the author of, among other work, *Oscar Wilde* (2007) and two other edited volumes with Martin Willis: *Jack the Ripper: Media, Culture, History* (2007) and *Repositioning Victorian Sciences* (also with David Clifford and Elisabeth Wadge, 2006). She is currently researching for a work on the importance of archaeology in Victorian culture.

Rhian Williams is a Postdoctoral Research Fellow on the AHRC project, 'The Brownings' Correspondence', based at De Montfort University. She has published on poetry by Tennyson, Elizabeth Barrett Browning and 'Michael Field' and has a volume forthcoming with Continuum, *The Poetry Toolkit*. Current research is directed at examining relationships between Victorian poetry and the theatre, following on from several projects investigating Shakespeare's nineteenth-century reception.

Martin Willis is Reader in English Literature at the University of Glamorgan. His research interests lie in the intersections between Victorian literature and science. His most recent work includes *Mesmerists, Monsters and Machines: Science Fiction and the Cultures of Science in the Nineteenth Century* (2006), *Jack the Ripper: Media, Culture, History* (edited with Alexandra Warwick, 2007), *Victorian Literary Mesmerism* (edited with Catherine Wynne, 2006), and *Repositioning Victorian Sciences* (edited with David Clifford, Elisabeth Wadge and Alexandra Warwick, 2006). He is presently writing a book on Victorian literature, science and vision, entitled *Hoodwinked: Vision in Victorian Literature and Science*.

Notes

Chapter 7

1 Tricia Lootens, *Lost Saints: Silence, Gender, and Victorian Literary Canonizations*, Charlottesville and London: University Press of Virginia, 1996, pp. 36–7.

2 See James Najarian, 'Canonicity, Marginality and the Celebration of the Minor', *Victorian Poetry*, 41(4); Winter, 2003, pp. 570–4.

3 Hugh Walker, *The Age of Tennyson*, London: G. Bell, 1914, p. 2.

4 Walker, p. 2.

5 Lytton Strachey, *Eminent Victorians*, London: Chatto and Windus, 1918; 1922, Preface.

6 Stewart M. Ellis, *Mainly Victorian*, London: Hutchinson and Co., 1924, p. 6.

7 Ellis, p. 4.

8 Oliver Elton, *A Survey of English Literature 1830–1880*, London: Arnold, 1920.

9 John W. Cunliffe, *Leaders of the Victorian Revolution*, New York: Russell and Russell, 1934; 1963, p. v.

10 Edith Batho and Bonamy Dobrée (eds); *The Victorians and After 1830–1914*, London: Croom Helm, 1938, p. 12.

11 Batho and Dobrée, p. 315.

12 Batho and Dobrée, p. 284.

13 John Holloway, *The Victorian Sage: Studies in Argument*, London: Macmillan, 1953, p. 1.

14 Holloway, p. 1.

15 Jerome Hamilton Buckley, *The Victorian Temper: A Study in Literary Culture*, Cambridge, MA: Harvard University Press, 1951; 1969, p. vii.

16 Buckley, pp. 2–3.

17 Buckley, p. vii.

18 Buckley, p. 3.

19 Ewbank (1966) cited in *Year's Work in English Studies*, 47, 1966, p. 277..

20 E. Wright, *Mrs Gaskell: The Basis for Reassessment*, London: Oxford University Press, 1965; R. Blake, *Disraeli*, London: Eyre and Spottiswoode, 1966.

21 Katherine L. Mix, *A Study in Yellow: The Yellow Book and its Contributors*, Lawrence, Kansas: Kansas University Press and Constable, 1960.

22 See Donald Thomas, 'My Secret Life: The Trial at Leeds', *Victorian Studies*, 12:4, 1969, pp. 448–51.

23 *Year's Work in English Studies*, 53, 1972, p. 337.

24 *Year's Work in English Studies*, 74, 1993, p. 388.

25 *Agenda*, vol. 10, nos 1–3, Spring–Summer, 1972; James Gibson (ed.), *The Complete Poems of Thomas Hardy*, Basingstoke: Macmillan, 1976.

26 *Year's Work in English Studies*, 63, 1982, p. 11.

27   *Year's Work in English Studies*, 63, 1982, p. 13.
28   See review of Fowler, Rowena, 'Cranford: Cow in Grey Flannel or Lion Couchant?', *Studies in English Literature, 1500–1900*, 24:4, in *Nineteenth Century* (1984), pp. 717–29 (719).
29   *Year's Work in English Studies*, 28, 1987, p. 438.
30   Joseph Litvak, 'Back to the Future', *Texas Studies in Literature and Language*, 30 (1988), pp. 120–49.
31   See Heidi Canner-Ruth, 'To be Continued? Sequels and Continuations of Nineteenth-Century Novels and Novel Fragments', *Year's Work in English Studies*, 64, 1983, p. 371.
32   Linda Hutcheon, *A Poetics of Postmodernism*, London: Routledge, 1988, p. 93.
33   *Year's Work in English Studies*, 74, 1993, p. 379.
34   *Year's Work in English Studies*, 71, 1990, p. 462.
35   Barbara Belford, 'Oscar Wilde Yet Again, and Why' in Frederick R. Karl (ed.), *Biography and Source Studies*, New York: AMS Press, 1998, pp. 31–40.
36   Strachey, Preface.
37   Philip Davis, 'Review of *A Companion to the Victorian Novel*, ed. Brantlinger and Thesing, and *A Companion to the Victorian Novel*, ed. Baker and Womack', *Victorian Studies*, 46:4, 2004, pp. 679–83.

Chapter 8

1   Michael Wolff, 'The Uses of Context: Aspects of the 1860s', *Victorian Studies*, 9, 1965, pp. 47–63.
2   Jerome Buckley, *The Victorian Temper: A Study in Literary Culture*, Cambridge, MA: Harvard University Press, 1951, rev. edn 1969, Preface.
3   Geoffrey Tillotson, *A View of Victorian Literature*, Oxford: Clarendon, 1978, p. 34.
4   A. W. Ward and A. R. Waller (eds), 'The Victorian Age, Part Two, The Nineteenth Century III', *Cambridge History of English and American Literature*, vol. XIV, Cambridge: Cambridge University Press, 1979, Prefatory Note.
5   George Levine, 'Victorian Studies' in *Redrawing the Boundaries: The Transformation of English and American Literary Studies*, New York: MLA, 1992, p. 143.
6   Rohan McWilliam, 'What is Interdisciplinary about Victorian History Today?', *19: Interdisciplinary Studies in the Long Nineteenth Century*, 1, 2005, www.19.bbk.ac.uk, p. 11.
7   Levine, p. 149.

Chapter 9

1   Thomas de Quincey, *Confessions of an English Opium Eater and Other Writings*, London: Penguin, 2003, pp. 134–7.
2   Josephine McDonagh, *De Quincey's Disciplines*, Oxford: Clarendon, 1994, pp. 68–9.
3   See McDonagh's readings of the psychology of political economy in de Quincey's work.
4   John Barrow's *The Infection of Thomas De Quincey* looks at the psychology of his imperialism.
5   See Isobel Armstrong's articles, 'Transparency: Towards a Poetics of Glass in the Nineteenth Century', in Francis Spufford and Jenny Uglow (eds) *Cultural Babbage: Technology, Time and Invention*, London: Faber and Faber, 1996, pp. 123–48, and 'The Microscope: Mediations of the Sub-Visible World', in Roger Luckhurst and Josephine McDonagh (eds) *Transactions and Encounters: Science and Culture in the Nineteenth Century*, Manchester: Manchester University Press, 2002, pp. 30–54.
6   See Gillian Beer, *Darwin's Plots: Evolutionary Narrative in Darwin, George Eliot and Nineteenth-Century Fiction*. London: Routledge and Kegan Paul, 1983.

7   In a recent issue of *Victorian Studies*, in a polemic focusing on the seemingly natural relationship between the methods of literary criticism and history in Victorian studies, Amanda Anderson, Matthew Rowlinson and James Vernon each (presumably independently) select and discuss a segment of this quotation to show the relationship between literature and history in the field, the field's dedication to interdisciplinary work and to examine the 'historiographical moment' of the founding of *Victorian Studies* (Vernon 275), respectively. See Rowlinson in particular for a more extended discussion of the ways *Victorian Studies* theorized and engaged with interdisciplinarity.

8   One can cite endless examples here. Each of the Armstrong essays I cite takes issue with Foucault's limitations either by addressing Foucault's work directly or via arguments with what she identifies as the Foucauldian aspects of the work of Jonathan Crary.

9   This is symptomatic of the globalization and Americanization of British university education. One pro-vice chancellor, who in the same article claimed his university was 'snapping at the heels' of the most highly funded universities (Oxford, Cambridge and London), recently suggested in the *Times Higher* that 'a key factor in [his] university's success was its readiness to cross old-fashioned disciplinary boundaries', having opened three interdisciplinary centres that year including one for the humanities (6).

10 It is interesting to note here that Beer cites Dickens's novels as a model for Darwin (6).

11 See Isobel Armstrong, 'Tennyson in the 1850s: From Geology to Pathology', in Philip Collins (ed.) *Tennyson: Seven Essays*, New York: St Martin's Press, 1992, pp. 102–40 and Michael Tomko, 'Varieties of Geological Experience: Religion, Body and Spirit in Tennyson's *In Memoriam* and Lyell's *Principles of Geology*', *Victorian Poetry* 42.2 (2004), pp. 113–33.

12 See Armstrong, 'The Microscope' and 'Transparency'.

13 See the first chapter, 'Theatre History Today', in Jacky Bratton, *New Readings in Theatre History*, Cambridge: Cambridge University Press, 2003.

14 The two books that Bratton cites as examples of this tendency are *The Melodramatic Imagination* by Peter Brooks and *Melodramatic Tactics* by Elaine Hadley.

15 For another mode of approaching the Victorian stage, see Gail Marshall's *Actresses on the Victorian Stage: Feminine Performance and the Galatea Myth*, which looks at acting manuals and the aesthetics of the statuesque female body on the stage for an approach that draws on the history of sculpture as well as literature and drama. For an examination of other forms of Victorian entertainment, see John Plunkett's article on optical entertainments: 'Optical Recreations and Victorian Literature', *Essays and Studies*, 58 (2005), pp. 1–28.

Chapter 10

1   Matthew Arnold, 'General Report for the Year 1852', in Sir F. Sandford (ed.), *Reports on Elementary Schools, 1852–1882*, London: Macmillan, 1889, pp. 19–29.

2   F. R. Leavis, *The Great Tradition*, London: Peregrine, (1948); 1962, p. 9.

3   Francis O'Gorman (ed.), *The Victorian Novel*, Oxford: Blackwell, 2002, p. 48.

4   Peter Barry, *English in Practice: In Pursuit of English Studies*, London: Arnold, 2003, p. 56.

5   Barry, p. 48.

6   John Sutherland, *Victorian Novelists and Publishers*, Chicago, IL: Chicago University Press, 1976, p. 6.

Appendix

1 The survey of 50 institutions records Dickens as appearing on Victorian modules offered by 39 universities, Eliot on 30, C. Brontë and Hardy on 27 each and Gaskell on 23. It is worth noting that, despite the equality of the data accrued for Hardy and Brontë, the former can be placed in fourth place rather than joint third due to the fact that a small number of instances recorded in Hardy's case actually represent the independent teaching of his poetry or short prose.

2 *Bleak House* and *Great Expectations* appear on syllabi at 15 institutions each, while *Hard Times* appears on 13.

3 *Middlemarch* and *The Mill on the Floss* were recorded on reading lists at 13 universities with the figures for Eliot's other works falling off dramatically: the next most popular of her novels was *Daniel Deronda*, itself taught at only 5 of the institutions surveyed.

4 *Jane Eyre* appears 17 times and *Villette* 13 times. *The Professor* and *Shirley* both appear very rarely with the former appearing three times and only a single instance recorded for the latter.

5 The survey recorded 12 instances for *Tess of the d'Urbervilles*, nine for *Jude the Obscure* and six for *The Return of the Native*.

6 *North and South* was recorded 11 times and *Mary Barton* eight times. The comparatively poor performance of Gaskell's other texts within the survey actually belies the breadth of her work currently studied: in addition to other of her novels such as *Ruth* and *Cranford*, the survey recorded teaching of a number of pieces of her short fiction as well as her biography of Charlotte Brontë, itself taught within the context of a specialist module dedicated to that author.

7 Thackeray was taught at seven institutions, Trollope at six and Emily Brontë at 13.

8 *Vanity Fair* was present on syllabi at six universities, Brontë's *Wuthering Heights* was present on 11 and specific references to her poetry were made on reading lists at three institutions, all of them American.

9 For ease of reference the 'top ten' texts are here provided in rank order: (1) *Jane Eyre*: 17 instances; (2) and (3) *Bleak House* and *Great Expectations*: 15 instances each; (4), (5), (6), (7) and (8) *Hard Times*, *Middlemarch*, *The Mill on the Floss*, *Villette* and *Lady Audley's Secret*: 13 instances each; (9) and (10) *Tess of the d'Urbervilles* and *The Strange Case of Dr Jekyll and Mr Hyde*: 12 instances each.

10 Tennyson is present on syllabi at 31 of the 50 universities surveyed, Christina Rossetti at 23, Elizabeth Barrett Browning at 22, Robert Browning at 21 and Mathew Arnold at 20. It is worth noting that a small number of references to Arnold as an author referred exclusively to his prose work, particularly in the USA. He does, however, retain his lead over the next ranked poet (D. G. Rossetti, present on syllabi at 17 institutions) by a small margin.

11 Tennyson's broad popularity is amply indicated by the fact that (if collating general references to a poet's poetry as a single 'text') Tennyson's poetry, with 28 instances recorded, becomes the single most taught text within the survey. Furthermore, the 17 specific references to *In Memoriam* recorded on reading lists actually equal those of *Jane Eyre*, itself the most popular novel within the survey's catchment.

12 Rossetti, Swinburne and Hopkins achieved frequencies of 17, 13 and 12 respectively. The specific statistics recorded for other writers are too numerous to economically list herein. However, a range of writers, many of them hitherto neglected female poets, are being taught in a limited capacity alongside more canonical figures and the survey recorded repeated references to Augusta Webster, Mary Coleridge, Coventry Patmore and Amy Levy, among many others

13 Specific data for these poems is as follows: *In Memoriam* is specified on reading lists at 17 of the institutions surveyed, *Goblin Market* at 13, *Aurora Leigh* at 11 and *Sonnets From the Portuguese* at six. As regards those long works taught less frequently:

Amours de Voyage was specifically recorded on three reading lists, *Modern Love* on three, *The Ring and the Book* on two and *Monna Innominata* on one.

14 A number of anthologies were utilized by the different courses surveyed, the most popular of these were: Francis O'Gorman's *Victorian Poetry: An Annotated Anthology* (Oxford: Blackwell, 2004); Bernard Richards' *English Poetry of the Victorian Period, 1830–1890* (London: Longman, 1988); Daniel Karlin's *The Penguin Book of Victorian Verse* (London: Penguin, 1997); Thomas J. Collins and Vivienne J. Rundle's *The Broadview Anthology of Victorian Poetry and Poetic Theory* (Peterborough Ontario: Broadview, 2000) and the relevant volumes from the *Norton Anthology of English Literature* and the *Longman Anthology of British Literature*, the latter two of which were particularly popular with institutions of the USA.

15 One worthy exponent of this approach is the recent *Broadview Anthology of Victorian Poetry and Poetic Theory* which, even in its 'concise' edition, reproduces the entirety of *In Memoriam, Maud* and *Monna Innominata* as well as providing three books of *Aurora Leigh*.

16 Specific data for the limited pool of dramatic authors and texts located by the survey is as follows: Oscar Wilde was present on 25 of the 50 syllabi surveyed, yet his dramatic work accounts for a relatively small number of these appearances. The survey recorded 8 references to *The Importance of Being Earnest*, making it the most widely taught drama on the courses examined. *A Woman of No Importance* and *Salome* were the only others of Wilde's plays mentioned by name on reading lists with one instance recorded for each. George Bernard Shaw was present on a mere four syllabi, with three references to his *Mrs Warren's Profession* and one general reference to his *Plays Unpleasant*.

An unspecified selection of Dion Boucicault's plays was referenced on one reading list.

17 *Lady Audley's Secret* was included on reading lists at 13 universities, *The Woman in White* at nine, *East Lynne* at six, *Aurora Floyd* at five and *The Moonstone* at four. Braddon's *The Doctor's Wife* also occurred on one course.

18 The survey provides the following data for Gothic fictions, reflecting presence on Gothic modules as well as on other more general courses: Stevenson's *The Strange Case of Dr Jekyll and Mr Hyde* appears at 12 institutions, with his short vampire fiction, 'Olalla', also appearing on two. Stoker's *Dracula* is mentioned at 11 and the associated short story 'Dracula's Guest' is also included on one. Oscar Wilde's *The Picture of Dorian Gray* appears 11 times. Rider Haggard's *She* appears five times. Henry James's *The Turn of the Screw* appears three times and his short story, 'The Beast in the Jungle', appears twice. Arthur Conan Doyle's *The Sign of Four* appears three times and *The Hound of the Baskervilles* appears twice. H. G. Wells's *The Time Machine* and *The Island of Doctor Moreau* are each included three times and *The Invisible Man* is included once. George Du Maurier's *Trilby* appears on two syllabi within the survey. Joseph Sheridan Le Fanu's *Carmilla, Uncle Silas* and 'Green Tea' are all referenced at one institution. Arthur Machen's *The Great God Pan*, Vernon Lee's *Hauntings* and Richard Marsh's *The Beetle* all appear once.

19 The following selected data for some of the other cultural documents most commonly studied within interdisciplinary approaches will hopefully serve to exemplify the wider range available. The survey recorded three references to Charles Darwin's *On the Origin of Species* and two to his *The Descent of Man*. Other documents specifically appropriate to the study of science and literature included T. H. Huxley's *Science and Culture*, which appeared four times, along with Matthew Arnold's *Literature and Science*, itself appearing on five syllabi. Sociological studies, documents and associated journalism were also well represented, with six appearances of Henry Mayhew's *London Labour and the London Poor* and one specific reference to W. T. Stead's *The Maiden Tribute of Modern Babylon*.

Thomas Carlyle's essays were particularly well represented, with eight appearances of his *Past and Present* and two each of his *On Heroes and Hero Worship, Sartor Resartus* and *Signs of the Times*. Several reading lists also included examples of Victorian aesthetic and literary theory: Matthew Arnold's *Culture and Anarchy* appeared five times, selections from John Ruskin's various essays appeared ten times and Walter Pater's *The Renaissance: Studies in Art and Literature* was included, in whole or in part, on syllabi at ten of the institutions surveyed. Political documents were also well represented, with five specific references to Engels's *The Condition of the Working Class in England* and several general references to Marx's writings.

Index